Contemporary Biographies in Business

Contemporary Biographies in Business

SALEM PRESS

A Division of EBSCO Information Services, Inc.

Ipswich, Massachusetts

GREY HOUSE PUBLISHING

∞ The paper used in these volumes conforms to the American National Standard for Permanence of Paper for Printed Library Materials, Z39.48-1992 (R1997).

Publisher's Cataloging-In-Publication Data

(Prepared by The Donohue Group, Inc.)

Contemporary biographies in business. -- [First edition].

   pages : illustrations ; cm. -- (Contemporary biographies in--)

Edition statement supplied by publisher.
Companion to book titled: Careers in business.
Part of a series that is supplemental to the Salem Press series: Careers in—
Contents extracted from the monthly magazine: Current biography.
Includes bibliographical references and index.
ISBN: 978-1-61925-541-8

  1. Businesspeople--Biography. 2. Biography. I. Title: Companion to (work) Careers in business. II. Title: Subseries of Careers in-- III. Title: Extracted from (work) Current biography.

HC29 .C668 2015
658/.00922 B

Contents

Publisher's Note

Contemporary Biographies in Business is a collection of 30 biographical sketches of "living leaders" in a variety of business environments. All of these articles come from the pages of *Current Biography*, the monthly magazine renowned for its unfailing accuracy, insightful selection, and the wide scope of influence of its subjects. These up-to-date profiles draw from a variety of sources and are an invaluable resource for researchers, teachers, students, and librarians. Students will gain a better understanding of the educational development and career pathways of the business leader.

The geographical scope of *Contemporary Biographies in Business* is broad; selections span the Eastern and Western Hemispheres, covering numerous major geographical and cultural regions. All of the figures profiled are still working at one or more of their specialties. This collection includes owners, founders, presidents, and CEOs, of professional sports teams, financial firms, media companies, manufacturers and retailers.

The articles in *Contemporary Biographies in Business* range in length from 1,000 to 4,000 words and follow a standard format. All articles begin with ready-reference listings that include birth details and concise identifications. The articles then generally divide into several parts, including Early Life and Education, and Life's Work, a core section that provides straightforward accounts of the periods in which the profiled subjects made their most significant contributions to the profiled businesses. Often, a final section, Significance, provides an overview of the person's place in history and their contemporary importance. Essays are supplemented by Selected Readings, which provide starting points for further research.

As with other Salem Press biographical reference works, the articles combine breadth of coverage with a format that offers users quick access to the particular information needed. Articles are arranged alphabetically by last name. An appendix consisting of ten historical biographies, culled from the Salem Press *Great Lives* series, introduces readers to professionals of historical significance in a variety of business roles.

The book ends with a general Bibliography that offers a comprehensive list of works for students seeking out more information on a particular individual or subject, plus a separate bibliography of Selected Works that highlight the significant published works of the professionals profiled. A Profession Index, listing subjects by profession is also included.

The editors of Salem Press wish to extend their appreciation to all those involved in the development and production of this work; without their expert contribution, projects of this nature would not be possible. A list of contributors appears at the beginning of this volume.

Contributors List

Campbell, Jennifer L.

Cullen, Christopher

Curry, Jennifer

Dewey, Joseph

Eniclerico, Ronald

Exum, Kaitlen J.

Hagan, Molly M.

Kim, David J.

Kiper, Dmitry

Padovano, Joanna

Polley, Michael

Rich, Mari

Roush, Margaret E.

Stanford, Claire

Suarez, Maria A.

Contemporary Biographies in Business

Bisciotti, Stephen

Businessman and owner, Baltimore Ravens football team

Born: 1960; Philadelphia, Pennsylvania

Although Stephen Bisciotti had founded one of the world's largest employment-staffing agencies and was one of the wealthiest businessmen in the U.S., he was largely unknown outside his own circle. That changed in 2000, when his purchase of the Baltimore Ravens football franchise thrust him into the media spotlight.

Education and Early Career

The youngest of three children, Bisciotti was born on April 10, 1960 in Philadelphia, Pennsylvania. The family moved to Baltimore, Maryland, when he was an infant. When Bisciotti was eight years old, his father, Bernard, who often took the family to local sports events, died of leukemia, leaving his wife, Patricia, to raise the children. On the Ravens Web site Bisciotti wrote, "I wasn't much of a high school athlete, but played football, baseball, and basketball all the time when I was growing up."

Bisciotti attended Salisbury State University in Maryland, graduating with a B.A. in 1982. After college Bisciotti was hired at a staffing agency but was laid off after a year, so in 1983 he and his cousin, James C. Davis, founded their own staffing company, Aerotek, which specialized in matching qualified engineers and other candidates with temporary work in the aerospace and technology industries. The cousins initially ran Aerotek from a basement in Annapolis, furnished with desks from Goodwill, but within their first year they had recorded more than $1 million in revenues. Bisciotti and Davis kept a relatively low profile over the years, but the company continued to expand. Now renamed the Allegis Group, it is—per the *Forbes* magazine list of the 400 wealthiest individuals— the biggest global privately-held staffing firm, with an estimated annual revenue of $10 billion.

Later Career

A lifelong fan of his local sports teams, Bisciotti put in a bid to buy the National Football League (NFL) Baltimore Ravens, and on March 27, 2000 he was granted the right to buy 49 percent of the team, with the option of purchasing the remaining 51 percent after four years. The initial purchase cost him almost $300 million. His initial investment gave the team funds to secure free agents, and largely as a result, the Ravens trounced the New York Giants, 34–7, in the 2001 Super Bowl.

As part-owner, Bisciotti was content to stay in the background, learning the ropes from Art Modell, who had purchased the team in 1961 when they were known as the Cleveland Browns. In April 2004 Bisciotti, who is often described as low-key and humble, purchased the remaining percentage of the team for an additional $325 million, making him the second-youngest owner in the NFL.

In 2014 Ravens running back Ray Rice entered an elevator at an Atlantic City, New Jersey casino with his fiancée (now wife), Janay Palmer. Rice—unaware the elevator was equipped with a security camera—was filmed striking Palmer unconscious and then lifting her off the floor and dragging her out into the hallway. The image horrified the American public and set off an impassioned debate on violence in the NFL and the wider problem of domestic abuse in general. Rice initially received a simple two-game suspension and was docked three game checks ($529,000).

But, as Peter King wrote in the July 25, 2014 *Sports Illustrated*, the penalty was "certainly light when compared to, say, recreational drug use." The fact that "a physical confrontation with a woman in which the woman was knocked unconscious—in a league courting women as fans and consumers, and talking up the horrors of domestic violence" had merited such a token punishment added to public outrage.

"I think what we're seeing is that the league never elevated domestic violence to the platform that it should have been on, relative to some of these other offenses: bar fights, marijuana possessions, and things like that."

Bisciotti and the NFL as a whole were accused of covering up the incident: "the worst crisis in his 10 years as principal owner of the Ravens," Childs Walker wrote in the *Baltimore Sun* (September 23, 2014). "After a life defined by immense successes, Bisciotti…stands accused of willfully obscuring the severity of Rice's assault…At the very least, he and the team knew Rice knocked out the woman he has since married, yet waited to act." Subsequently, Rice's contract with the Ravens was terminated. Bisciotti—"an embattled owner," in the words of Rick Maese, writing in the *Washington Post* (September 22, 2014)— eventually expressed a measure of contrition: "I think what we're seeing is that the league never elevated domestic violence to the platform that it should have been on, relative to some of these other offenses: bar fights, marijuana possessions, and things like that." For many, though, it was too little, too late. Football's often brutal climate—on and off the field—can be expected to engender debate for some time to come.

Further Reading:
Baltimore Business Journal Jan. 2, 2004
Baltimore Sun Mar. 28, 2000; Sept. 23, 2014
Baltimore Ravens Web site
Sports Illustrated July 25, 2014
Washington Post Sept. 22, 2014

Branson, Richard

Founder and chairman, Virgin Group, Ltd.

Born: 1950; Surrey, England

Since 1970 Sir Richard Branson has been expanding his tiny, discount mail-order music operation, Virgin Records, into a multinational, billion-dollar conglomerate of more than 200 diverse businesses, in such fields as travel, tourism, television, finance, and health. Through a process that Branson calls organic expansion, in which his Virgin Group, Ltd. grows by launching new companies based on the ideas spawned by the old ones rather than by acquiring existing businesses, Virgin has become one of the world's most recognized brands. In addition to his successful business ventures, Branson is known for his flamboyant personality and fondness for undertaking daredevil stunts in pursuit of free publicity.

Education and Early Career

One of the three children of Eve Branson, a former ballet instructor, glider pilot, and flight attendant, and Ted Branson, a lawyer, Richard Charles Nicholas Branson was born on July 18, 1950 in a suburb of London. "My parents brought me up with this philosophy," Branson has said, as quoted by Fred Goodman for *Vanity Fair* (May 1992): "'You must do things—you mustn't watch what other people are doing; you mustn't listen to what other people are doing.'" Taking that advice to heart, he spent much more time participating in sports than he did studying, until he was sidelined by a knee injury. "Having played sports since I was seven and never having looked at a book," he told Paul Mansfield for *Woman's Journal* (January 1985), "I realized I'd be hopeless at studying, so I quit to do something I knew I could do and which interested me." That something was *Student*, an "alternative culture" magazine that the 15-year-old Branson launched while he was at Stowe, an exclusive English boarding school. "I didn't like school, and I wanted to put the world right," he explained to Keith H. Hammonds for a *New York Times* (June 5, 1984) profile.

Branson's career as a journalist, however, was short-lived; he soon became immersed in the role of publisher, handling the day-to-day operations of the magazine and selling advertising space. "I never had any interest in being a businessman," he told a reporter for *BusinessWeek* (June 30, 1986). "I started out wanting to edit this magazine. But the business side became all-important, and I realized that if I didn't get all that sorted out I wouldn't be able to be an editor." With the combination of tenacity and informality that would become his trademark, Branson turned *Student* into a huge, albeit brief, success. From his makeshift office (a corner telephone booth), he sold $10,000 in advertising space for the first issue; persuaded the writers Jean-Paul Sartre, Alice Walker, and John le Carré to contribute articles; and landed interviews with the likes of the actress Vanessa Redgrave and the novelist and essayist James Baldwin. The first issue of *Student* reportedly sold 50,000 copies. Branson dropped out of Stowe when he was 16 to commit himself full-time to the magazine.

When *Student* began to lose money in the late 1960s, Branson devised a plan to raise capital by selling discount records by mail. Christening the operation Virgin Records in 1970, he caught the country's retail-record industry off-guard with the success of his business model, the first of its kind in Britain. *Student*, however, remained unprofitable, and later that year he was forced to cease publication. The following year, when a postal strike threatened the mail-order operation, Branson responded by opening the country's first discount record store; he also purchased a recording studio. Strapped for cash to keep his growing enterprises afloat, he devised a number of innovative money-saving schemes. One illegal scheme—selling tax-exempt export records on the domestic market—landed him in jail for a night on charges of tax fraud, an experience that had a profound effect on the young entrepreneur. After his parents mortgaged their home to post his bail, Branson pleaded guilty, eventually paying some $85,000 in fines. "In one sense I'd recommend that everyone go through that experience," he told Echo Montgomery Garrett for *Success* (November 1992). "One night in jail teaches you that sleeping well at night is the only thing that really matters. Every single decision since has been made completely by the book."

Later Career

In 1973 Branson and his cousin and new business partner Simon Draper produced the first original album under the Virgin Records name, launching what would become one of the biggest labels in the world. "Tubular Bells," a haunting instrumental album by the then-unknown artist Mike Oldfield, became one of the most popular records in Britain. It eventually sold more than 7 million copies worldwide, and its opening theme was used on the soundtrack of the hit movie *The Exorcist*. Branson capitalized on the unexpected success of "Tubular Bells" to hammer out lucrative worldwide distribution and marketing deals, earning the respect of many in the record business and attracting the attention of an apprehensive British financial community. "People thought that because we were twenty-one or twenty-two and had long hair, we were part of some grander ideal," Branson told Mick Brown for the *London Sunday Times* (June 8, 1986). "But it was always 99.5 percent business."

Virgin Records experienced phenomenal growth over the next several years, as Branson earned a reputation for taking chances with unknown artists and developing raw talent. In 1977, for example, he signed the punk-rock group the Sex Pistols, whose controversial BBC appearance had alarmed other record companies. The gamble paid off, and the Sex Pistols made two successful records on Virgin, firmly establishing the company's position as a hot new independent label. After a lull during the late 1970s and early 1980s, Virgin reemerged in 1982, when Branson signed Boy George and Culture Club, a band unknown outside the London nightclub scene. The group became a major sensation on both sides of the Atlantic, selling millions of records. As Virgin Records' coffers bulged and its roster grew to include such artists as the Human League, UB40, and Phil Collins, Branson again looked to expand his empire.

In 1984 the California-based lawyer and businessman Randolph Fields contacted Branson to request financial backing for his planned airline, British Atlantic. Fields, who was having trouble persuading the British government to approve his proposed all-business-class London-to-New York route, asked Branson to finance the venture in return for a 75 percent stake in the operation. Uneasy at the prospect of deviating from Virgin's successful strategy of expanding into related fields, Branson's advisers opposed the plan, fearing their fledgling empire could be destroyed by head-to-head competition with British Airways (BA), the most traveled international airline in the world. Branson, however, agreed to the deal, reasoning that the volatile airline business was, in fact, closer in spirit to the entertainment industry than conventional wisdom allowed. "Obviously you've got to make sure you've got somebody running it who can safely get your airplane from A to B," Branson explained to Fred Goodman. "But once you've sorted that out, the airline business has everything to do with entertainment."

Industry observers, who criticized Branson's lack of experience in the field, and Britain's financial community, which felt he was spreading his empire too thin, predicted the quick demise of what many insiders referred to derisively as "the airline Boy George built." Branson's initial plan for the airline, renamed Virgin Atlantic Airways, was modest: to build the type of carrier that he would like to fly on and to offer an alternative to the high fares and burdensome restrictions imposed by the major airlines. Launched in less than four months, Virgin Atlantic initially consisted of a single leased Boeing 747 flying round-trip daily between Gatwick Airport, just south of London, and Newark International Airport in New Jersey. Branson distinguished his airline by offering perks that would be uneconomical for large carriers, including more leg room and a seat-back video screen for each passenger.

"Obviously you've got to make sure you've got somebody running it who can safely get your airplane from A to B. But once you've sorted that out, the airline business has everything to do with entertainment."

Lacking an advertising budget comparable to those of the large international carriers, Branson found himself in the unfamiliar position of serving as Virgin Atlantic's spokesperson. "Up until four or five months ago, I wouldn't do interviews," he told Paul Mansfield. "I wanted a completely private personal life. It was only when I decided to do the airline that I realized finally that we just had to go out there and sell it." To distance his airline from the often stodgy image of his larger competitors, Branson staged outrageous daredevil stunts to gain media coverage. In his first such foray, in 1985, he attempted to break the transatlantic speed record for powerboats; on schedule to surpass the record, his craft crashed and sank just 150 miles short of his goal. Undeterred, he attempted the stunt again the following year, and on that occasion he succeeded in setting a world record.

Branson made headlines again in 1987, when he and the Swedish aeronaut Per Lindstrand became the first people to cross the Atlantic in a hot-air balloon. (It had been done in a helium balloon.) Although the 3,400-mile voyage nearly ended in disaster when the pair crash-landed in the Irish Sea, the record-setting flight proved to be a major public-relations success. In 1991 Branson and Lindstrand attempted a Pacific crossing, from Japan to California, in a record-size, 196-foot-tall balloon. Although they accomplished their goal of crossing the Pacific Ocean, they missed their destination by some 1,800 miles and landed instead on a frozen lake in the desolate Northwest Territories of arctic Canada, where they were stranded for six hours before rescue helicopters arrived. "It's a tremendous personal challenge and a wonderful distraction from running an empire," Branson said of his attention-getting exploits in an interview with Marc Frons for *BusinessWeek* (June 30, 1986). "And it gives us millions of dollars of free publicity."

Encouraged by the phenomenal growth of the Virgin Group (as he had dubbed his empire), which had quadrupled in size in just four years, Branson set out in 1986 to expand his record label into the United States. To finance the venture, he decided to go public with Virgin's record-label and retail holdings. Although the sale was a success, several unforeseen events—including the October 1987 stock-market crash and a lack of institutional support for Branson's brash style—took their toll on Virgin stock, prompting Branson to take his companies private again within two years, with a vow to never again put himself at the mercy of "shortsighted" investors.

Eager to generate cash for a planned expansion of Virgin Atlantic, Branson focused on creating joint ventures and outside partnerships. Although the entire company had been valued at $440 million, within months of the stock buy-back he sold a 25- percent stake in the record label to the Fujisankei Communications Group of Japan for $170 million. A year later he sold a 10-percent share in the airline to another Japanese company, Seibu Saison International, for $60 million. The deals with Japanese companies not only supplied Virgin with cash but also helped open the door to profitable Asian markets. By 1989 Branson had created about 20 major partnerships and had sold outright several small chunks of his empire, fueling speculation that Virgin was in financial straits. Branson insisted that, on the contrary, he was restructuring his empire to shift his attention almost exclusively to the airline.

With Virgin Atlantic's London-Newark and London-Miami routes operating at an industry-leading 80-percent capacity, Branson's first step in the planned expansion was to continue to compete on BA's most profitable routes. By 1991 he was well on his way to realizing his goal of flying to the world's 12 largest cities. The British government strengthened Virgin's competitive position by awarding the airline highly coveted spots at London's Heathrow Airport, approving new flights to New York's Kennedy Airport, and granting permission for a lucrative London-Tokyo route. By 1992 Virgin Atlantic had also gained routes to Singapore, Hong Kong, and Sydney, as well as to Los Angeles and other American cities. Virgin's biggest coup came later that same year, when the government awarded its airline a London-Johannesburg route, the world's most lucrative, ending British Airways' and South African Airways' long-held monopoly.

On the retail front, the enterprise that had begun in 1971 as an extension of Branson's discount record mail-order operation had matured into the Virgin Retail Group, which oversaw Virgin Megastores: huge home-entertainment emporiums packed with music recordings, videotapes, and computer games. Intended to fuse shopping with entertainment, the megastores contained listening and viewing booths, condom-vending machines, supervised play areas for children, and cafes, and they extended shopping hours beyond those typical of retail outlets. By 1992 there were more than 30 megastores in Britain, on the European continent, and in Australia and Japan, many of which were funded by local partners. The Virgin retail operation entered the U.S. market in 1992, with the opening of a 30,000-square-foot megastore on Hollywood's Sunset Boulevard. The Hollywood outlet was modeled after the huge Virgin Megastore on the Champs- Élysées in Paris, which attracted more people each year (7 million) than the Eiffel Tower and which, with $130 million in annual sales, had the highest revenue of any record store in the world.

While the Virgin Megastores exhibited tremendous growth, in 1992 Branson's Virgin Atlantic fleet still consisted of only eight planes, compared to BA's 240. Nevertheless, Virgin Atlantic's successful blend of quality customer service and publicity-driven trendiness steadily lured hundreds of customers away from BA. With its popular Upper Class service, which featured first-class perks for business-class fares, Virgin was costing BA an estimated $250 million a year in profits. For about half the price of BA's first-class service, Upper Class passengers were treated to comfortable sleeper seats, on-board stand-up lounges, free neck massages and manicures, personal video screens, menus prepared by some of London's finest chefs, free standby transatlantic coach tickets, and, on certain routes, limousine service to and from the airport. The astounding success of its Upper Class service enabled Virgin Atlantic to offer competitive economy service as well. Troubled by its dwindling market share, British Airways accused Virgin Atlantic of unfair business practices, citing its strategy of muscling in on BA's prime routes. Branson, on the other hand, regularly cited what he regarded as BA's monopoly as an example of why small carriers had difficulty surviving. As the feud between the two airlines escalated, Branson responded with legal action. In his complaints to the European

Commission and the Civil Aviation Authority, Branson contended that BA had waged an all-out "dirty-tricks campaign" to force Virgin Atlantic out of business. Among other things, he accused BA of instituting unfair pricing policies, flooding the market with discount tickets, overcharging Virgin Atlantic for maintenance services, and gaining access to its computerized booking system in a concerted effort to steal Upper Class customers. Claiming that BA had hired private detectives and a public relations firm whose task was not only to discredit Virgin but to defame him personally, Branson also filed a libel suit against the carrier.

Although BA initially dismissed Branson's allegations as a publicity stunt, the High Court ruled in his favor, awarding Virgin Atlantic nearly $1 million in damages as well as compensation for legal fees. Still not satisfied, Branson used the threat of further litigation—including an antitrust suit in the United States and action under the Data Protection Act—as leverage in his attempts to gain a formal public apology, a substantial cash settlement as compensation for commercial damage, prime takeoff and landing slots at Heathrow Airport, and assurances that BA would not again engage in unfair practices. Although BA formally apologized and offered Virgin Atlantic a large sum of money to prevent further litigation, it balked at any other concessions and tried to persuade Branson to drop the subject forever. Unwilling to accept such an agreement, Branson initiated another round of lawsuits.

As the turf battle between the two airlines dragged on, Branson solidified his commitment to Virgin Atlantic in March 1992 by selling the Virgin Music Group to Thorn EMI for $980 million. The deal was considered a major coup for Branson. After the sale, which left him with nearly $700 million to reinvest into his airline, he made it clear that Virgin Atlantic intended to become a major player in international air travel. With plans to increase his fleet to 16 planes by the end of 1995, Branson finally had the resources to set up several new routes and the ability to compete with BA on more equal terms. (During the Persian Gulf war, Branson donated the services of his Virgin Atlantic fleet to aid refugees.)

The sale of the Virgin Music Group did not, however, signify Branson's abandonment of the entertainment industries. In June 1995 Virgin, which had sold its film distribution and production arm, Virgin Vision, several years earlier, reentered the film industry with the purchase of the 116-theater MGM United Kingdom cinema chain.

Branson's Virgin Group continued to expand into other markets. In 1996, for example, the company launched Virgin Brides, a wedding-apparel business. For the event, Branson shaved his beard and donned a wedding dress. (Virgin Brides was sold in 2008.) Virgin also teamed up with the bus and rail company Stagecoach to create Virgin Trains. In 1997 Virgin Trains won the franchises for the West Coast Main Line and Cross Country sectors of British Rail.

Virgin founded nine new companies in 2000 alone, including a financial-services concern (Virgin Money), an online wine merchant (Virgin Wines), and a low-cost Australian airline (Virgin Blue). The year 2004 marked the founding of Virgin Galactic, which sought to produce privately funded spaceships that would allow commercial passengers to take trips into space. Virgin Galactic commissioned the famed aerospace designer Burt Rutan to build the vessels needed: the mother ship, dubbed *WhiteKnightTwo*, and the spacecraft, *SpaceShipTwo*.

Branson announced the Virgin Earth Challenge in February 2007. He pledged a $25-million prize to the first scientist who could develop technology to extract harmful greenhouse gases from the atmosphere. Later that year Branson and the musician Peter Gabriel formed the Elders, a group of former world leaders that pool their combined wisdom to resolve global problems. Members of the Elders included the late Nelson Mandela, former UN secretary-general Kofi Annan, and Jimmy Carter.

In August 2007 the Virgin Group launched Virgin America, an airline based in California. Despite the airline's limited routes, it was lavishly praised by the travel press and industry insiders. In his spare time Branson continued to attempt feats of daring. In June 2004 he set a new record (one hour, 40 minutes, and six seconds) for the fastest crossing of the English Channel in an amphibious vehicle. The previous record, held since the 1960s, had been six hours. Four years later, in September 2008, Branson and his two children attempted to beat the record for the fastest crossing of the Atlantic Ocean in a single-hulled sailboat. Starting just south of New York City and sailing toward England's Lizard Point, the trip was abandoned after two days when 40-foot waves damaged the vessel.

Branson has authored many books, including his best-selling 1998 autobiography *Losing My Virginity: How I've Survived, Had Fun, and Made a Fortune Doing Business My Way*; *Screw It, Let's Do It: Lessons in Life* (2006); *Business Stripped Bare: Adventures of a Global Entrepreneur* (2008), *Screw Business As Usual* (2011), and *The Virgin Way: Everything I Know About Leadership* (2014). He has also made cameo appearances on several television series, including the popular sitcom *Friends*, as well as such films as *Around the World in 80 Days* (2004), *Superman Returns* (2006), and *Casino Royale* (2006). Queen Elizabeth II knighted Branson in 1999 for his services to entrepreneurship.

Virgin Galactic suffered a horrific setback when SpaceShipTwo crashed into California's Mojave Desert on October 31, 2014. According to Joel Glenn Brenner in the November 4, 2014 Washington Post, "video from the cockpit of SpaceShipTwo shows co-pilot Mike Alsbury"—who was killed— "making a fatal error in the first 10 seconds of the flight, prematurely unlocking a critical mechanism that reconfigures the ship's wings to provide drag."

Following a divorce from his first wife, Kristen Tomassi, in 1976, Branson married his current wife, Joan Templeman, in 1989. They have two grown children. Branson, who owns homes in Oxford and London, also owns Necker Island, a private, 74-acre property in the British Virgin Islands.

Further Reading:

BusinessWeek June 30, 1986

London Guardian Apr. 28, 2006

London Sunday Times June 8, 1986

New York Times June 5, 1984

People Nov. 2, 1998

Success Nov. 1992

Vanity Fair May 1992

Virgin.com

Washington Post Nov. 4, 2014

Women's Journal Jan. 1985

Selected Books:

Losing My Virginity: How I've Survived, Had Fun, and Made a Fortune Doing Business My Way, 1998

Screw It, Let's Do It: Lessons in Life, 2006

Business Stripped Bare: Adventures of a Global Entrepreneur, 2008

Screw Business As Usual, 2011

The Virgin Way: Everything I Know About Leadership, 2014

Bravo, Rose Marie

CEO, Burberry Ltd.

Born: 1951; New York City

Had it not been for the efforts of Rose Marie Bravo, the ubiquitous brown, red, white, and black plaid that is synonymous with the fashion house Burberry might still be glimpsed only in the linings of raincoats. Today, it adorns a wide variety of the company's very popular fashion accessories. After becoming chief executive officer (CEO) of the London-based, British firm Burberry Ltd. in 1997, Bravo revived the company—turning the once-floundering firm into an upscale label with products perceived as symbols of both high socioeconomic status and street cred, attracting a new, younger clientele without losing older, established customers, and helping to double the company's profits.

Education and Early Career

The fashion executive was born Rose Marie LaPila on January 13, 1951 in New York City. Her parents were Italian immigrants; her father, Biagio, owned a hair salon on 181st Street in the Bronx, and her mother, Anna Bazzano, was a Sicilian-born seamstress. Bravo attended the elite Bronx High School of Science, graduating in 1969. She then enrolled at the all-female Thomas More College, on the Rose Hill campus of Fordham University, also in the Bronx, where she earned a B.A. in English in 1971. The dean of Fordham College of Rose Hill, Reverend Jeffrey P. von Arx, told Michele Snipe for the Fordham Web site (May 20, 2000) that when Bravo "arrived on the Rose Hill campus . . . she was a young woman in a hurry," displaying "the energy and sense of direction that have distinguished her business career."

Following her graduation, Bravo began her career in retail at the now-defunct Abraham & Straus, in Brooklyn, where she served as a department manager from 1971 to 1974. Later in 1974 she moved to the famed Macy's, where she started out as an associate buyer and had ascended to the position of senior vice president of merchandising by 1988. During her time at Macy's, Bravo worked primarily in cosmetics, forming a high regard for the feminist sensibilities of major figures in the field. She told Kristina Zimbalist for *Time* (February 9, 2004), "In cosmetics, which is where I particularly grew up, we had these wonderful role models. Estee Lauder, Helena Rubinstein and Elizabeth Arden are all women who created companies. . . . If you've been given this road map and you see that others have gone before you and achieved, you never have in your mind the notion of failure. You have the notion that you can do it too, if you're good enough and smart enough and make the right decisions."

In 1988 Edward Finkelstein, then chairman of Macy's, promoted Bravo to chairman and CEO of I. Magnin, a no-longer-extant chain of specialty stores that Macy's had recently acquired. Bravo headed to San Francisco to rejuvenate the stores' fading image. One of her first acts was to ask a local fashion reporter for a list of names and telephone numbers of women who frequented I. Magnin; she then invited the women to lunches, asking them for suggestions as to how to improve the store. When, for example, one woman proposed that I. Magnin might carry shawls to cater to tourists unused to San Francisco's variable weather, Bravo saw to it that shawls appeared in the accessory department before the end of the same week. To promote an air of exclusivity, she closed several I. Magnin locations and installed designer boutiques in the remaining stores. Bravo also arranged for a variety of personal appearances by designers, attracting the likes of Hubert de Givenchy, Emanuel Ungaro, Bob Mackie, Bill Blass, Gianfranco Ferre, and Oscar de la Renta, among others. While in that position, Bravo was known for her personal attention to designers, her pursuit of positive publicity, and her friendly but businesslike manner. According to Mandy Behbehani in *Mirabella* (December 1990), Robert A. Nielsen, chairman and president of Revlon at the time, called Bravo "one of those very rare individuals who combine conceptual thinking with execution. If anyone can turn I. Magnin back to its former glory days, she can."

While Bravo was credited with making significant improvements at I. Magnin, Macy's as a whole was suffering. The company filed for bankruptcy in 1992. Only a few months later, riots broke out in Los Angeles, sparked by the acquittal of four white police officers whose beating of a black man, Rodney King, had been captured on videotape; in the midst of the rioting, the Los Angeles I. Magnin store was looted. Bravo, who had just completed a $40 million renovation of that store, lamented to Richard Fletcher for the *London Sunday Telegraph* (October 5, 2003) that the rioters "looted everything except our rare books and our soaps. Every single thing." Later that year Bravo accepted the position of president of Saks Fifth Ave. In that capacity she was responsible for merchandising, overseeing the store's fashions, and developing private-label goods. "She's a brilliant merchant and a great leader of people," Philip Miller, who hired Bravo when he was vice chairman of Saks, said to Cathy Horyn and Suzanne Kapner for the *New York Times* (July 12, 2002). "She has a very good rapport with designers and the fashion market. She understands the whole world of luxury. And she works like a demon."

"But above all, love what you do. Love the people, the team, have passion for the product, the category, the industry, the selling dynamic, the company. Without this special ingredient, you won't be as great as you can be."

Demon-like determination may have been necessary for Bravo's next job: CEO of Burberry's Ltd., a post she assumed in 1997. (In 1999, for aesthetic reasons, the company dropped the apostrophe and "s" from its name.) Thomas Burberry, as a 21-year-old apprentice to a country draper, founded the brand in 1856 in Hampshire, England, where it became a favorite of sportsmen and hunters, who appreciated Burberry's new fabric--gabardine. Gabardine, which received a patent in 1888, was both breathable and waterproof and went into wide use, particularly once Thomas Burberry was commissioned to design the uniforms and trench coats for the British army, in 1901. In 1920, the famous Novacheck plaid lining was created. Since then, although such legendary figures as the Antarctic explorer Sir Ernest Shackelton had sported Burberry designs, the brand had lost its cachet, relying primarily on exports--ranging from suits to whiskey to biscuits--for its profits. Charged with injecting life into what was generally seen as a stodgy British raincoat company, Bravo found herself based in the company's seedy headquarters, located above its raincoat factory in Hackney, an unfashionable area of London's East End. When her parents went to visit her in London, they expressed concern for her well-being. Bravo recalled to *BusinessWeek* (January 12, 2004), "They said, 'You're leaving Fifth Avenue for this?'"

Within weeks of her arrival, Bravo secured the photographer Mario Testino and the model Stella Tennant for a fashion shoot that was meant to change the Burberry image; however, as no new clothes had yet been created for the brand, Bravo had to make do with what was available. "All we had [were] raincoats," she told

Richard Fletcher. "I remember saying 'just get me some pretty pictures of the coat.'" Soon another model, Kate Moss, began endorsing the brand, which by that time consisted of more than just raincoats. By 2003, three fashion lines had been created: Burberry London, the basic collection, which accounted for 85 percent of the company's sales; Prorsum, a higher-end international line; and Thomas Burberry, a more casual collection geared toward younger consumers. Additionally, Burberry has marketed fragrances, a line of baby clothes and accessories, pet items, and other accessory collections, such as shoes and handbags. In 1999 Burberry held its first catwalk show in London. These successes allowed Bravo to relocate Burberry's head offices to a more presentable location: the newly converted flagship store in London's Haymarket, which had originally opened in 1891. "The concept," Bravo explained to Horyn and Kapner, "is a British lifestyle, and we've stayed very committed to it for five years. It's family, friends, dogs, wit. Everybody getting together, in sort of this zany British setting."

Now that Burberry Novacheck plaid can be seen on items from baby carriages to dog coats to bow ties, the question that some fashion pundits have pondered is whether Bravo has done her job too well. Imitations of Burberry goods are rampant, and some predict that since the brand's identity is based so firmly on the easily identifiable plaid, the products' current position as status symbols might prove to be just a fad. Bravo saw such popularity in a positive light, though, as she told Matthew Goodman for the *London Sunday Times* (June 30, 2002): "By its very nature, the brand has broad appeal. It appeals to everyone from children to grandparents. I only see that as positive." Still, to avoid overdoing the emphasis on plaid, Bravo announced that less than 10 percent of the 2002 line of products would feature the Novacheck pattern. That decision may have been due to the revelation that some British pubs had banned Burberry-wearing customers because of U.K. gang members and soccer hooligans who had begun sporting the trademark plaid. While these developments might have kept some harmless Burberry-wearers out of pubs, the phenomenon has also lent the brand further street cred.

In 2013 Bravo wrote a piece for *Women's Wear Daily* on the new challenges facing businesses such as Burberry. "[T]he globalization of American companies with major profit centers outside the U.S. adds to the complexity of the business," she stated. "Spending real time across the globe to better understand the dynamics of a unique market takes stamina and energy. Becoming a student of the cultural nuances and preferences of each market and special business models therein, is a vital prerequisite.

"....the digital revolution and new technology has made change a part of a company's life and has changed life in every company. The online business has forced management to constantly review their financial formulas, business models and strategies. The economics of a category, a collection, a product, a brand or a business model, can change rapidly. What worked last year may not work this year or the next."

Bravo ended the piece on an interestingly inspirational note. "But above all," she concluded, "love what you do. Love the people, the team, have passion for the product, the category, the industry, the selling dynamic, the company. Without this special ingredient, you won't be as great as you can be."

Further Reading:

BusinessWeek Web site
London Sunday Telegraph Oct. 5, 2003
London Sunday Times Jun. 30, 2002
Mirabella Dec.1990
New York Times Jul. 12, 2002
Time Feb. 9, 2004
Women's Wear Daily Jan. 14, 2013

Drexler, Millard S.

Former executive, The Gap and J. Crew

Born: 1944; the Bronx, New York City

In the early 1980s the Gap was a moderately successful apparel chain that sold ho-hum casual wear at bargain-basement prices. By the next decade, the company had mushroomed into a $2.5-billion fashion empire comprising over 1,200 stores known for selling hip, designer-quality clothing to millions of Americans of all ages from all walks of life. The man responsible for the Gap's metamorphosis was Millard S. ("Mickey") Drexler.

Education and Early Career

An only child, Millard S. Drexler was born August 17, 1944 in the New York City borough of the Bronx. As a boy, he knew he wanted to be a businessman, though he felt no special affinity for the world of fashion. The apparel industry, however, was the central professional activity in his family's life: His father bought leather and buttons for a coat manufacturer in New York's garment district, and his uncle, for whom Drexler worked for a time as a teenager, operated a laundry.

On graduating from the Bronx High School of Science, Drexler attended City College of New York and later enrolled at what is now the State University of New York at Buffalo, where he earned an undergraduate degree in business. He continued his education at Boston University, where he received an M.B.A. in 1967. Although he failed to distinguish himself as a student (when asked for his recollections of Drexler, one of his former classmates responded, "Never heard of him"), Drexler had already begun to carve a niche for himself in the business world. During his summer vacations, he worked as an intern at the department-store chain Abraham & Straus, and it was there that Drexler, in his words, "fell in love with the business."

Later Career

Drexler's first job after he graduated from business school was in the junior sportswear department at Bloomingdale's; six months later he was promoted to buyer of women's swimsuits and sweaters. His boss at Bloomingdale's remembers him as an unusually talented young man. "He had a sense of style," he told Russell Mitchell, who profiled Drexler for *Business Week* (March 9, 1992). "You could see there was a spark there....It might have taken someone else two to three years for that kind of promotion."

After working briefly at R. H. Macy & Company, Drexler returned to Abraham & Straus. But even as he rose through the industry ranks, he felt increasingly stifled by the bureaucratic red tape that he invariably encountered whenever he tried to bring a new product to market. "The more I was advancing in the business, the less fun I was having," he told Jonathan Van Meter in an interview for *Vogue* (June 1990). "I wasn't dealing with merchandise as much as dealing with bureaucracy." He was ready for a change when, in 1980, he was tapped to become president of Ann Taylor Stores, an unprofitable chain selling somewhat dowdy career clothes for women. Over the course of the next three years, Drexler transformed the chain into a chic specialty store catering to working women.

Meanwhile, Donald G. Fisher, the president of the Gap, Inc., a 500-store apparel chain that sold a wide assortment of brand-name jeans and sweat suits at steeply discounted prices, was searching for a merchandising expert who would be able to breathe new life into his company. Fisher, who had founded the company in 1969, had seen the Gap's fortunes soar throughout the 1970s, when the baby-boom generation had a seemingly unquenchable thirst for denim. But by the early 1980s, the craze for faded denim had begun to subside, and Fisher realized that his company would have to redefine itself if it were to continue to prosper. Fisher discussed his concerns with several leaders in the industry, but it was not until he spoke to Drexler, whose accomplishments at Ann Taylor had captured his attention, that he felt that his vision of the Gap's future had been understood. Fisher subsequently offered to make Drexler president of the division responsible for the Gap's stores; Drexler accepted, and in 1983 he relocated to San Francisco, where the company was head-quartered.

> **"At the end of the day, the thing that we all try to do best is please the customer. The ones that please them the most, win."**

What Drexler "understood," apparently, was that the Gap's strategy of stocking its no-frills outlets with large quantities of jeans and selling them at low prices was out of sync with the needs of the consumer market of the 1980s. He based his reasoning on the fact that baby boomers, who had grown up with the Gap in the 1970s and therefore comprised an important market for the company, were now entering middle age and thus were less interested in price than in quality and style. "What troubled me especially was that the taste level of the merchandise was, well, just plain ugly," he explained to Isadore Barmash in an interview for the *New York Times* (June 24, 1991). "The stuff was trendy but not tasteful and the quality was not what I would have liked. The problem was that we were running a margin-driven business based on price. There was no real, bright future in that."

With such thoughts rooted firmly in his mind, Drexler assumed his new post determined to make classic designs and quality fabrics the hallmarks of Gap clothing. He quickly discovered, however, that in order to realize his goals he would first have to convince his employees that jeans and T-shirts, which they considered outmoded, could be stylish as well as comfortable. Drexler enjoyed telling the story of his first day as president, when he walked around Gap headquarters waving a magazine profile of Giovanni Agnelli, the chairman of Fiat, before his incredulous employees. "They're looking at the guy, they're wondering who he is, they're wondering who I am," Drexler recalled to Jonathan Van Meter. "And I say, 'He's the chicest guy in the world and he's wearing a Levi's chambray shirt,' which they hated at the Gap because they said, 'It's downscale, it's not right for us.' I took in pictures of Ralph Lauren. He was always in jeans and a jean jacket. And they'd say, 'We thought people weren't wearing jeans and jean jackets anymore.' And I'd just say, 'But this is the right kind of denim to wear now.' And they would say, 'What? Is he nuts?'"

As it turned out, Drexler had to overcome more than the protestations of his employees, for during his first year as president, the Gap's profits tumbled to $12 million, down from $22 million the year before, and the price of Gap stock plummeted to slightly more than $1 per share, down from $3. "We were all scared," Drexler recalled to Russell Mitchell, "and I was more scared than anyone the first year and a half." Fortunately for Drexler, Fisher had faith in his president's vision and sanctioned the reorganization that would allow that vision to unfold. That reorganization entailed replacing the Gap's old and "ugly" merchandise with colorful, classically designed separates made out of all-cotton fabric; reducing the number of brands of jeans from 14 to two—Levi Strauss and Gap brands—and offering a greater variety of clothing, from jeans and sweat suits to skirts, sweaters, jackets, dresses, backpacks, and handbags. To encourage multiple purchases, Drexler also directed manufacturers to produce the most popular styles in many different colors.

Drexler also looked for ways to improve the public's image of Gap products. His most successful technique was creating the illusion that Gap clothing was produced by a single designer, in the same way that designer clothing is. He decided, for example, that the Gap label would be sewn onto each garment and that a new Gap "collection" would be introduced approximately every two months. Each collection, moreover, would feature a different palette; one season pastels might predominate, the next might feature bright jewel colors. All of Drexler's efforts were directed toward the goal of creating classic yet stylish clothing—"not too far to the left, not too far to the right," as he has described it—that appealed to a broad spectrum of the consumer market. "Everybody can wear these clothes," Drexler has often been quoted as saying. "We want to provide the basic pieces for anyone's closet."

In keeping with his desire to burnish the Gap's public image, Drexler also redesigned the stores' interiors. Until Drexler came on board, the stores had exuded a somewhat claustrophobic atmosphere, for the merchandise had for the most part been displayed on circular pipe racks clustered closely together. The racks were among the first casualties of Drexler's reorganization; he replaced them with white modular shelves on which neatly folded articles of clothing were carefully stacked. He also ordered the installation of light wood floors, which were to be polished every three to four days, and declared that the stores' white walls were to be touched up once a week. "Hopefully, when a customer sees a Gap store," Drexler told Beatrice Motamedi in an interview for the *San Francisco Chronicle* (November 12, 1990), "they'll see a picture that's been very well painted: everything flows together."

By 1985 Drexler's revolution had begun to reap financial rewards. In that year the Gap posted a 127 percent increase in profits over the previous year, and sales rose 25 percent. That upward trend continued throughout 1986, at the end of which the Gap's sales totaled $849 million—or 40 percent more than the company's sales just three years earlier. But despite the Gap's good fortunes, Drexler was convinced that the company could do better, and in 1986, acting on a hunch that other parents shared his frustration at not being able to find attractive and durable clothes for their children, he launched GapKids, which would sell Gap clothing designed for children under 12.

Drexler's hunch earned the company millions of dollars: In its first year, GapKids saw revenues of $2 million, and as more GapKids stores opened, sales continued to boom, reaching $260 million in 1991. Meanwhile, in early 1990, Drexler pounced on the infant-clothing market by introducing the babyGap line, which offered classic Gap designs for children under two. That line, which was sold at GapKids stores, also proved a success. "It's very difficult to find good-looking, durable baby clothes that aren't baby blue or have those little doggies all over them," one satisfied babyGap customer told Russell Mitchell.

If an obsession with order and simplicity was the driving force behind Drexler's efforts to improve the appearance of the stores and create more attractive clothing, it also informed his management style. Indeed, soon after taking over as president, Drexler fired those buyers, regional managers, and merchandise distributors who based their decisions on complex quantitative analysis or whose responsibilities were so esoteric that they could not explain to him what they did. In their place he hired individuals who took a more intuitive approach to the business of designing and selling clothing—an approach based on the philosophy that a piece of clothing is successful if it is one that Gap employees themselves would want to wear.

Drexler also encouraged his staffers to come up with creative ideas that would increase the company's profitability. "There are no memos here," Richard Crisman, the company public relations director, told Jonathan Van Meter. "Mickey's a firm believer in, when you're out in the hallway, when you're talking, that's when things get done. And everyone here has input. Mickey or Maggie [Maggie Gross, the Gap's senior vice president in charge of advertising] will walk through and ask everyone, 'What do you think of this shirt? What do you think of this idea for an ad?'" Drexler's management style, in turn, helped to create an environment in which employees appeared to be unusually enthusiastic about their work. "I've never worked in a company where no one bitches about their jobs," Richard Crisman told Van Meter. "It's unnatural."

Drexler's ability to recognize the talents of staff members, coupled with his willingness to entrust them with making important decisions, occasionally had startlingly favorable consequences. In 1988, for instance, Drexler agreed to launch an innovative print advertising campaign, called "Individuals of Style," which had been conceived by Maggie Gross. Under her direction, the company hired such celebrated photographers as Annie Liebovitz and Herb Ritts to produce striking black-and-white shots of Americans from all walks of life, including famous actresses, athletes, and musicians as well as ordinary people. What the subjects had in common was that each was wearing his or her favorite piece of Gap clothing together with other, not necessarily Gap-brand, garments. The message of the campaign was twofold: Not only can Gap clothes be worn by everyone, but they can be mixed and matched with other garments to fit the personal style of any individual. Moreover, by placing the ads in such trendy magazines as *Vanity Fair* and *Rolling Stone* rather than in fashion magazines, the company reinforced its belief that its clothing has more to do with comfort and lifestyle than with fashion.

The campaign also contributed to the success of the now-famous Gap T-shirt. Although the Gap's version of the American classic differed little from those sold in department stores around the country, over one million were sold after the appearance of an ad in which the actress Kim Basinger was featured wearing a long white T-shirt with a string of pearls. The campaign was also noted for its artistry, winning, among other prizes, an award from the Council of Fashion Designers of America.

The Gap's emergence as an industry-wide model of excellence was a testament not only to Drexler's expertise as a merchandiser and a marketer, but also to his philosophy that in order to build a company, one must dare to take risks. While some of his ventures—such as the GapKids stores and the babyGap line—turned out to be highly profitable, others have not. In 1987, for instance, Drexler established Hemisphere, a chain of stores catering to more affluent customers; the company was forced to close the division in 1989. But Drexler had no regrets over his ill-fated effort to enter a new market. "We took the risk, and it didn't work," he told Louis Trager in an interview for the *San Francisco Examiner* (February 11, 1990). "I will never mark us down for that attitude. We made the judgment it didn't work. It wasn't a thing where our egos were tied up in the business."

Drexler also waged an uphill battle in trying to revive Banana Republic, which Fisher had purchased in 1983 when it consisted of two stores and a mail-order catalogue business selling the khaki surplus of European armies. Sales of the stores' safari-inspired clothes boomed from 1985 until 1987, thanks in large part to the release of *Out of Africa* and other films set in exotic locales. When "khaki fever" subsided, however, Banana Republic lost its appeal among customers, and its sales and profits plummeted. Drexler, in the years since becoming the Gap's corporate president in 1987, tried to reinvent the stores as upscale Gap stores; his strategy included toning down the jungle theme and selling such items as expensive bomber jackets and suede skirts. Although its comeback has been slower than Drexler had hoped, Banana Republic eventually became profitable.

Notwithstanding such setbacks, the Gap, thanks in large measure to Drexler, secured its place in retailing history as one of the most successful operations of the late 1980s and early 1990s.

Success in retail, of course, is cyclical. "In May 2002," Meryl Gordon wrote in the May 21, 2005 *New York* magazine, "Drexler found himself in trouble…" having "made a series of bad calls"—and was ousted from the Gap. Nothing if not resilient, Drexler then took the helm of retailer J. Crew in 2003 and, in this capacity, proved to be a resounding success. In a profile for the *Business of Fashion* Web site (April 30, 2014), Imran Amed and Lauren Sherman wrote, "A big part of what makes J. Crew the most compelling American retail—dare we say it, fashion—success story of the past 10 years is Drexler's uncanny ability to pick up on market trends and patterns incredibly quickly, consult data to back up his observations, then bring those trends to the masses. It's perhaps the core reason he was able to transform a once-promising, long-struggling catalogue business [J. Crew] into a powerful arbiter of taste. Indeed, the only thing Drexler seems to fear is missing out on the next big thing. And he uses his unique mix of instinct and information to figure out exactly what that is and act upon it."

"At the end of the day, the thing that we all try to do best is please the customer," he told Beatrice Motamedi. "The ones that please them the most, win."

Further Reading:

Business of Fashion Apr. 30, 2014

Business Week Mar. 9, 1992

New York May 21, 2005

New York Times Jun. 24, 1991

San Francisco Chronicle Nov. 12, 1990

San Francisco Examiner Feb. 11, 1990

Vogue Jun. 1990

Who's Who in America, 1992–93

Duke, Michael T.

Former president and CEO, Wal-Mart

Born: 1949; near Fayetteville, Georgia

Michael T. Duke became president and CEO of Wal-Mart Stores Inc. in 2009. (Although an individual store is referred to as a "Walmart," the parent corporation includes a hyphen in its name.) As the fourth CEO of the company, which is the world's largest retailer—boasting more than 8,650 big-box stores in 15 countries, $405 billion in annual sales in 2010, and more than two million employees—Duke has been credited with pushing Wal-Mart to become more environmentally responsible and socially conscious. Jim Tharpe wrote for the *Atlanta Journal-Constitution* (December 26, 2009), "Those who know Duke say his mix of people skills, logistics savvy and business toughness make him a good fit for his job, which comes with responsibility for all that is respected and reviled about the retail giant. Some analysts have equated running Wal-Mart to governing a small country."

Education and Early Career

Michael Terry Duke was born on December 7, 1949 and raised, along with his three younger sisters, in a middle-class family outside of Fayetteville, Georgia. Both his father, a truck driver, and his mother, a housewife, emphasized the merits of hard work. "There weren't a lot of financial resources or time," Duke told Tharpe. "Even my dad's vacation time was spent fixing up the house or farming."

Duke was the captain of the football team at Fayette County High School, but he didn't consider himself skilled enough to win an athletic scholarship to college. On the advice of his physics teacher he applied to the Georgia Institute of Technology (Georgia Tech) in Atlanta, where he majored in industrial engineering—although he has admitted to having always been a "retailer at heart," as quoted by Diane Bullock for *Minyanville* (May 28, 2010). Duke graduated from Georgia Tech with a bachelor's degree in 1971 and took a job as a manager at Rich's Department Stores in Atlanta. He worked for the company for 23 years, spending much of that time in the logistics department. (Rich's was later involved in a string of mergers and is now part of Macy's Inc.)

Later Career

In 1995 Duke joined Wal-Mart Stores Inc. as a senior vice president of distribution and logistics in Bentonville, Arkansas. In March 2000 he was promoted to executive vice president of logistics. Later that year Duke became the company's executive vice president of administration, and in 2003 he became president of Wal-Mart Stores USA and executive vice president of Wal-Mart Stores Inc. In October 2005 he became CEO of Wal-Mart International, as well as vice chair of Wal-Mart Stores Inc. During his tenure as CEO of Wal-Mart International, the company opened some 8,000 retail units in 15 countries.

The appointment of Duke as CEO of Wal-Mart Stores Inc. was announced in November 2008, and the following February he replaced Lee Scott, who had served as CEO since 2000. The company was often criticized during Scott's tenure for its controversial health-care and wage policies, which led to decreases in the company's stock prices. Duke took over the position in the midst of a global recession, when the company's low retail prices were more appealing to customers. Given Duke's previous success in expanding the company's retail units abroad, observers interpreted his selection as CEO as evidence of the company's intention to focus on international expansion.

"I'd want Sam Walton to be proud. I came here because of the culture of the company and what we stand for ... the basic beliefs and values of our company."

Duke redesigned the layout of the stores, expanding aisle size and improving lighting and other features. He also increased the company's donations to nonprofit organizations and continued Scott's efforts to create a more green-friendly entity by establishing programs to measure the sustainability of its global suppliers by selling food grown by local farmers, and by funding a consortium consisting of government and university leaders, corporations, and nonprofit organizations. Wal-Mart, in cooperation with the Environmental Defense Fund, has also agreed to work toward eliminating 20 million metric tons of greenhouse gas from its global supply chain.

"I'd want Sam Walton to be proud," Duke said in Jim Tharpe's profile. "I came here because of the culture of the company and what we stand for ... the basic beliefs and values of our company. Do we serve more customers? Do we help out around the world with people living better? Do we make a difference in issues like sustainability and health care?"

Duke was named one of "the global elite" by *Newsweek* in 2008 and was ranked number eight by *Forbes* magazine on its 2009 list of most powerful people in business. Also in 2009, the Ethisphere Institute, a think tank devoted to improving business practices and ethics, named Duke to its list of influential leaders, and in 2010 *Fortune* magazine ranked Wal-Mart first among retailers in a survey of most admired companies. According to Bullock, "Duke has earned [his company] the reputation as a 'Green Giant.'" In May 2010 Wal-Mart Stores Inc. reclaimed the top spot on the *Fortune* 500 list of America's largest corporations from ExxonMobil, which had taken over the spot in 2009.

Mike Duke retired from Wal-Mart in early 2014. He sits on the advisory board of several schools, including the University of Arkansas and the Tsinghua University School of Economics and Management in Beijing, China.

Duke and his wife, Susan, have two daughters.

Further Reading:

Atlanta Journal-Constitution Dec. 26, 2009
Minyanville May 28, 2010

Eyler, John

President and CEO, Toys "R" Us

Born: 1948; Seattle, Washington

In 1992, when John Eyler became president and CEO of FAO Schwarz, one of the most prestigious and well-known toy-store chains in the world, Stephanie Strom wrote in the *New York Times* (May 14, 1992) that the appointment was "something akin to being crowned king of Toyland." After an almost eight-year reign there, Eyler accepted the position as president and CEO of the industry giant Toys "R" Us, Inc. Although less upscale than FAO Schwarz, Toys "R" Us, with almost 1,500 stores, is acknowledged to be the world's largest retailer of toys, clothing, baby items, and other children's products.

Education and Early Career

Little is known about the early years of John Eyler, who was born in 1948 and graduated from Seattle's University of Washington and then received a master's of business administration from the Harvard University School of Business in Cambridge, Massachusetts. He began his retailing career at May Department Stores Co., which had been founded in 1877 with one store in the silver-mining town of Leadville, Colorado. By the time Eyler joined the company, in 1979, it had developed into a large conglomerate with several affiliates, including Hecht's and Kaufmann's.

Later Career

In 1980, at the age of 32, Eyler became the president and CEO of the Denver-area May D&F division of May Department Stores. He oversaw May D &F's stores until 1983, when he left the company to become the chairman and CEO of Main Street, the family-apparel branch of Federated Department Stores. During his six-year tenure, Main Street expanded to 27 stores with 4,000 employees and $250 million in annual sales, but the division later disbanded.

Eyler next joined the Hartmarx Corp., a clothing manufacturer that also operated 27 small retail chains, which sold a mixture of brand-name and private-label apparel and accessories. He was appointed chairman and CEO of the company's specialty-stores division. The entire firm had been suffering badly when he arrived, due to a drop in the market for men's tailored suits—a significant segment of its sales—and Eyler set out to revitalize the retail stores. In 1991, instead of mailing a conventional holiday catalog to all the customers on Hartmarx's mailing list, he had a specially made video sent to the 150,000 consumers who had purchased the most merchandise during the past year. Titled *A Picture Perfect Christmas*, the 12-minute video depicted a photogenic family and their guests, all wearing clothing from Hartmarx stores. Eyler's move was considered fairly innovative at the time, and though that holiday season was not very profitable for most of the nation's retailers, industry analysts applauded Eyler's fresh approach to slumping sales. Eyler stayed with the ailing firm for three years, until Hartmarx merged the specialty-store business with Kuppenheimer, its retail division for men's discount clothing.

On May 13, 1992 Eyler was appointed president and CEO of FAO Schwarz. "I think it's going to be sort of like a second childhood," he told Stephanie Strom. "When you look at the store environment, these are the most exciting, most playful, most fun places to shop you can find anywhere in the world." FAO Schwarz, named for its founder Frederick August Otto Schwarz, had been in business since 1870 and had established itself as one of the all-time leading retailers of specialty toys. Its flagship shop on New York City's Fifth Avenue is visited yearly by more tourists than either the Statue of Liberty or the Empire State Building. The store has been the setting for several movie scenes—perhaps most memorably in the film *Big*, when Tom Hanks's character dances on a giant piano keyboard. But it appeared to analysts as though Eyler had jumped from one floundering company to another. FAO Schwarz had been purchased by the Dutch retail group Koninklijke Bijenkorf Beheer (KBB) in 1990, and in the year before Eyler's arrival, the toy store's losses were greater than they had ever been before. Eyler blamed the poor performance on the series of owners before KBB, who had lacked sufficient capital to keep the chain competitive.

"...these are the most exciting, most playful, most fun places to shop you can find anywhere in the world."

With the support of the Dutch conglomerate, Eyler began implementing what he has called a "back to the future" policy. "It was a matter of looking at what had made FAO Schwarz great in the past--its capacity to create 'magic' for people," he told Marguerite Rigoglioso for a profile on the Harvard Business School Web site, "and restoring it to its former glory." To that end, Eyler initiated renovations of many of the chain's stores, including the one on Fifth Avenue, to which he added an elevator shaped like a huge robot. He changed the stock so that almost 70 percent of the toys were either totally exclusive to FAO Schwarz—such as the FAO Schwarz Barbie, who wore a sweatshirt bearing the store's logo—or hard to find. He decreed that rather than stock any toys on high shelves, all toys had to be displayed so that they could be readily demonstrated by specially trained sales associates or tried by customers. "The whole environment of FAO Schwarz encourages people to interact with the merchandise, not just take it off the shelf and pay for it and be out the door in 10 minutes," Eyler told Strom. "We beg our customers to play." He also announced plans to open several new stores overseas, explaining to Strom, "Around the world, everyone likes fantasy. And entering an FAO Schwarz store is making fantasy a reality."

Although Eyler kept close watch on trends in the toy industry, even FAO Schwarz was caught unaware by the popularity of the Tickle Me Elmo doll in 1996. The next year, in anticipation of a similar phenomenon, Eyler was careful to stock the New York store with 15,000 Sing and Snore Ernie dolls. He made frequent appearances at store functions, working the crowd at the opening of a new Star Wars boutique, for example, and showing up at the launch of a new line of dolls. Although FAO Schwarz's instantly recognizable name and carefully crafted image made it an undisputed marketing success, during his tenure the store posted several quarters of operating losses and diminishing profits.

When the retail giant Toys "R" Us asked Eyler to take the place of president and CEO Robert Nakasone, who had resigned unexpectedly amid dissension about the company's future direction and problems with its fledgling Web site, Eyler agreed. The company, founded in 1948, also operated a chain of children's-clothing stores called Kids "R" Us, and a separate chain of stores for baby items called Babies "R" Us. Eyler assumed his new responsibilities on January 17, 2000. At the time Toys "R" Us was facing stiff competition from the retailing behemoth Wal-Mart, and in the previous 12 months its stock prices—which had been weak for a decade—had fallen more than 25 percent. They fell even further after Eyler's appointment was announced. Some industry analysts believed that the drop stemmed from Eyler's reputation of working with losing companies. Others blamed the fact that he had been working for the most part with specialty toys rather than the mass-market items that Toys "R" Us carried.

In a statement quoted on *TheStreet.com* (January 11, 2000), Eyler said, "I look forward to working with the Toys 'R' Us family to help the company reach its potential of being the premier retailer for toys and children's products." Industry insiders agreed that Eyler's task was formidable. In addition to falling stock prices (which would plummet another 27 percent during his first quarter at the company), problems with the Web site, and increased competition from other retailers, Toys "R" Us had experienced shortages of many of the 1999 holiday season's most popular toys, such as Pokemon and Game Boy systems. Eyler immediately announced plans to expand and diversify the stores' inventory, remodel aging stores, and repair the Web site. He also initiated an IPO in Japan of shares of Toys "R" Us-Japan; with 93 stores, Toys "R" Us-Japan accounted for 10 percent of the parent company's worldwide sales. Believing Toys "R" Us stock to be undervalued given the relative strength of its brand name, Eyler also instituted a new $1 billion share-repurchase plan to buy back shares of common stock in open-market or private transactions. By March 20, 2000, according to Anne Newman in *Business Week*, the company's last earnings announcement exceeded all estimates, and she theorized that a turnaround for the company, while not assured, was at least a possibility. She quoted the investment analyst John Taylor as saying, "[Toys "R" Us] is not in damage-control mode any more." In May 2000 the chain's earnings rose for the first time in two years, a gain that Eyler attributed to better customer service and inventory control.

In *Worth* magazine (January 1994), James Kaplan described him as "gray-haired but boyish, smooth-faced, and cool-eyed…the very model of the modern young chief executive." Kaplan noted that Eyler did not "bear any resemblance to some avuncular—or even flinty with a heart of mush—ideal of a toy-store boss."

Further Reading:

Business Week Mar. 20, 2000

FAO Schwarz Web site

Harvard Business School Web site

New York Times Oct. 9, 1991; May 14, 1992

TheStreet.com Jan. 11, 2000

Worth magazine Jan. 1994

Fudge, Ann M.

Former executive, General Mills

Born: 1951; Washington, D.C.

Reaching the top echelons of corporate power in the United States has traditionally been a struggle for women and members of minority groups. One of the few who has done it is Ann M. Fudge, an African-American who has spent most of her career breaking though glass ceilings.

Education and Early Career

Born Ann Marie Brown in Washington, D.C., on April 23, 1951, Ann M. Fudge is the elder of the two children of Malcolm R. Brown, who was an administrator with the U.S. Postal Service, and Bettye (Lewis) Brown, who was a manager at the National Security Agency. Her parents impressed upon her the value of getting a good education. At the Catholic parochial schools that she attended through high school, Fudge has said that she was also motivated by nuns who taught her to always do her best. After graduating from high school, she enrolled at Simmons College, a women's school in Boston, Massachusetts. During her sophomore year, she married Richard E. Fudge, who worked as an educational and training consultant to businesses and nonprofit agencies. While still a student, she gave birth to her first son, Richard Jr. She and her husband juggled their class schedules to care for the baby and hired other students to babysit when necessary. "I paid them with food," Fudge recalled to Judith Dobrzynski. She graduated with her class in 1973 and the couple had a second son, Kevin.

Fudge's first corporate job was at General Electric in Bridgeport, Connecticut, where, for two years beginning in 1973, she worked in the human resources department. In 1975, she began studying at the Harvard University Graduate School of Business, in Cambridge, Massachusetts. After she earned an M.B.A. in 1977, she was hired by General Mills, in Minneapolis, Minnesota, as a marketing assistant. Part of her job involved the development and marketing of brand items. She was a member of the team that developed Honey Nut Cheerios, which became one of the most popular cereals in the country.

Later Career

Fudge climbed the corporate ladder quickly at General Mills. She was promoted to assistant product manager in 1978 and product manager in 1980. Then, in 1983, she was thrilled to learn that she had been named marketing director—becoming the first woman and first African-American to hold that title at General Mills. "I came home all excited," Fudge told Judith Dobrzynski in the *New York Times* (May 11, 1995), "and was telling my family, and [Kevin, who was then nine,] said, 'What's the big deal, Mom? So now instead of one brand, you have four.' He was right. My sons have helped keep things in perspective."

In 1986, Fudge left General Mills to become director of strategic planning for General Foods, a division of the Philip Morris Corp., in White Plains, New York. Three years later, she was named marketing director, and a year after that she became vice president of marketing and development. Fudge's forte as a marketer was "resuscitating older brands," as she once put it. She has been credited with breathing life into the sales of the powdered, fruit-flavored drink Kool-Aid, by launching a "Wacky Warehouse" ad campaign that invited youngsters to mail in coupons for novelty toys. She was also responsible for the manufacturing, sales, and promotions of such venerable brands as Minute Rice and Stove Top Stuffing. "Under Fudge's leadership, the division reached double-digit growth in an already tight market," Rhonda Reynolds reported in *Black Enterprise* (August 1994). Another success story was Fudge's revival of Shake 'N Bake; her team's "Why Fry?" campaign and strategy of special promotions and coupons resulted in a near doubling of sales.

In 1991 General Foods named Fudge executive vice president and general manager. Three years later, the company merged with Kraft Foods, and she became executive vice president of the new conglomerate as well as president of one of its top divisions, Maxwell House Coffee, the makers of Maxwell House, Brim, Yuban, and Sanka coffees. With responsibility for a $1.5 billion operation, Fudge had risen to a level in the corporate world "where, for women, the oxygen gets decidedly thin," Dobrzynski noted. At the time Fudge took over Maxwell House, the century-old company was facing stiff competition from specialty brands, especially Starbucks. To learn more about specialty products, Fudge spent her first days as Maxwell House president in Seattle, talking to the owners of that city's many coffee shops and sampling coffees of different flavors.

To attract younger consumers, many of whom like flavored coffee, Fudge introduced a new line of Maxwell House coffees, with such names as Irish Cream, Swiss Cocoa, and French Vanilla. Her aggressive marketing and advertising campaign included the revival of the company's once-famous "Good to the last drop" slogan. In three years, the company's earnings doubled, according to a report in *Black Enterprise* (August 1997), and Maxwell House accounted for almost a third of the U.S. coffee market. In September 1997, Fudge was promoted to executive vice president of Kraft Foods and president of the company's newly created Coffee and Cereals Division.

According to Robert S. Morrison, the former president of General Foods USA, which merged with Kraft in 1994, "As a business leader, Ann combines a very forceful personality with a great sensitivity to people. She relies heavily on a team approach to achieving business goals. Ann has positively affected every area she's been in."

"I wanted to do something that black people hadn't done before. When I hit roadblocks, that was what kept me going."

In 2003, Fudge became CEO of the "giant Young & Rubicam Brands, a global group of advertising, communications, public relations, branding, and marketing companies. She also became chair and CEO of Young & Rubicam Advertising, making her the first black woman to head a major American advertising firm." (Ashley Carr, AAUW Web site, March 31, 2009). She has since retired and now sits on numerous boards, including the Council on Foreign Relations. Fudge was a member of President Barack Obama's National Commission on Fiscal Responsibility and Reform (commonly referred to as the Simpson-Bowles commissions).

When asked about instances of racism that she had experienced or witnessed on her way up the corporate ladder, Fudge said to Dobrzynski, "I choose not to talk about it." She did reveal, however, that the riots she had lived through in Washington, D.C. after the assassination of the Reverend Martin Luther King Jr. in 1968, had been "hurtful" but ultimately motivating. "They made me incredibly determined," she said. "I wanted to do something that black people hadn't done before. When I hit roadblocks, that was what kept me going."

Further Reading:

AAUW Web site Mar. 31, 2009

Black Enterprise Aug. 1994; Aug. 1997

New York Times May 11, 1995

Who's Who in America, 1998

Gass, Michelle

Former president, Starbucks Europe, Middle East, and Africa

Born: 1968; Lewiston, Maine

CEO Howard Schultz may be the driving force behind the Seattle-based Starbucks Corporation, the world's largest coffeehouse company, but Michelle Gass was perhaps the coffee juggernaut's greatest asset. During her many years there, Gass had been responsible for orchestrating some of Starbucks's most successful ventures and for leading the company through sweeping changes.

Education and Early Career

Michelle Gass, born Michelle Petkers in 1968, grew up in Lewiston, Maine. Her parents, Bob and Claire Petkers, raised her with traditional Maine values and taught her the importance of hard work and humility. "The Maine work ethic is still deep inside me," Gass recalled to Kathryn Skelton in the *Lewiston* (Maine) *Sun Journal* (Nov. 28, 2011). After graduating from Lewiston High School as class valedictorian in 1986, she attended Worcester Polytechnic Institute (WPI) in Worcester, Massachusetts, where she studied chemical engineering.

During her time at WPI, Gass interned at Proctor & Gamble, a *Fortune* 500 company based in Cincinnati, Ohio, that specializes in the manufacturing of consumer goods. Her experience working in the research-and-development group of the company's health-care products group ultimately helped her discover her passion for working with people and her interest in consumer behavior. Gass, who had originally planned on a technical career in research and development, told Eileen McCluskey for WPI's quarterly magazine, *Transformations* (spring 2005), "I was introduced to the world of the consumer and loved it."

After receiving a degree in chemical engineering from WPI in 1990, Gass moved to Cincinnati to accept a full-time position with P&G's health-care products group. She held a variety of roles in marketing and product development over the next six years, during which she observed consumer trends and helped launch several varieties of Crest toothpaste. Gass has said that P&G allowed her to utilize both her analytical and creative skills. "P&G really sparked my curiosity—that there are real people who create real insights around better laundry detergent and toothpaste and products that people interact with every day," she explained in an interview with *Foster Business Magazine* (fall 2008), the biannual magazine of the University of Washington's Michael G. Foster School of Business. "It took my engineer's analytical bent and problem-solving mind and applied that to the customer. That's where I found my passion. And there was no turning back."

In 1996 Gass left P&G and relocated to Seattle, Washington, after her husband, engineer Scott Gass, received a business opportunity there. That year Gass returned to school, enrolling at the University of Washington, where she received her MBA in 1999. It was during her first year at the school that she starting working for Starbucks. A classmate who worked at the rapidly growing coffeehouse chain had persuaded Gass to apply for a job there, and in September 1996 she was hired as the marketing manager for the company's line of Frappuccino blended beverages. Commenting on her decision to work for the company, Gass told Kathryn Skelton, "Even though I was in a very safe place at P&G, it felt like there was something else bigger out there calling. And surely there was, little did I know, a coffee company called Starbucks."

Later Career

As marketing manager for Starbucks's Frappuccino line, a position she held until 2001, Gass was charged with developing a growth strategy for the new product. First launched in 1995 in two flavors as part of Starbucks's efforts to expand into nontraditional coffee beverages, the Frappuccino—a creamy, frozen concoction of coffee, milk, and ice—had won instant popularity among customers but had yet to tap into its growth potential. In order to realize that potential, Gass began talking with customers in Starbucks stores to understand why they were buying the drink. In her interview with *Foster Business Magazine*, she said, "The big insight was that people were not just drinking it for the coffee. They were drinking it as an indulgence."

Working with a team of three, Gass overhauled the marketing of the Frappuccino brand to reflect its perception as an indulgent novelty treat. She introduced new flavors, such as caramel, and made the drink more visually attractive to customers by adding green straws, a domed clear-plastic lid, whipped cream, and caramel-syrup drizzles. Although those changes were initially met with resistance from baristas and top-level executives who were concerned the added accoutrements would hinder operations and service, Gass refused to relaunch the product without all of the modifications. She explained to Kate Macarthur in *Advertising Age* (June 1, 2007), "If you don't do it in its full concept, then you can't have it." She added, "I'm a quantitative person, but when it comes to decisions and conviction, I'm more about passion and gut. If you take the easy road all the time, if you go with 'Squirt a little bit of syrup in it,' it might be a hit but won't be a big innovation. If we had not done that, I don't know if we'd have the Frappuccino business we have today."

"I'm a quantitative person, but when it comes to decisions and conviction, I'm more about passion and gut."

Gass's instincts proved to pay off in grand fashion. Since Frappuccino's makeover the product has become one of Starbucks's most successful products. The Frappuccino brand, which also includes a line of bottled coffee beverages sold in retail stores and vending machines, brought in more than $2.5 billion in annual sales and made up nearly a quarter of Starbucks's total annual revenue. Frappuccinos are offered in numerous flavors and versions. In addition to developing and expanding the Frappuccino brand, Gass helped launch numerous other Starbucks products, including seasonal and holiday drinks such as the pumpkin-spice latte, Black Apron Exclusives coffees, Tazo tea beverages, Ethos bottled water, and breakfast and lunch sandwiches.

Gass began earning a series of promotions, rising from vice president of the company's beverage category in 2001 to senior vice president of its category management division in 2004. In the latter role, which she held for four years, she supervised a 150-person department that was responsible for developing many of the retail offerings at Starbucks. Although some of those were flops, Gass became known for her willingness to work closely with members of her team to understand the reasons behind such failures.

That kind of urgency led Starbucks Corporation founder, chair, and CEO Howard Schultz to appoint Gass in January 2008 as senior vice president of global strategy. Responsible for much of Starbucks's global expansion, Schultz had returned to the helm that month in response to falling stock prices and sales due to a dwindling economy and increased competition. Gass was brought on board to serve as Schultz's chief strategist in a special two-person office of the CEO and began working with him on restructuring plans for the company. "Howard set the agenda, drove the vision," she told *Foster Business Magazine*. "I was there to shape the narrative, bring the entire organization around it. It was an exhilarating challenge." As part of the "Starbucks Transformation Agenda," which was highlighted by seven major initiatives, Gass and Schultz closed nine hundred Starbucks shops worldwide and reduced costs by nearly $600 million. They also launched a new advertising campaign that focused on the quality of Starbucks coffee, and in late February 2008 closed down every shop in the United States for three hours to retrain baristas as part of efforts to re-create an emotional attachment with customers. "We were courageous and disruptive," Gass told Melissa Allison for the *Seattle Times* (May 22, 2011). "I felt unleashed, with [Schultz's] energy and vision and willingness to be courageous. For someone like me who thrives on that, it was like, 'Wow! This is going to be a ride.'"

In July 2008 Gass was named executive vice president of Starbucks's marketing and category division. In that role she was in charge of overseeing the implementation of the company's other transformation initiatives, one of which was the chain's bold move into instant coffee with the launch of Starbucks VIA Ready Brew. Gass organized and led the team that helped develop the product, which underwent months of test marketing before its launch on September 12, 2009. Although the very idea of the company tapping into the instant coffee market caused skepticism—stemming from instant coffee's widespread reputation for tasting bad—Starbucks VIA Ready Brew proved to be a great success and generated $100 million in sales within ten months of its launch.

Many credited Gass, who was responsible for coming up with the more marketable "Ready Brew" name, with playing a vital role in that success. Chris Bruzzo, former online-marketing executive for Starbucks, told Jenna Goudreau, "It was audacious. It got people nervous. But it took someone like Michelle to see the opportunity and then bring an entire organization through the curve of believing." By the end of March 2011, sales of Starbucks VIA Ready Brew had exceeded $200 million.

After driving other reorganization efforts—including overhauling the company's food menu, launching its loyalty-rewards program, and strengthening its online presence—Gass was called upon by Schultz to lead Seattle's Best Coffee, a chain that had failed to gain much market traction since being acquired by Starbucks in 2003. She recalled to Goudreau, "I was drawn to it. There were no rules here. With a smaller brand in a nascent stage, I had the opportunity to create everything."

As president of Seattle's Best, a role she held from September 2009 to July 2011, Gass helped expand the chain by creating partnerships with fast-food chains such as Burger King and Subway, AMC Theaters, and Delta Airlines, thus increasing its distribution network from three thousand to more than fifty thousand locations in the United States and Canada. Gass developed a new logo and identity for the brand. She also simplified its packaged coffee business with the unveiling of Seattle's Best Coffee Levels System. Introduced in early 2011, the Levels line, which consists of five roasts differentiated by numbers and colors, proved to be a major success; by August of that year, it had experienced a double-digit increase in sales. Seattle's Best, meanwhile, also experienced double-digit sales growth under Gass. She explained to *Seattle Times* reporter Melissa Allison that one of her main goals at Seattle's Best was to "create an emotional connection around fun and optimism and a level of approachability and simplicity," in efforts to help the chain distinguish itself as a separate entity from Starbucks. Commenting on Gass's motivational influence, Chris Bruzzo told Allison, "She gets people to work stronger, harder, to be more committed and have an 'everything matters' mentality."

Describing her to Jenna Goudreau for *Forbes* (Nov. 21, 2011), Schultz called Gass "a courageous leader with a rare combination of business and interpersonal skills," and one of her collaborators, Jack Anderson, CEO of the brand-design agency Hornall Anderson, stated that she was the company's "greatest kept secret."

In June 2011 Gass was named president of Starbucks's Europe, Middle East, and Africa (EMEA) division, as part of Schultz's reorganization of top-level executives to focus on international growth. As head of Starbucks EMEA, Gass oversaw twenty thousand employees and seventeen hundred stores in more than thirty countries, where she was responsible for developing the Starbucks brand. The division makes up one of four entities of Starbucks's foreign operations (the others are Asia Pacific, Greater China, and the Americas), which bring in roughly a quarter of Starbucks's $10 billion-plus annual revenue. Starbucks executives plan to double those international revenues. In late 2011 Starbucks had over seventeen thousand stores worldwide, making it the largest coffeehouse chain in the world. Gass told Kathryn Skelton, "No matter where you go, there's a level of awareness and love of this brand. People are waiting for Starbucks to arrive." And, as quoted by Eileen McCluskey, Gass said, "I feel very proud to be associated with Starbucks. If I didn't feel absolutely impassioned about my work, I wouldn't be here."

"One of the things I strive to be is a very approachable leader, a real person," she explained to Kathryn Skelton. "I want everybody to feel very comfortable that they can talk to me about everything."

In 2013 Michelle Gass ended her long tenure at Starbucks and joined Kohl's, the nation's third-largest department-store chain. Gass was tapped to be "responsible for marketing, e-commerce and omnichannel experiences." (*Advertising Age*, May 23, 2013). Gass, according to Stacy Vogel Davis in the *Milwaukee Business Journal* (March 24, 2014), "received $1 million as a signing incentive" and "$12.1 million in compensation in her first year, putting her as the highest-paid Kohl's executive in fiscal year 2013."

Further Reading:

Advertising Age Jun. 1, 2007; May 23, 2013

Forbes Nov. 21, 2011

Foster Business Magazine fall 2008

Lewiston Sun Journal Nov. 28, 2011

Milwaukee Business Journal Mar. 24, 2014

Seattle Times May 22, 2011

Transformations spring 2005

Wall Street Journal Mar. 18, 2008

Gorman, James P.

Executive, Morgan Stanley

Born: 1958; Melbourne, Australia

In January 2010 James P. Gorman became the chief executive officer (CEO) of Morgan Stanley, one of the world's biggest financial-services companies. When he agreed to join the firm, in the summer of 2005, Morgan Stanley was perceived by some analysts as inefficient and was in reality the least profitable brokerage on Wall Street. But Gorman soon faced bigger challenges, stemming from the international economic crisis caused in large part by careless and highly risky use of various investment tools and strategies. In 2008 Morgan Stanley's stock price fell drastically, and along with several other major investment firms, the company reached the brink of collapse. But during the first three months of 2010, under his leadership, the company reported a $1.8 billion profit. Gorman has been commended for his calm, honest approach to leadership.

Education and Early Career

The sixth of the 10 children of Kevin Gorman, an engineering consultant, and Joan Gorman, James P. Gorman was born on July 14, 1958 in Australia and raised in Glen Iris and Armadale, Melbourne suburbs. In an interview with the Melbourne daily *The Age* (2005), quoted by Clive Mathieson in *The Australian* (September 12, 2009), Gorman said that as a member of such a large family, he learned tolerance, because "you have to decide whether you want to fight your whole life, or fit in. . . . Rather than fight, we talked a lot, particularly over the evening meal, where each had to contribute something specific to a designated topic for discussion. . . . That meant from an early age we were all exposed to the very full range of behaviors, personalities and political beliefs that you could ever expect to get over dinner from a family of 12 very extroverted Australians of Irish descent in Melbourne. We are competitive to a point. We all like to win but none of us particularly enjoys seeing others lose." Gorman described himself as "probably the most shy" of all the siblings.

Gorman attended Xavier College, an all-boys Roman Catholic high school in Kew, another Melbourne suburb, and after his graduation enrolled at the University of Melbourne, where he received a bachelor's of law degree in 1982. He then worked as an insurance litigator at the law firm Phillips Fox & Masel (now called DLA Phillips Fox), in Melbourne. "Those were hectic years" for him, Leonie Wood wrote for *The Age* (October 20, 2001), referring to the large number of lawsuits that followed the devastating, wind-driven bushfires that broke out in Victoria on February 16, 1983 (known ever since in Australia as Ash Wednesday) after a long drought; 75 people died and thousands of homes and huge swathes of forest burned. Since a large number of the fires were traced to electricity power lines' coming in contact with trees or with one another, many of the suits were filed against the State Electricity Commission. Gorman first worked to defend the commission against individual claims and then represented the commission in its attempt to gain compensation from its insurers.

"Absorbed as he was by the intellectual challenge of law," Wood wrote, "Gorman found he had developed a taste for business management, and craved a leadership role." Gorman decided to study business and in 1985 moved to New York City, where he attended the Columbia University Graduate School of Business. He welcomed instruction from businessmen as well as professors. "If you want to be a financier, it's the place," Gorman told

Wood. "I didn't want to just learn; I wanted to enjoy the whole New York world-experience." Gorman received his M.B.A. in 1987.

Later Career

That year Gorman joined the international management-consulting firm McKinsey & Co. as an intern. In 1992 he was made a partner and was named co-head of the North America division of personal financial services. He served as chairman of the New York personnel operating committee from 1996 to 1999 and concurrently, for two years starting in 1997, as both a member of the partner election committee and a senior partner. Earlier, in 1990, he had taken on Merrill Lynch & Co. as one of his clients, and in time he took charge of the whole Merrill Lynch account. During his time with McKinsey, Gorman lived at various times in countries including Mexico, Germany, Japan, China, England, and France, as well as the U.S.

In 1999, when David H. Komansky, then the CEO of Merrill Lynch, recruited him, Gorman already had a detailed knowledge of the firm's strengths and weaknesses. His first position at Merrill Lynch was that of executive vice president and chief marketing officer. His responsibilities included developing the firm's Internet-initiated business. A joint venture for online banking and investment he negotiated with HSBC proved to be unprofitable and ended in 2002. Earlier, in 2001, Gorman had been appointed head of the U.S. private-client group, a branch of the brokerage division, which was headed by E. Stanley O'Neal, Merrill's CEO. His promotion raised some eyebrows among his colleagues, because Gorman's expertise was in marketing and advising; he had never worked as a broker. Over the next two years, as a cost-cutting measure, he closed one-fourth of the company's retail branches. He also fired one-third of Merrill Lynch's brokers, retaining those whose clients invested the greatest amounts. In shifting the firm's focus to wealthier clients, he ruled that calls from investors whose accounts totaled $100,000 or less must be shunted to call centers. In 2002 Gorman was appointed head of Merrill's global private-client group, a position in which he managed the firm's 14,000 financial advisers. According to the Morgan Stanley Web site, under Gorman's leadership from 2002 to 2004, the global private-client group more than doubled its pretax profits and "led the industry in terms of revenue and profits per broker."

In the summer of 2005, John J. Mack—who had returned to Morgan Stanley a few weeks earlier as CEO and chairman after an absence of four years—asked Gorman to leave Merrill Lynch and join Morgan Stanley. Mack had been with the firm from 1972 until 2001; that year, after holding the post of president for seven years, he left in the wake of a fierce power struggle that followed Morgan Stanley's 1997 merger with Dean Witter Reynolds, another major brokerage house, and Discover Inc., Sears Roebuck's financial-services spin-off. Landon Thomas Jr. wrote for the *New York Times* (July 1, 2005) that Mack's recruitment of Gorman represented "his first substantial hiring of an executive who had no previous ties to him. More important, it signals to investors and the firm's employees that Mr. Mack is committed to turning the much maligned business around, as opposed to just sprucing it up for a quick disposal." Gorman came on board as president and chief operating officer of Morgan Stanley's individual-investment group in February 2006, after his contractual obligations to Merrill Lynch ended.

As president of Morgan Stanley, Mack had been dubbed "Mack the Knife," for his "cost-cutting prowess and obsessive focus on efficiency," Kamelia Angelova wrote for *Business Insider* (September 14, 2009). When he returned, Morgan Stanley was the least profitable of Wall Street's major brokerage houses. In his first two months as CEO and chairman, he laid off about 10 percent of the company's brokers whom he considered to be underperforming. Gorman too promptly fired 500 brokers who he believed showed little promise, and he replaced 27 of the top 30 managers.

Within months the effects of those changes were palpable. "By the spring, Mack was starting to see signs of progress," Emily Thornton wrote for *BusinessWeek* (July 2, 2006). "Gorman was making real strides in overhauling the retail brokerage business." In particular, Gorman had begun laying off an additional 700 employees and set about changing numerous aspects of day-to-day business, from the training of brokers to customer statements. Among other moves, he also instructed his team to attract wealthy clients through new investment initiatives and expanded the company's services with regard to retail banking and small-business lending programs. But there were also problems: The firm, Graham Bowley wrote for the *New York Times* (January 16, 2010), was engaged in too much high-risk trading and "factional disputes and internal debates over strategy." Furthermore, Bowley wrote, "Under Mr. Mack, Morgan Stanley made errant mortgage bets and commercial property gambles that cost it billions of dollars and almost destroyed it." The company survived in large part because of funds from Asian investors and $10 billion from the U.S. government (a portion of its October 2008 financial-bailout package). In the summer of 2009, Gorman coordinated Morgan Stanley's acquisition of 51 percent of Citigroup Inc.'s wealth-management firm Smith Barney (for $2.75 billion), which made Morgan Stanley Smith Barney—with its 20,000 financial advisers—one of the world's biggest wealth-management firms.

"...You have to decide," as a member of a large family, "whether you want to fight your whole life, or fit in. . . . Rather than fight, we talked a lot, particularly over the evening meal, where each had to contribute something specific to a designated topic for discussion. . . . That meant from an early age we were all exposed to the very full range of behaviors, personalities and political beliefs..."

As Morgan Stanley's CEO, Mack engaged in risky financial activities, in part to keep up with Goldman Sachs and its other competitors. In 2006 he was suspected by the Securities and Exchange Commission of insider trading with his former employer, Pequot Capital Management, but no official charges were filed. Between 2005 and the fall of 2009, when Mack announced that he would be stepping down as CEO, the value of the company's stock fell more than 30 percent. Despite the firm's extensive risk-taking, in the summer of 2009 Mack attributed Morgan Stanley's near-collapse to its being too cautious.

On January 1, 2010 Gorman became the company's CEO. He was unanimously selected by the board, not only for his intellect but also for his calm, thoughtful temperament. (John Mack stayed on as company chairman.) Speaking to Bowley, Gorman acknowledged that Morgan Stanley had "periods of management turmoil" and "misplaced trading positions." The immediate focus, he said, would be well-grounded advisory services for clients, not big, risky trading. But as Bowley pointed out, Gorman and his firm had a huge task ahead. "Some analysts remain tentative about Morgan Stanley's prospects in a financial landscape littered with corporate wreckage and dominated by a handful of wily survivors. While the firm's traditional investment banking franchise has emerged strongly from the crisis—topping JPMorgan and Goldman in some of its businesses—it has shrunk its fixed-income division and taken piles of money off the table in its broader institutional securities business." In January 2010 Morgan Stanley reported its second annual loss—the second fiscal year during which it did not make a net profit. However, it had earned profits during the last two quarters of 2009.

Gorman expressed his displeasure with the firm's overall performance in 2009. With the new year some good news came: During the first three months of 2010, Morgan Stanley reported a profit of $1.8 billion. Under his leadership as CEO, Gorman has sought to reduce the company's general risk levels. Overall, there was notable growth (for example, in its asset-management business) and some big losses (among others, a $932 million loss on an abandoned casino-hotel project). In the second quarter of 2010, Morgan Stanley reported a profit of $1.4 billion. According to Antony Currie and Rob Cox, writing for the *New York Times* (July 22, 2010), what made the firm stand out among its competitors was Gorman's traders, who showed "greater resilience" than traders at, for example, Citigroup and JPMorgan Chase. Currie and Cox added: "By sidestepping the latest trading pitfalls, Mr. Gorman showed admirable restraint. He didn't give in to the all-too-common Wall Street temptation of chasing the outsize results of rivals. That should give shareholders comfort that the firm's 18-month-old pledge to keep risk in check is more than just talk."

The six-foot two-inch Gorman is "cerebral, circumspect and analytical," according to Bowley. Gorman and his wife, Penny, have two teenage children.

Further Reading:

The Australian Sept. 12, 2009

Bloomberg.com Sept. 11, 2009

The (Melbourne, Australia) *Age* Oct. 20, 2001

Business Insider Sept. 14, 2009

BusinessWeek Jul. 2, 2006

Morganstanley.com

New York Times Jul. 1, 2005; Aug. 17, 2005, Jan. 16, 2010; Jul. 22, 2010

Gorman, Leon A.

Former president, L. L. Bean

Born: 1934; Nashua, New Hampshire

One day, more than 100 years ago, Leon Leonwood Bean, an outdoorsman from Freeport, Maine, got fed up with returning from his fishing and hunting expeditions with his feet sodden and aching from the heavy leather hunting boots that he wore for such activities, and so he decided to make a better boot by combining lightweight leather with thick rubber soles that would keep his feet dry. Before long, he had sold 100 pairs to like-minded men through the mail—and thus was born L. L. Bean, which he launched as a mail-order company in 1912. Eventually, many of those first boots were returned because the stitching had given out. Not easily discouraged, Bean refunded his customers' money and set to work to improve the quality of his boots. This is the origin of L. L. Bean's guarantee of 100 percent customer satisfaction, still in effect today, which allows customers to return products for any reason, no matter how long ago they were purchased. By 1917, so many visitors were coming to Bean's workshop in Freeport to buy his boots that he decided to open a showroom, which became the L. L. Bean retail store. He eventually added more products to his line; by the early 1950s, the catalog had become well known and the company eventually gained true iconic status.

Education and Early Career

Bean's grandson, Leon Gorman, was born in 1934 and attended Bowdoin College in Maine, later serving in the military on a U.S. Navy destroyer. He started working at his grandfather's company in 1961, after a job as a trainee at a Boston branch of the department-store chain Filene's. When Bean died in 1967, the ownership of his business was split equally among his children and grandchildren, creating about 15 principal shareholders. Phyllis Austin, a reporter for the *Maine Times*, said of the Bean family, as quoted by *Forbes* (July 6, 1992), "They are ordinary, old-fashioned people with ordinary jobs. None of them is showy and many of them are eccentric or extremely timid." Gorman was the only one who was interested in running L. L. Bean, and he took over as president.

Later Career

While the company was doing well enough, it had stopped growing in the 1950s. In an article that appeared in *Forbes*, Gorman said that when he arrived at the business, "L. L. was quite old and there wasn't much vigor in the company. Fifty percent of our product line was obsolete." Gorman saw opportunity in the increased interest in outdoor recreation that was sweeping the country, and so he added new products and started using lighter materials and improving the quality of existing items. He also introduced Christmas and summer catalogs, in addition to the ones for spring and fall, and began renting other companies' mailing lists to broaden his customer base. Mail-order sales, which accounted for the bulk of L. L. Bean's revenues, grew an average of 24.5 percent every year between 1974 and 1979. By 1980, the company was receiving 2.2 million mail orders and 500,000 telephone orders yearly for items from the catalog, and the profit margin was averaging 6 percent after taxes—unusually high for a retailer, according to industry specialists. And between 1981 and 1988, revenues rose 20 percent a year, on average. The

Bean family made numerous appearances on the *Forbes* 400 list of the richest Americans, having amassed a net worth of about $500 million.

Another reason the company thrived throughout this period is that Gorman made sure the company retained its commitment to customer service. For example, the company employed workers who repaired L. L. Bean products. Reportedly, customers have been known to use their Bean purchases for decades; among them are owners of Bean boots who have had the company resole them three times. Refunds are made with no questions asked, even if the item being returned appears to have been worn. The company even stocks buttons for the items that they sell, sending them to customers free of charge upon request. L. L. Bean also has customer-service experts who deal with special inquiries, such as which boots would be best for a hiking trip, or for a customer with extra-large feet. Most products are marked up only 70 percent, well below the industry average of 100 percent. For many years, the company's generous return policy and low prices were possible because it kept its inventory limited, offering relatively few styles and colors.

The company also retained its longstanding policy of having hunters, fishermen, climbers, and outdoor guides test its products. Gorman himself was a graduate of Outward Bound, an organization that offers trips on which participants learn self-reliance and wilderness survival skills, and he was also an avid cyclist, skier, and outdoorsman who took up hiking when he joined L. L. Bean. After skiing a 29-mile trail through the Colorado Rockies in 1994, he turned in five pages of notes to the company's product manager, commenting on the snow build-up in his boot bindings and the fit of his ski pants, among other things. Gorman also required that his marketing staff and other employees participated in outdoor sports. The company conducted clinics in cross-country skiing, canoeing, and other activities. One longtime marketing director displayed the spoils of his hunting expeditions—the heads of a white Dall sheep and a mule deer—above his desk.

After two decades of solid growth, the company took a downward turn that began in the late 1980s. In 1989, L. L. Bean's growth slowed drastically to 3 percent; the company stagnated in 1990, and over the next two years was forced to lay off 200 of its 3,500 hourly workers. Its failure to grow stemmed partly from a recession in retailing, and partly from its traditional way of doing business. Unlike its competitors, L. L. Bean had not charged customers for shipping, making the company vulnerable to continually rising postal and trucking rates. In the early 1990s, it changed this policy (still charging less than other mail-order retailers, however). Another problem was that L. L. Bean's products were so durable; the classic clothing and footwear that customers owned didn't need to be replaced often. In addition, Gorman had been forced to expand the traditionally limited inventory to spark the interest of customers who already owned L. L. Bean staples, and attract younger, more trend-conscious buyers.

"We've no intention of being the hottest or trendiest. The soundest strategy is to be more like L. L. Bean."

At the same time that the company was expanding its inventory and growth was slowing, customer returns suddenly jumped to 14 percent of products sold, up from a usual 5 percent. Competition was also getting more fierce from mail-order companies such as Eddie Bauer, J. Crew, and Lands' End, which were targeting markets for outdoor clothing and activewear that had traditionally belonged to L. L. Bean. The company was also having difficulties expanding its mailing list. At 15 million names, Bean's list was already one of the world's largest, and any new mailing list the company purchased inevitably overlapped it.

Gorman decided to combat these problems by reinforcing L. L. Bean's ties to sports and outdoor activities. He created positions for experts in skiing, biking, and fly-fishing to answer customers' questions about products over the phone. To limit inventory, he discontinued some of the company's dress clothes and its special women's clothing catalog. By having managers focus on either products or business operations, he made it possible for product managers to spend more time with customers and manufacturers. He has worked to cut costs by making catalog mailings more efficient and also expanded into foreign markets as well.

By the time Gorman stepped down in 2013, he had transformed his grandfather's company into "a multi-channel marketer with more than $1.5 billion in revenue, 5,000 employees and a globally known brand" (*Bangor* [Maine] *Daily News*, May 20, 2013). J. Craig Anderson, writing in the *Portland* (Maine) *Press Herald*, reported that the company's"220-square-foot retail campus in Freeport is open 24 hours a day, 365 days a year, and has more than 3 million visitors annually." Gorman is reportedly the richest single individual in the state of Maine. "We've no intention of being the hottest or trendiest," Leon Gorman said to *Business Week* (December 18, 1994). "The soundest strategy is to be more like L. L. Bean."

Further Reading:

Bangor Daily News May 20, 2013

Business Week Dec. 19, 1994

Contemporary Newsmakers, 1987 (Peter M. Gareffa, ed.)

Forbes July 6, 1992

New York Times Aug. 31, 1980

Portland Press Herald May 20, 2013

Selected Books:

Gorman, Leon. *L.L. Bean: The Making of an American Icon* (Boston: Harvard Business School Publications, 2006).

Ivey, Susan M.

President, Reynolds American, Inc.

Born: 1958; Schenectady, New York

As president, chief executive officer, and chairwoman of Reynolds American Inc., Susan M. Ivey is one of only 15 women leading companies included on the 2009 *Fortune* 500 list of the nation's top corporations. She has spent nearly three decades in the tobacco industry, working her way up from a job as a sales representative in Kentucky. "People ask me how it feels to be a woman CEO," Ivey told Edward Martin for *Business North Carolina* magazine (April 2005). "I say I don't know, because I have no idea what it feels like to be a male CEO."

Education and Early Career

Born Susan Marie Hickok on October 31, 1958 in Schenectady, New York, Ivey was raised in Fort Lauderdale, Florida. Her father, Allan Hickok, worked as a manager for the General Electric Co., while her mother, Harriett (Mathis) Hickok, was a part-time secretary and school volunteer. Ivey graduated in 1976 from Fort Lauderdale High School, where she was voted "most likely to succeed," then enrolled at the University of Tennessee at Knoxville. Soon deciding to return to her home state, she transferred to the University of Florida at Gainesville, where she earned a B.S. in marketing in 1980. Shortly afterward Ivey followed her then-boyfriend to Louisville, Kentucky. To make ends meet she sold office supplies. "I hated it," she told Brian Lewis for the *Winston-Salem* (North Carolina) *Journal* (November 16, 2003), "because I had no affinity for the product category whatsoever."

Six months later, in 1981, Ivey began working in the tobacco industry by chance, after she was unable to obtain a carton of Barclay Menthol cigarettes—her favorite brand—which were manufactured by Brown & Williamson. "I couldn't find them anywhere, so I called [Brown & Williamson marketing officials] and they told me that they couldn't find a distributor for them locally," Ivey told Brent Adams in an article that appeared in the Louisville, Kentucky *Business First* (November 15, 2002). "They asked me if I would be interested in coming on board as a trade marketing representative, and that's how it all started. Believe it or not, I'm still smoking those cigarettes today." As a trade marketing representative, Ivey distributed cigarettes to retail outlets in Kentucky's Jefferson and Bullitt Counties. In 1983 she was promoted to district sales manager.

Ivey continued her education at Bellarmine University (then Bellarmine College) in Louisville, earning an M.B.A. in 1987. She had worked her way up to become the Far East marketing director at B&W when, in 1990, Brown & Williamson's parent company—British American Tobacco—offered her a position as brand director in London, where the company was headquartered.

Later Career

With only a day to decide, Ivey accepted, serving in that post until 1994. She then moved to Hong Kong (now part of China), to become director of marketing for British American Tobacco. After two years she moved back to London to become manager of international brands for Brown & Williamson. She married an Englishman, Trevor Ivey, in 1997. "There was a period from 1994 to 1997 where I didn't think I'd ever come back to the States," Ivey told Adams. "I had gotten married . . . and I was content living abroad."

Nonetheless, Brown & Williamson lured Ivey back to the U.S. in 1999, when they offered her the position of senior vice president of marketing, as well as a spot on the company's executive committee. She returned to Louisville, where she was charged with promoting the company's cigarette brands, including Kool, Pall Mall, Lucky Strike, Capri, Barclay, Raleigh, and Viceroy. In November 2000 Brown & Williamson's CEO, Nick Brookes, and president, Earl Kohnhorst, announced their intentions to leave the company at the end of the year. Ivey was named to both posts, effective January 2001, becoming the first woman ever to run a major U.S. tobacco company.

"People ask me how it feels to be a woman CEO. I say I don't know, because I have no idea what it feels like to be a male CEO."

Ivey took the helm at a time when Brown & Williamson was working to reduce its workforce and attract a larger number of consumers. The third-largest tobacco company in the nation at the time, it had suffered in previous years from a series of lawsuits. Brown & Williamson had come under fire in 1994 when it was discovered that the company had worked with a biotechnology firm, DNA Plant Technology Corp., to develop a genetically engineered tobacco plant, nicknamed Y-1, with twice the amount of nicotine found in other tobacco. When Congress investigated the matter, then-CEO Thomas Sandefur promised that the company would stop using genetically altered tobacco, though he denied manipulating nicotine levels. (Tobacco companies continue to dispute the fact, which is otherwise universally accepted, that nicotine is highly addictive.) It was discovered four years later that Brown & Williamson had continued to use the engineered tobacco in three of their cigarette brands and that Y-1 was being grown in Brazil and shipped into the U.S. In January 1998, during a government investigation into the tobacco industry, the DNA Plant Technology Corp. pleaded guilty to conspiring to grow high-nicotine tobacco abroad secretly so that Brown & Williamson could increase nicotine levels in its cigarettes. Brown & Williamson, however, denied that it had conspired secretly to manipulate nicotine levels in its products. Despite cooperation by DNA Plant Technology Corp. during the investigation, charges were never filed against Brown & Williamson. The following year, however, the Food and Drug Administration (FDA) filed suit against the tobacco industry, claiming that since the agency has the authority to regulate drugs, it should have the legal right to regulate cigarettes and smokeless-tobacco products, since they contain nicotine, an addictive substance. The 1999 U.S. Supreme Court case *Food and Drug Administration v. Brown & Williamson Tobacco Corp.* was the culmination of years of court battles between the FDA and the tobacco industry. (*Brown & Williamson* was the only company named in the FDA's lawsuit, due to its association with Y-1.) On March 21, 2000 the Supreme Court voted 5-4 in the tobacco industry's favor, ruling that the FDA did not have the jurisdiction to regulate tobacco products under the Food, Drug, and Cosmetic Act. The FDA, responsible for allowing only products they deem safe and healthy in the marketplace, had asserted that if tobacco products—which the FDA views as dangerous— were within its jurisdiction, the agency would ban the products entirely. That assertion, together with Congress's having passed several laws in recent years regulating tobacco—thus showing no intention to ban the product—shaped the decision by the Court, which judged that the FDA sought to overstep the authority it had been given by Congress. (In June 2009, however, President Barack

Obama signed the Family Smoking Prevention and Tobacco Control Act, which grants the FDA permission to regulate tobacco products but not ban them entirely.)

Prior to the Supreme Court case, Brown & Williamson, along with the three other top cigarette companies—Philip Morris USA, R.J. Reynolds, and Lorillard Tobacco Co.—agreed to pay a total of $206 billion to 46 states through the year 2025 as part of the Tobacco Master Settlement Agreement (MSA), adopted in November 1998. The settlement was reached after several court battles between the states and tobacco companies over who was responsible for the cost of smoking-related health care. (The four states not included in the MSA—Florida, Minnesota, Mississippi, and Texas—had already reached similar deals with the companies in the preceding year.) In addition to the monetary compensation, the tobacco industry agreed to invest money in anti-smoking campaigns, particularly ones aimed at youth, and to limit the marketing of their products. (Tobacco advertisements on billboards, apparel, and all forms of transportation were banned as part of the deal.)

The legal battles were part of the reason Ivey had been reluctant to return to the U.S. "I . . . had been watching the litigation craze and the court battles over limited personal responsibility in the U.S., and I was really apprehensive about what was happening," she told Adams. "I thought the whole place had gone mad." In an effort to compensate for the damage to sales after the MSA, Philip Morris and R.J. Reynolds heavily discounted their cigarettes. Brown & Williamson, which was not in a position to do so, saw its sales dip. When competition within the industry intensified and cost-cutting became a priority, R.J. Reynolds, the second-largest U.S. tobacco company at the time, struck a deal with British American Tobacco PLC in July 2004 to acquire Brown & Williamson for $4.1 billion. Together, R.J. Reynolds and Brown & Williamson created a new publicly traded parent company, Reynolds American Inc. (British American Tobacco received a 42 percent stake in the new company.) After the merger, Reynolds American controlled about 30 percent of the tobacco market. (Altria Group, which owns Philip Morris, continues to hold the top spot, with 50 percent of the market.)

Ivey was named president and CEO of the new company, based in Winston-Salem, North Carolina. She made it clear to Edward Martin that her appointment was entirely due to her experience. "I'd spent 23 years in the industry and been successful as CEO of Brown & Williamson," she said. "In no way was it a gender-based decision."

"It is a real accomplishment to be a woman in this position, but the thing that drives me is my desire to see the company succeed," Ivey told Brent Adams. "A lot of employees and their families rely on the decisions I make, and as someone who has worked her way from the ground up, I want to see things [in the tobacco industry] turn around."

Reynolds American employed more than 6,600 people and is the parent company of R.J. Reynolds Tobacco Co., American Snuff Co. LLC, Niconovum AB, and Santa Fe Natural Tobacco Co. Inc. The second-largest tobacco company in the U.S., R.J. Reynolds produces five of the nation's 10 top-selling cigarette brands: Camel, Kool, Pall Mall, Doral, and Winston. American Snuff (formerly Conwood Co.) is the second-largest manufacturer of smokeless tobacco products in the U.S., and Santa Fe Natural manufactures Natural American Spirit additive-free tobacco products.

Reynolds American acquired Conwood for $3.5 billion in May 2006. Citing 4 to 5 percent growth over the past five years in smokeless-tobacco products—which include chewing tobacco and snuff—due to smoking bans in public areas, Ivey stated, "We are excited about the growth prospects Conwood brings to Reynolds

American. Conwood's strong, well-positioned brands are gaining share in the growing moist snuff market, and its high margins will enhance our ability to continue to provide an excellent return to our shareholders."

The following year Reynolds American garnered some criticism for launching a new line of cigarettes aimed at women. Given the slogan "Light and luscious," the brand, Camel No. 9, came in fuchsia and teal packaging. Anti-smoking advocates were angered by Camel No. 9's aggressive marketing campaign, which included advertisements in several women's magazines, such as *Cosmopolitan* and *Glamour*, and lavish parties in bars and clubs that offered women sample cigarettes, massages, and take-home gift bags. Though Reynolds American officials said they were careful to gear their message toward adults, critics argued that their tactics were aimed at younger people as well.

In 2010 Ivey unexpectedly announced that she would be retiring as chairwoman of Reynolds American Inc. at the end of October; Thomas C. Wajnert was named as her replacement. And just as suddenly, Ivey—who remarried and now goes by the name Susan Cameron—returned to the helm in 2014. Shortly after her return, Patricia Sellers wrote in the October 6, 2014 *Fortune* that "Reynolds announced its plan to buy Lorillard [tobacco] for $27.4 billion. The deal is history-making, and not just for its size: It is the largest acquisition ever led by a female CEO."

Ivey, who is reported to have earned $8.8 million in 2008, has been named many times to *Forbes*'s list of the "100 Most Powerful Women in Business" and *Fortune*'s "50 Most Powerful Women in Business." She has long been an active member of the United Way; she is currently a member of the Women's Leadership Initiative for the United Way of America. Ivey is also a member of the Committee of 200, an international organization of female business leaders who provide mentoring, education, and support for aspiring female business executives, and she is on the board of trustees of Salem College, a private liberal-arts institution for women in Winston-Salem. In 2007 she created the Susan Ivey Professorship, an endowed chair, at the University of Florida's Warrington College of Business Administration.

Further Reading:

Business North Carolina Apr. 2005

(Louisville, Kentucky) *Business First* Nov. 15, 2002

Reynoldsamerican.com

Winston-Salem (North Carolina) *Journal* Nov. 16, 2003; Oct. 16, 2010

Kamprad, Ingvar

Founder, IKEA

Born: 1926; Pjatteryd, Sweden

The Swedish company IKEA, which sells home furnishings, is a global phenomenon, with megastores spread throughout the world. IKEA is the brainchild of Ingvar Kamprad, who founded the company in 1943, when he was just 17, by selling pens and other small items out of his home. Kamprad developed his company with the idea of providing affordable quality furnishings to the masses. He has accomplished that mission with notable success, and in the process, has influenced other retailers with his innovative approach to retailing.

Education and Early Career

Ingvar Kamprad was born in 1926 in Pjatteryd, a town in Almhult, a district in Sweden. He was raised on his family's farm, Elmtaryd, in the small village of Agunnaryd, in the portion of southeastern Sweden known as Smaland. His high school was "what I guess you would call a trade school," he told Claudia Dreifus for the *New York Times Magazine* (April 6, 1997). "And it was there that I started to be interested in the way factories turn out products for the consumer." In 1943, with his father's help, Kamprad established his own company, through which he sold matches, ballpoint pens, and other sundries. To name it, he combined his first and last initials with the first letters of "Elmtaryd" and "Agunnaryd," and thus came up with the acronym IKEA.

Later Career

Some years later, Kamprad traveled outside Sweden for the first time: He went to Paris, at the invitation of IKEA's ballpoint-pen supplier. The trip inspired him to expand his business through advertisements in local newspapers and a primitive mail-order catalog. In 1950, Kamprad began selling locally manufactured home furnishings through his nascent mail-order business. Before long, encouraged by positive customer response, he became a furniture vendor on a much larger scale. In 1951, the first official IKEA catalog was published, and Kamprad soon discontinued all products except low-priced furniture.

Kamprad opened the first IKEA furniture showroom in Almhult in 1953. In 1961, at the suggestion of his designers, he adopted the concept of customer-assembled furniture. Such furniture would be shipped unassembled in flat packages, rather than in finished form in large, cumbersome crates. By reducing his shipping and storage costs, Kamprad could keep retail prices lower than could his competitors. Over the next three decades, IKEA continued to expand. Showrooms opened in Australia, Canada, Singapore, France, Iceland, and the Netherlands, among other places. In 1985, the first IKEA store in the U.S. opened, outside Philadelphia. By 1994, IKEA was operating 125 stores in 26 countries and employing 25,000 people. Total sales were $4.7 billion.

Kamprad's success has been attributed to many factors. First, there is his zeal as a provider of affordable furniture. In *Forbes* (March 21, 1988), Peter Fuhrman reported that in a description of the IKEA company philosophy that was issued to all senior company executives, Kamprad wrote, "Too many new and beautifully designed products can be afforded by only a small group of better-off people. We have decided to side with the many."

Kamprad was also known for being extremely cost-conscious. To get to airports, he took public transportation, and neither he nor IKEA executives flew first-class. Today, as Sam Webb wrote in the U.K. *Daily Mail* newspaper (March 29, 2013), "the founder of global juggernaut IKEA lives in an unassuming bungalow, favors the meatballs sold by his stores and only ever flies economy class, even though he could own a private jet without it even denting his personal fortune."

Innovation is another key to Kamprad's success. One of his innovations was to drastically reduce the number of salespeople on the floor of a typical IKEA store. Without any salesperson hovering nearby, a shopper may simply wander about, trying out, say, various chairs or couches. After making a selection, within a short time that same day, the merchandise—unassembled, in flat boxes—is ready to be picked up from the shipping department. There are unquestionably inconveniences associated with the dearth of salespeople and the job of assembling the furniture oneself, but low prices make them palatable. Kamprad's stores also feature facilities designed to make shopping easier and more pleasant. There are lockers for public use, bathrooms, an in-store restaurant, and even a play area dubbed the "ballroom," where parents can leave their children while shopping. The store in Almhult even boasts a hotel, complete with swimming pool and sauna. "We want to make it easy for young families to get their homes started," Kamprad told Claudia Dreifus. "Or, put another way, we do nothing to stop people from buying from us."

Another of Kamprad's distinguishing characteristics is his foresight. Apparently anticipating the ever-increasing population flight to the suburbs, he placed his stores in vast suburban lots, away from urban shopping districts but near major thoroughfares. The typical IKEA store lies on the outskirts of a major city and is easily accessible from a major expressway. Its trademark facade—with stripes of blue and yellow, the colors of the Swedish flag—beckons all who drive past.

"Too many new and beautifully designed products can be afforded by only a small group of better-off people. We have decided to side with the many."

In keeping with his reputation for prescience, Kamprad has made preparations to ensure that his brainchild will continue to thrive even after he is gone. In 1982, to limit "death duties"—estate taxes that would be levied at the time of his death—he transferred ownership of IKEA to a private foundation based in the Netherlands. And in 1986, he stepped down as president of IKEA and appointed as his successor Anders Moberg, a 37-year-old who had joined IKEA at 19, immediately after high school. To ensure that his vision carried into the future, Kamprad prepared a written record of his corporate philosophy. Not surprisingly, one of Kamprad's directives in the text, known as "Instructions for the Future," was "No effort shall be spared to keep the price picture down." Even though Kamprad is no longer president of IKEA, he has continued to play an active role in the running of the company.

Kamprad's image was tarnished in November 1994, when a Stockholm newspaper, *Expressen*, reported their discovery of Kamprad's name in the archives of Per Engdahl, a Swedish ultra-rightist and pro-Nazi activist who had died. The archives revealed that Kamprad had contacts with Engdahl's pro-Nazi group between 1942 and 1950 and had befriended Engdahl himself. According to a profile by the *London Observer* (November 13, 1994), Kamprad responded to the allegations by sending to IKEA employees worldwide a letter in which he called the alleged activities "a part of my life which I bitterly regret." Describing his association with Engdahl as "the most stupid mistake of my life" and one of "the sins of my childhood and youth," he explained that he had, in part, been influenced by his grandmother, a German who had fled the Sudetenland in Czechoslovakia before World War II, and been drawn to Engdahl's vision of a "non-Communist, Socialist Europe." The revelations about his activities during the 1940s reportedly dampened IKEA's business little, if at all.

In 2013, the British *Telegraph* newspaper reported that Kamprad, who "left Sweden in the 1970s in protest at the country's high taxes, setting up residence in Switzerland," was returning to his homeland. "Moving back to Sweden," Kamprad said, "gets me closer to my family and my old friends. After my dear wife… died about a year and half ago, there is less that keeps me in Switzerland."

Further Reading:

Daily Mail Mar. 29, 2013

Forbes Mar. 21, 1988; Jul. 22, 1991

(London) *Observer* Nov. 13, 1994

New York Times Nov. 9, 1994

New York Times Magazine Apr. 6, 1997

Telegraph Jun. 26, 2013

Time Jul. 27, 1987

Kanter, Rosabeth Moss

Management consultant; writer; educator

Born: 1943; Cleveland, Ohio

"In a sense, the theme of all my work has been how we have to break down categories and boxes, and create better connections that allow people to move freely between the different parts of their lives," Rosabeth Moss Kanter told Susan McHenry in an interview for *Ms.* magazine (January 1985). "That's what I've always wanted personally, too, because I never felt I fit neatly into anybody's category; I cut across so many." As a sociologist, professor, consultant, and writer, Kanter brings a fresh, multidisciplinary perspective to the study of organizations.

Education and Early Career

Born on March 15, 1943 in Cleveland, Ohio, Rosabeth Moss Kanter is the daughter of Nelson Nathan Moss, an attorney and small-business owner, and Helen (Smolen) Moss, a teacher. After graduating from Cleveland Heights High School in 1960, Kanter enrolled at Bryn Mawr College in Pennsylvania, where she majored in sociology and minored in English literature. From 1962 to 1963 she attended the University of Chicago as a "special student." On June 15, 1963 she married Stuart A. Kanter (who died in 1969), and she graduated magna cum laude in 1964 from Bryn Mawr, with a bachelor's degree in sociology. While working toward her master's degree (awarded in 1965) at the University of Michigan at Ann Arbor, she specialized in social organization and completed a minor specialization in social psychology. Two years later she successfully defended a doctoral dissertation at the same institution. While completing her education, she worked at the university from 1965 to 1967, first as a research assistant, then as a teaching fellow, and ultimately as an instructor in sociology.

Later Career

Combining the research she had performed for her doctoral dissertation—on 19th-century utopian societies—with five years of intermittent communal living and further research, Kanter wrote her first book, *Commitment and Community: Communes and Utopias in Sociological Perspective* (1972). While teaching sociology as an assistant professor at Brandeis University in Waltham, Massachusetts from 1967 to 1973, she had visited numerous communes and had participated in several social experiments, among them Cumbres, a personal-growth community in New Hampshire; the Cambridge Institute New Cities Project, whose goal was to design and build an urban-style commune—a "new city"—in rural Vermont (a goal that was never realized); and the NTL Institute in Bethel, Maine. Drawing on those experiences and on the results of a questionnaire completed by the members of 20 communes, she sought in *Commitment and Community* to explain why certain communal and utopian experiments have either succeeded or failed. Viewing these living environments as large-scale social-science "laboratories," Kanter wrote in her preface to the book that "the study of utopian communities in America can. . . contribute to the understanding of social life in general. Communal orders represent major social experiments in which new or radical theories of human behavior, motivation, and interpersonal relations are put to the test."

Her examination of the organizational structure of communes inspired Kanter to produce several other works on the subject. She edited and contributed to *Communes: Creating and Managing the Collective Life* (1973). With

Marcia Millman, she edited *Another Voice: Feminist Perspectives on Social Life and Social Science* (1975), to which she also contributed. Her pamphlet, *Work and Family in the United States: A Critical Review and Research and Policy Agenda*, was published by the Russell Sage Foundation in 1976. Meanwhile, after taking a leave of absence from Brandeis in 1973–74 to teach at Harvard University in Cambridge, Massachusetts as an associate professor at the Graduate School of Education, she returned to Brandeis in 1974 as an associate professor of sociology. Although she remained on the faculty of Brandeis until 1977, she was also associated with Harvard Law School, where she was a fellow in law and sociology in 1975–76 and a visiting scholar in the following academic year.

In her groundbreaking book *Men and Women of the Corporation* (1977), Kanter applied sociological research techniques to a detailed analysis of the corporate environment of a fictional midwestern company called the Industrial Supply Corporation, or Indsco. Examining all levels of the company—from secretarial and clerical up through management positions to the executive "power elite"—Kanter studied employees' and managers' behavioral patterns, which, as she wrote in her introduction to the book, "can only be fully understood when there is adequate appreciation of the self-perpetuating cycles and inescapable dilemmas posed by the contingencies of social life." She found that the corporate structure's effect on the morale and performance of employees is often obscured by erroneous assumptions about gender roles in the workplace. "Findings about the 'typical' behavior of women in organizations," she wrote in her introduction, "that have been assumed to reflect either biologically based psychological attributes or characteristics developed through a long socialization to a 'female sex role' turn out to reflect very reasonable—and very universal—responses to current organizational situations." *Men and Women of the Corporation*, which won the C. Wright Mills Award for the year's best book on social issues, is still regarded as a classic treatise on the subject.

"Confidence isn't optimism or pessimism, and it's not a character attribute. It's the expectation of a positive outcome."

In 1977 Kanter joined the faculty of Yale University in New Haven, Connecticut, as a tenured associate professor of sociology. She was promoted to full professor of sociology and of organization and management in the following year. She remained at Yale until 1986, additionally teaching at the Sloan School of Management at the Massachusetts Institute of Technology in Cambridge, where she was a visiting professor of organizational psychology and management in 1979–80.

The year 1977 was a milestone in many ways for Kanter, who at that time founded the consulting firm Goodmeasure, Inc. with Barry Stein, then a consultant with two decades of experience, whom she had married in 1972. In addition to teaching and writing, she had begun consulting on the side in about 1970. Goodmeasure came about partly as the result of the success of *Men and Women of the Corporation*, which enhanced her reputation as someone who was knowledgeable about the special opportunities and challenges presented to corporations by a rapidly changing labor force. The book also provided a focal point for her consulting skills.

Consulting was but one of the areas where Kanter and Stein found fruitful collaboration possible. She and her husband edited a compilation of essays entitled *Life in Organizations* (1979) and wrote *A Tale of "O":*

On Being Different in an Organization (1980). Filled with cartoonlike illustrations and humorous prose, *A Tale of "O"* (also available as a video) explored "the pressures of living as a token, the dilemma faced by the single O in a roomful of Xs," as Susan McHenry wrote in her profile of Kanter for *Ms.* magazine. Lamenting the number of women who choose to leave the fast, or most direct, track to success within an organization to pursue their careers through alternate routes, she told McHenry that it is often due to frustration that "many [women] go into their own entrepreneurial activities, or join consulting firms." Moreover, she later noted that those who do move up in line jobs, as opposed to staff positions, could no longer count on being automatically promoted to the top levels. "It's a wonderful irony that, just as we get in, it doesn't mean anything," Kanter said at a New Orleans gathering of the Academy of Management in 1987.

Having gradually shifted her perspective from that of outsider to that of a high-profile adviser to CEOs, Kanter wrote *The Change Masters: Innovation for Productivity in the American Corporation* (1983), a highly acclaimed collection of case studies of some 100 American corporations (including 50 that she had personally visited). Ranking the companies in terms of their "progressiveness" in corporate policies and management strategies, she compared the financial performance of the most progressive companies and the least progressive corporations. She controlled for size by comparing only those companies that fell within set ranges of net sales, assets, and number of employees. She concluded, in part, that those companies that were found to be the most "integrative"—that encourage employees to collaborate across organization boundaries—were more profitable than those deemed to operate in a "segmentalist," or "antichange" fashion—by compartmentalizing, for instance, information, people, problems, and solutions.

When the Harvard Business School hired her as a fully tenured professor of business administration in 1986, Kanter became only the second woman in the business school's history to be tenured. Kanter and the Harvard Business School enjoyed a mutually advantageous relationship, in which each enhanced the other's visibility and reputation. Kanter's growing clout also afforded her greater access to the political realm. In 1986 she served as an adviser to Senator Gary Hart of Colorado, who was gearing up for his second presidential campaign in the Democratic primaries. She also became closely associated with the eventual 1988 Democratic presidential nominee, Governor Michael S. Dukakis of Massachusetts, whom she had met in 1985 during a tour of 30 of the state's most innovative companies. "We have compatible visions," Kanter explained to Bruce Nussbaum in an interview for *Business Week* (May 30, 1988). "His attitude on how you get welfare recipients back to work is linked to his attitude about how you help ailing industries. You don't artificially support them. You give them a chance to revitalize with temporary import restrictions."

Together, Kanter and Dukakis wrote *Creating the Future: The Massachusetts Comeback and Its Promise for America*, which was published in 1988 to coincide with Dukakis's campaign against the Republican nominee, Vice President George Bush. For her next book, *When Giants Learn to Dance: Mastering the Challenges of Strategy, Management, and Careers in the 1990s* (1989), Kanter studied more than 80 companies whose management styles ranged from the "corpocratic" sluggishness of multilayered bureaucracies to the "cowboy" mode pioneered by fast-growing newer ventures. She found that companies were becoming aware of the need for a managerial reaction to recent technological advances and the globalization of markets, a "post-entrepreneurial response," as she labeled it in *When Giants Learn to Dance*, "that marries the entrepreneurial spirit to discipline and teamwork." For workers, she coined the notion of "employability," or the ability to acquire transferable skills and the flexibility required to advance one's career by moving from company to company rather than by moving up in a single firm. Reflecting the large increase in corporate mergers—and the resulting layoffs—which occurred during the late 1980s, *When Giants Learn to*

Dance included various tips and pointers to help companies strengthen the corporate bottom line while still achieving employee satisfaction and reducing employee burnout. Addressing the latter goal, she suggested that managers and subordinates view work cyclically, with periods of intense productivity to be followed by stints of tackling the less stressful components of their jobs.

With a few exceptions, *When Giants Learn to Dance* was very well received by reviewers and by the business community. "Without minimizing the problems that arise in implementing post-entrepreneurial strategies," Nancy Jackson wrote in the *HBS Bulletin* (April 1989), "her book conveys a sense of hope that U.S. companies are discovering a way to manage large organizations without heavy-handed command-and-control systems." In an evaluation for the *Training & Development Journal* (November 1989), a reviewer noted, "This book requires thought and deliberation on the part of the reader. Kanter has already done both. Without providing right or wrong answers, she asks tough-minded, perceptive questions about many of today's most critical issues." The book, which has been translated into 10 languages, earned Kanter the Johnson, Smith & Knisely Award for new perspectives on executive leadership.

In 1989 Kanter was appointed the first female editor of the *Harvard Business Review*, a 67-year-old bi-monthly scholarly journal that was in the process of broadening its audience to include more industry leaders and corporate decision makers. During her three years as editor, Kanter elaborated on the changes set in motion by her predecessor, Theodore Levitt, who tried to make the magazine more accessible. She added cover illustrations and longer article summaries, converted a book-review section into an idea review, and instituted a feature called "Four Corners," which was dedicated to international business concerns, a field that Kanter had become more involved with in her own research. In 1991 the *Harvard Business Review* was a finalist for a National Magazine Award for general excellence.

Although subscription renewals to the *Harvard Business Review* increased under her leadership, Kanter was criticized by some disgruntled employees—in many cases, anonymously—for managing her editorial staff ineffectively, according to Joan Vennochi's 1993 article for *Working Woman*. Some employees complained that her speaking engagements and frequent traveling prevented her from being available and responsive to their concerns, while others said that several issues of the *Review* were perceived to have been delayed by an extensive reader survey Kanter commissioned on international business trends. Kanter's supporters have pointed out that many of the problems she encountered at the *Review* were the result of the pressures any faculty editor with outside demands would face in trying to expand the audience of the nation's most prestigious business journal. Others contended that sexism played a role in her difficulties and that her activities, policies, and decisions would probably be admired if she were a man. Under the terms of a reorganization in 1992, the *Review* brought in a full-time, professional editor—a move that some staff members, as well as Kanter herself, had been advocating long before Kanter's arrival—and Kanter became vice-chair of the newly created Harvard Business School Publishing Group.

With Barry Stein and Todd Jick, Kanter wrote *The Challenge of Organizational Change: How Companies Experience It and Leaders Guide It* (1992), whose premise is that change within corporate organizations arises from three sources (the general business environment, the company's own aging and development, and individuals within the company competing for power), which in turn produce three forms of change (identity-related product-line expansion, a redesigned corporate hierarchy, and departmental reorganization). Accordingly, the authors argued that three managerial roles are called for to manage such changes (top-down strategic planning, middle-management implementation of new policies, and lower-level motivation tactics that give incentives to employees to be responsive to new corporate obligations).

Kanter's 1995 book *World Class: Thriving Locally in the Global Economy*, in which she emphasized the alternatives to the disorientation, job insecurity, and economic chaos that had been wrought by (among other factors) the increasing globalization of industry. Envisioning new opportunities and the revitalization of certain regions, she argued that local companies—and even entire cities—could benefit from globalization by becoming "world class" at thinking, manufacturing, or trading. As a successful exemplar of each skill, she selected Boston; Spartanburg-Greenville, South Carolina; and Miami, respectively. "This book is about how business leadership and community leadership can work together," she wrote in *World Class*, which found a far-flung audience overseas and in nonacademic fields. Although Stephen Baker argued in *Business Week* (October 16, 1995) that "it would have made for better reading had the author compared a winner and a loser city instead of just heaping praise upon her three cosmopolitans," a reviewer for *The Economist* (September 9, 1995) concluded, "*World Class* is carefully researched and soberly argued."

Confidence: How Winning Streaks and Losing Streaks Begin and End was published in 2004. "Confidence," Kanter said in a *New York Times* profile (September 19, 2004), "isn't optimism or pessimism, and it's not a character attribute. It's the expectation of a positive outcome."

SuperCorp: How Vanguard Companies Create Innovation, Profits, Growth, and Social Good, "a timely and captivating assessment of what it takes" for corporations "to succeed in the face of rapid technological, cultural and economic change" (*Publishers Weekly)* was published in 2009.

The recipient of numerous grants and awards, including a Guggenheim Fellowship in 1975–76, Kanter holds numerous honorary doctoral degrees. She has been named Woman of the Year by *Ms.* magazine (1985), and she has been inducted into the Working Woman Hall of Fame. Boston College offers a Rosabeth Moss Kanter Award for excellence in work-family research.

"[Kanter is] an entrepreneur in the best sense of the word—applying ideas to problems," Robert B. Reich, the secretary of labor during the administration of President Bill Clinton, told Joan Vennochi for *Working Woman* (February 1993). "She is a fount of insights into how the economy actually works, rather than how theoreticians say it works."

Further Reading:

Ms. Jan. 1985

Contemporary Authors rev. vol. 14 1985

New York Times Sept. 19, 2004

Who's Who in America, 1996

Working Woman Feb. 1993

Selected Books:

Commitment and Community: Communes and Utopias in Sociological Perspective, 1972

Men and Women of the Corporation, 1977

The Change Masters: Innovation for Productivity in the American Corporation, 1983

When Giants Learn to Dance: Mastering the Challenges of Strategy, Management, and Careers in the 1990s, 1989

The Challenge of Organizational Change: How Companies Experience It and Leaders Guide It (with Barry Stein and Todd Jick), 1992

World Class: Thriving Locally in the Global Economy, 1995

Confidence: How Winning Streaks and Losing Streaks Begin and End, 2004

Supercorp: How Vanguard Companies Create Innovation, Profits, Growth, and Social Good, 2009

Kao, John J.

Businessman; writer; political consultant

Born: 1950; Chicago, Illinois

Before he became a prominent expert on creativity, the author of two best-selling books on innovation, and the founder of a company that advises such businesses as IBM, Nokia, and Intel on how to encourage creativity and innovation in their employees, John Kao had already pursued careers as a professional keyboardist, psychiatrist, college professor, and movie and theater producer. "It is only in the last 10 or 15 years that it's become clear to me that I was filling out a pattern," Kao told Cornelia Dean for the *New York Times* (June 24, 2008), referring to the connection between his nonlinear career path and his passion for innovation. Kao has proposed implementing a national program that would efficiently and creatively address problems in such areas as health care, energy, and education. "The problem in America is not that we don't have lots of good ideas," he told Matthew Bandyk for *U.S. News & World Report* (October 29, 2007). "The problem is aligning our innovative capabilities to pay off on big ideas and big challenges of the day so that we can have innovation operate at a national level."

Education and Early Career

Kao's parents left China shortly before the Communist takeover of the country in 1949 to attend Northwestern University in Chicago, Illinois. His father, who trained as a physician, had received a university research fellowship just before the borders closed. An only child, John J. Kao was born on December 14, 1950 in Chicago and raised in Garden City, New York. As a youth, he tried to absorb American culture while maintaining his Chinese heritage. "I was like a little astronaut," Kao told Laura Silverman for *Transpacific* (March 1, 1997). "I'd go out every day into the American world and then come home at night to this very different world, and it was up to me to make the connections between the two." When he was nine years old, Kao started a literary magazine at his school, putting together an editorial board and organizing a school-wide literary contest. "I just kind of figured out that it was more fun being in the principal's office, organizing a contest, than it was learning whatever I was supposed to be learning in fourth grade," Kao told Silverman. "And that's pretty much been par for the course all the way through."

Though his parents encouraged him to become a research scientist, Kao dreamed of becoming a psychoanalyst. He was also a talented student of jazz piano. Kao attended Yale University in New Haven, Connecticut and majored in behavioral science and philosophy. At one point during his studies, a professor introduced him to the iconoclastic composer and guitarist Frank Zappa. Kao told Zappa how much he revered his work and ended up playing the keyboards on tour with Zappa's band, the Mothers of Invention, for three months in 1969. At the end of the summer—in a year that saw the height of the Vietnam War—he was motivated to return to school to avoid being drafted and graduated in 1972. Though he recalled to Dean that his decision to attend the Yale School of Medicine was partially driven by "some family pressure," Kao greatly enjoyed his medical-school experience. His interest in human behavior led him to study Jungian psychoanalysis, but during his psychiatry residency he realized that he was interested in pursuing neither clinical nor academic medicine. He obtained a fellowship from Harvard University in Cambridge, Massachusetts, which allowed him to enroll in the business school while finishing his psychiatry residency; he had a vague notion of using his business degree and his training in psychiatry to help CEOs or "people who were developing new things," as Kao told Silverman.

Kao received his M.B.A. in 1982, and shortly thereafter he began teaching at the Harvard Business School. In 1983, as a junior faculty member, he proposed teaching a course on creativity and entrepreneurship. It was unprecedented for a professor teaching for less than two years to make such a proposal, and most of his colleagues opposed the idea on the grounds that creativity could not be taught in a classroom setting. Kao offered to do all the necessary preparatory work himself in addition to the regular work for his classes and was ultimately granted permission. The course—Entrepreneurship, Creativity, and Organizations—proved to be extraordinarily popular, attracting 200 students in its first session. During the course Kao presented corporate case studies and asked his students to resolve the businesses' problems by trial and error, using creative strategies. He emphasized expanding and invigorating the businesses through improvisation and innovation. In 1989 he published many of his case studies in a textbook (also titled *Entrepreneurship, Creativity, and Organizations*). Kao continued to teach popular courses on corporate creativity for 14 years at Harvard, as well as at schools including the Massachusetts Institute of Technology and Denmark's University of Copenhagen.

Later Career

In 1986 Kao heard about the work of Howard Green, a professor at the Harvard Medical School, who was doing research on growing sheets of skin in the lab for use on burn victims. Recognizing a business opportunity, Kao helped launch BioSurface Technologies, a company that commercialized the manufacturing of skin, cartilage, and other human tissue, for medical replacement procedures. "I did everything," Kao told Silverman. "I wrote a business plan, I raised the money, I recruited a CEO, I kind of whipped it all together—and then there was this magical day when we had money in the bank and investors and a management team, and I walked into this lawyer's office and signed my name 400 times, and we had a company." Kao later sold BioSurface Technologies to Genzyme, one of the most successful biotech companies in the country. He subsequently launched several other successful companies, including another biotech company, K.O. Technology (now called Variagenics), which focused on cancer treatment, and Advanced Video Communications, which provided such services as video conferencing.

"My job is to put a container around an idea so that it has tangibility, resources are attracted to it and it starts to have a life."

While attending business school, Kao had become interested in the film industry, and in the mid-1980s he began to network aggressively in Hollywood. Through various connections, he met the writer and director Steven Soderbergh, then a newcomer. Soderbergh had written a screenplay called *sex, lies, and videotape*, about four young adults and their complicated, intertwined sex lives. Kao helped produce the movie, which Soderbergh directed, for $1.2 million. Released in 1989 to great critical acclaim, it won the Palm d'Or, the highest prize at the Cannes International Film Festival, and James Spader, who played one of the main characters, won best-actor honors. (Soderbergh was later nominated for an Academy Award for best screenplay.)

Kao next had the idea to make a movie about an American baseball player in Japan. As executive producer, he raised money, commissioned a screenplay, and oversaw the production of *Mr. Baseball* (1992), a modest hit starring Tom Selleck. While busy with other ventures over the next few years, Kao remained interested in the entertainment field, and in 1998 he produced the stage play *Golden Child*, which was written by David Henry Hwang and was nominated for three Tony Awards.

In 1996 Kao published *Jamming: The Art and Discipline of Business Creativity*. In that book he advocated a management system in which employees work within a defined structure but are encouraged to be creative in developing new ideas and products. He likened the creative process needed in business settings to that used by jazz musicians in jam sessions. "[You] must ruthlessly trash outmoded obstructions to creativity: standard operating procedures, protocols, norms of behavior, a confining brand image, rules, the revered memory of old successes, and so on," Kao wrote in *Jamming*, as quoted by Stephen G. Minter for *Occupational Hazards* (August 1996). "This is always difficult because it obliges people continuously to revise their sense of themselves and their place in the organization." He suggested that managers create office environments that encourage playful and productive interaction and that they be careful not to stifle their employees' creative impulses. Published in 12 languages, *Jamming* reached number 14 on the *BusinessWeek* bestseller list and was generally hailed as a useful resource. Some critics, however, found fault with the book. "Kao makes jamming seem too easy," Ronald Henkoff wrote for *Fortune* (September 9, 1996). "He owes it to his readers to consider the sometimes darker complexities of creativity. Innovation can be destabilizing, unpredictable, and threatening."

In 1997 Kao left Harvard and moved to San Francisco. That year he co-edited *Innovation: Breakthrough Thinking at 3M, DuPont, GE, Pfizer, and Rubbermaid*. In each of the book's five chapters, a business leader described the ways in which his or her company incorporated innovation into its organizational structure. That year Kao also produced a short companion film to *Jamming*, which combined video and audio recordings of jazz musicians with various business case studies. In a critique for *Training Media Review* (November 1997), Jeanne Baer praised the video for its entertaining qualities and concluded, "There are a few cases of circular logic and jargon-laden explanations that may set an analytical viewer's teeth on edge, but on the whole, *Jamming* presents a convincing argument for the need to become more 'improvisational.'"

In 1997 Kao also founded the Idea Factory, a firm that consulted with major corporations on fostering business creativity, planning strategically for the future, and using intuition to make better decisions. The Idea Factory helped develop software and other online tools to support collaboration, participated in redesigning businesses' physical space to foster creativity, and offered training programs and workshops, among other services. Initially, the Idea Factory's central office was located in San Francisco, in a large, high-ceilinged loft that contained a grand piano. (The firm's headquarters eventually moved to Singapore.) Kao served as the Idea Factory's CEO until 2001, opening several branch offices throughout Europe and Asia; raising millions of dollars to establish Idea Factory Capital Partners, a venture fund; and developing a number of start-up companies.

n 2000 Kao, along with a group of partners, purchased Ealing Studios in London, England. Since then Kao worked to convert Ealing, the oldest film studio in the world, into a cutting-edge digital entertainment company. "My job is to put a container around an idea so that it has tangibility, resources are attracted to it and it starts to have a life," Kao told Andrew Davidson for *Management Today* (April 1, 2001).

In the early 2000s Kao found himself in great demand as a lecturer on subjects related to innovation: He spoke, for example, about the ways in which the U.S. health-care system could be improved through creative means and the ways in which the innovations of East Asian corporations were changing the global economy. During that time he founded Kao & Co., whose services included, according to the company Web site, "helping an organization to clarify its desired future state, generating ways of communicating its desired future state to a variety of constituents, designing an innovation strategy, and supporting the efforts of innovation teams and senior leadership to execute in a variety of ways."

In 2007 Kao published *Innovation Nation: How America Is Losing Its Innovation Edge, Why It Matters and What We Can Do to Get It Back*, a book that discusses the global trends behind the shift of economic dominance from the United States and Western Europe to Asia. One reason for the shift in power, according to Kao, is the recent improvement of educational institutions in Asia, coupled with the declining quality of science and math education in the U.S. Furthermore, Kao blames the restrictive immigration policies instituted by the federal government after the terrorist attacks of September 11, 2001 for the inability of American corporations to recruit highly educated Asian scientists and engineers. "The rest of the world is getting smarter about innovation," Kao told Bandyk. "We've gone from an arms race in the Cold War to a brain race in the 21st century."

Kao, who intentionally published the book just before the 2008 U.S. presidential-election cycle, suggested the creation of a Department of Innovation, overseen by the U.S. Congress, which would coordinate 20 regional groups made up of CEOs, scientists, cultural leaders, policy makers, and technologists, focused on finding creative approaches to specific national problems. He envisions research centers at which young people would study in "regionally strategic fields such as agricultural biotech in Iowa, energy in Montana and aerospace in California," as quoted by Heidi Benson in the *San Francisco Chronicle* (November 24, 2007).

Without action, Kao told Cornelia Dean, "[The U.S.] will have an elite class of educated, cosmopolitan, global citizens who have a ticket of entry to the major leagues and a much larger group of marginally employable people who have been sold a bill of goods by a consumption economy." Dubbed "scary, insightful, and ultimately very useful" by Bruce Nussbaum, writing for *BusinessWeek* (October 22, 2007), *Innovation Nation* was critically acclaimed, and its premises have been endorsed by such organizations as the National Academy of Sciences and the Brookings Institute. It was chosen by the editors of *BusinessWeek* as one of the ten best books of the year.

Kao had met Senator Hillary Rodham Clinton in 2004, when both were members of a Defense Department advisory group. In 2006 Kao served as an adviser on Clinton's Senate reelection campaign, and the following year he was a consultant on her presidential bid. Clinton became the target of some derision for working with an innovation expert. In the *Huffington Post* (May 16, 2007), E. A. Hanks criticized Clinton's decision to hire Kao and noted that it was "alarming" that his "faux-inspirational babble" might influence Clinton's or any other political campaign. "Innovation doesn't come from a pamphlet, even a $70,000 one," Hanks wrote, referring to the amount Clinton paid Kao, "and it can't be squeezed into a stump speech here or there."

Despite skepticism from some quarters regarding his methods, Kao remains optimistic about the country's ability to address its problems creatively. He believes that because Americans do not attach lasting stigma to failure, the U.S. is an excellent place to try new ideas. "The world needs us, even if it does not believe it does," he told Dean.

In 2012 Kao spearheaded the creation of the San Francisco–based EdgeMakers company, created (as per its Web site) "with the mission of empowering young people everywhere to become innovators and make a difference."

Kao lives in San Francisco with his wife, Lauren, and their three children.

Further Reading:

BusinessWeek Oct. 22, 2007

Fortune Sep. 9, 1996

Management Today Apr. 1, 2001

New York Times June 24, 2008

San Francisco Chronicle Nov. 24, 2007

Transpacific Mar. 1, 1997

U.S. News & World Report Oct. 29, 2007

Books:

Jamming: The Art and Discipline of Business Creativity, 1996

Innovation Nation: How America Is Losing Its Innovation Edge, Why It Matters and What We Can Do to Get It Back, 2007

(as co-editor)

Innovation: Breakthrough Thinking at 3M, DuPont, GE, Pfizer, and Rubbermaid, 1997

Lampert, Edward S.

CEO, ESL Investments

Born: 1962; Roslyn, Long Island, New York

According to a list compiled by *Alpha* magazine, Edward S. Lampert, the chief executive officer (CEO) of ESL Investments, was the highest-paid hedge-fund manager in 2004, becoming the first to take home more than $1 billion in a single year. Lampert thus unseated the billionaire George Soros, primarily because his shares in the Kmart Holding Corp.—which he had nursed back from bankruptcy in 2003—more than tripled in value when the company acquired Sears, Roebuck & Co. to form Sears Holdings Corp., now the nation's third-largest retailer. The merger of those once-iconic retailers, each of which had struggled to stay afloat on its own, was considered by observers of the retail industry to be an audacious move. As Andrew Ross Sorkin and Riva D. Atlas noted in the *New York Times* (November 18, 2004), "The deal catapults Mr. Lampert, a virtual unknown several years ago, to one of the most powerful people in retailing and a major player on Wall Street."

Education and Early Career

Edward S. Lampert was born July 19, 1962 in Roslyn, on Long Island, New York. His father, Floyd M. Lampert, was a senior partner at a New York law firm and his mother was a homemaker. Raised in privileged circumstances, Lampert played with the children of the wealthy, including the son of Fred Wilpon, who later became part owner of the New York Mets baseball team. He developed an interest in the stock market at an early age thanks to his grandmother, whom he often visited at her home in Miami Beach. "She was retired and I would sit on the bed with her going through the stock pages," he told Brett D. Fromson for the *Washington Post* (September 10, 1995). "She and I would go to the public library and look up stocks in the S&P [Standard & Poor's] guides to understand a little bit about the companies in the stock pages. But I really didn't know what I was doing. I was just curious."

When Lampert was 14 years old, his father died unexpectedly of a heart attack. Afterward, to help support the family, his mother went to work as a clerk at the New York store Saks Fifth Avenue. Lampert told Brett D. Fromson, "I felt a responsibility to my mother and my sister to help them get through." To buy a car and help pay for his college education, he found jobs in the summers and during his senior year of high school. Lampert was accepted at Yale University in New Haven, Connecticut, where he majored in economics and joined the Skull and Bones Society—an elite, secretive club to which many of the most powerful American men of the past century have belonged. In his sophomore year he took a seminar in investment banking taught by a partner at the prestigious investment firm Goldman Sachs, and he landed an internship there the summer before his senior year. During his three-month stint in the sales-and-training program at Goldman, he grew interested in risk arbitrage, the practice of trading the stocks of companies involved in mergers or acquisitions.

After earning his bachelor's degree in economics from Yale in 1984, Lampert wanted to return to Goldman Sachs, but his mother urged him to apply to law school. "It was my mother's dream that I become a professional," he told Brett D. Fromson. "It represented security, a nice life, [respect] in the community. . . . She didn't know what Goldman Sachs was." Despite her wishes, and his being accepted at the prestigious Harvard and Yale law schools, Lampert took a position as a junior research analyst in Goldman's risk-arbitrage division in 1984. "My mother thought I was a little crazy," he told Fromson. While at Goldman Sachs he worked for Robert E. Rubin, who was later appointed Secretary of the Treasury during the Clinton administration. "I found risk arbitrage intellectually stimulating," Lampert told Fromson. "You needed to analyze the situation in a short period of time, and you needed to understand the relationship between the risks and rewards—how much money you could make and how much you could lose…It appealed to me because you made the decisions. You were committing the partners' capital and could see immediately whether you were right or wrong simply by the facts. It was definite and not subject to other people's opinions."

> **"I didn't want to have to ask permission to do a deal. . . . If I was the quarter-back, I didn't want the coach calling the plays."**

While working in risk arbitrage, Lampert grew interested in value investing. The practice—in which the investor buys shares in companies that he or she thinks are being traded for less than they are actually worth—was made famous by the investor Warren Buffet, whom Lampert had long revered. "I liked the idea of buying something at $30 if it's worth $60 as opposed to buying it at $59 to sell at $60," he told Fromson. Goldman was not in the business of value investing, and so, with the encouragement of the investor Richard Rainwaterw—who years earlier had worked at Goldman himself—Lampert quit in 1988 and opened his own investment partnership, ESL Partners (later changed to ESL Investments), in Fort Worth, Texas. (E, S, and L are Lampert's initials.) Rainwater provided him with $28.8 million in financial backing for the enterprise. "[Rainwater] gave me a huge vote of faith, and I respond very well to that," Lampert told Fromson. "He really took me under his wing." ESL saw excellent returns from the beginning: The overall value of its stock went up 39 percent in 1988 and another 21 percent in 1989. Despite that promising start, Rainwater pulled his money out of ESL in 1989 due to growing conflicts with Lampert over control of the partnership. "I view my investors as partners. They are not just money," Lampert said to Fromson. "But what I have always wanted to do, and the reason I set up my own business, is to make the investment decisions in whatever areas I thought I understood and made sense. I didn't want to have to ask permission to do a deal. . . . If I was the quarterback, I didn't want the coach calling the plays."

Later Career

In the early 1990s Lampert returned to the East Coast, moving the headquarters of ESL to Greenwich, Connecticut. By building substantial positions in a few heavily researched holdings, ESL earned one of the best track records in the investment business—with returns from 1998 to 2004 averaging a 29 percent gain per year. Today Lampert manages around $10 billion, for a blue-chip roster of investors that includes the Ziff family of publishing fame, the entertainment mogul David Geffen, the Fischer family of the Gap retail chain, and Michael Dell of Dell Computers.

Lampert is often described as a private and secretive man, and despite his success, he received little coverage in the mainstream media until he was abducted at gunpoint from the parking garage of his ESL office on January 10, 2003. Four captors kept him handcuffed in a bathtub at a Days Inn motel in Hamden, New Jersey, and demanded a $5 million ransom for his release. Lampert's years of experience in negotiating on Wall Street apparently paid off: He managed to convince his abductors that he would pay them the $5 million ransom if they released him first. The abductors dropped him off at an I-95 exit ramp around 2:50 a.m. on January 12. Three of them were captured at the motel shortly thereafter (authorities were able to track them down because they had used Lampert's credit card to order a pizza, which they had delivered to the motel room); the fourth suspect was arrested in Toronto, Canada, a week later.

In May of that same year, Lampert was elected chairman of the board of the Troy, Michigan–based Kmart Holding Corp. Once an icon in American retailing, Kmart had been suffering under the competition from other big-box retailers, such as Wal-Mart and other very big stores. When the company filed for bankruptcy protection in 2002, Lampert began buying its bonds, eventually purchasing a controlling share for slightly less than $1 billion. Lampert had already established a reputation for activism as an investor—he closely monitored the internal management of the companies in which he invested—and even before his appointment to chairman, he had overseen an overhaul in Kmart's management and helped the company cut costs and improve the logistics of its operations. Under his stewardship Kmart climbed out of debt, slowed the decline of its sales, and turned a $1.1 billion profit in 2004. When the company emerged from bankruptcy in May 2003, its stock was valued at $15 per share. By November 2004 the figure had risen to $109.

Sales at Kmart were still declining, though, and most of the profit was due to the sale of some of Kmart's real estate. During the summer of 2004, the company sold 18 of its stores to Home Depot for $271 million and 54 stores to Sears for $621 million (some sources say that 50 were sold to Sears for $576 million). Some analysts on Wall Street began to wonder if Lampert actually intended to revive Kmart's sagging retail business. "Lampert is more inclined to sell off Kmart's real estate assets for his monetary purposes," Kurt Barnard, president of Barnard Retail Consulting, told Michael Rudnick for *HFN* (September 20, 2004). "Kmart has some marvelous real estate in prime markets. But does he want to make retailing a goal of his life? Probably not."

That statement notwithstanding, in 2004 Lampert masterminded the acquisition of another failing retailer, Sears, Roebuck & Co. He had begun buying shares in the company around the same time that he had begun investing in Kmart stock, eventually becoming the largest single shareholder of each company. In November 2004 Kmart announced a $12.3 billion acquisition (some sources say $11 billion) of Sears to create Sears Holdings Corp., the country's third-largest retailer—after Wal-Mart and Home Depot—with 3,800 stores in Canada and the United States and a projected $55 billion in revenue. The deal was finalized on March 24, 2005, when 69 percent of the shareholders of both companies voted to approve the deal. Before the creation of Sears Holdings Corp., Lampert was known within the financial industry as a master of value investing, or capitalizing on companies whose stocks were undervalued. Industry observers noted his activism as an investor; rather than spreading his investments over a vast array of firms, he staked out positions of influence in a handful of well-researched companies and then closely monitored their day-to-day operations. In an interview with Robert Siegel for National Public Radio's *All Things Considered* (November 17, 2004), Andy Serwer, an editor at large of *Fortune*, said, "Lampert has a track record of going into companies, especially retailing companies, when they're down and out and providing them with capital, with money, and then helping them get back on their feet and, in the process, making a ton of money for himself and for his hedge fund."

Some analysts questioned whether combining two struggling retail chains could help to salvage either of them. Lampert believed, however, that each retail chain had something to offer the other: Kmart needed more higher-margin products, such as the Craftsman tools and Kenmore appliances sold at Sears, and Sears needed to expand beyond its traditional outlets in malls to stand-alone stores. After the merger, Sears Holdings announced plans to convert approximately 400 Kmart stores to a new "Sears Essentials" format over the next three years. Those midsize, stand-alone stores would stock snacks and convenience items in addition to the usual Sears offerings. "[Kmart has] this enormous store base that's not easily differentiated from Wal-Mart and Target," Lampert admitted to Becky Yerak for the *Chicago Tribune* (March 28, 2005), "but it can be by virtue of Sears services, home delivery, installation and repair, as well as the product lines that are proprietary to Sears."

Lampert set to work cutting overhead costs. Around 1,400 jobs at Kmart were eliminated or relocated, and Lampert told the remaining employees that in order to do well at the company they needed to demonstrate the commitment shown by employees at dot-coms and technology firms. He said to Susan Chandler for the *Chicago Tribune* (March 25, 2005), "We can't compete against the Wal-Marts, the Home Depots, the Targets, etc. without that level of passion."

As a result of the acquisition, Kmart lost market share in its stores, but profits increased. Lampert's ESL fund saw a 69 percent return in 2004—compared with the 8 percent growth that hedge funds generally saw that year—due largely to its stake in Kmart, which had tripled in value. Lampert, who earned an estimated $1.02 billion in 2004, was the highest-paid hedge-fund manager of the year, according to *Alpha* magazine. Knocking George Soros from the top of the list, Lampert became the first to pass the $1 billion mark since the list had been created four years before. (By comparison, James Simons, second on the list, earned $607 million.) According to *Forbes* magazine, Lampert ranked as one of the world's richest people.

When Lampert announced the creation of Sears Holdings Corp., he made it clear that he would focus on the long-term profitability of the company instead of worrying about quarterly earnings reports. Unlike most retailers, the company does not provide earnings forecasts or release monthly sales reports, and the posting of its first quarterly earnings report, on June 7, 2005, came without any announcement beforehand. In its first quarter Sears Holdings Corp. lost $9 million after the company was charged a $90 million after-tax fee due to its having changed accounting procedures for certain inventory costs. Before the accounting adjustment, the company's income was $81 million, compared with $91 million during the same period from the year before. Same-store sales and total sales at Kmart decreased 3.7 percent and 2.3 percent, respectively. Days before the earnings report, the investment company's stock had reached its highest levels, but it had lost nearly 10 percent of its value by the Friday after the report. Investors saw great potential for long-term investment in the company but a high level of immediate risk. "Given Mr. Lampert's track record . . . we expect a high level of success," Robert Drbul, an analyst at Lehman Brothers, told Vicki M. Young for *WWD* (June 8, 2005), adding nonetheless that Sears Holdings Corp. "remains several years away from being a formidable competitor in the industry."

Lampert reversed his position on retailing to some extent in 2005, deciding to assume personal control of marketing, merchandising, design, and online operations of Sears Holdings. He demoted the chief executive officer of Sears stores, Alan J. Lacy, and replaced him with Aylwin B. Lewis, who had been serving as Kmart's chief executive. (Lacy remained at Sears, as a director and vice chairman.) Lampert told shareholders that he had made the changes in order "to make the company more responsive to our customers," and he said that his new responsibilities notwithstanding, would take no salary or stock options, according to Jeff Bailey in the *New York Times* (September 9, 2005). Commenting on the reactions to Lampert's move, Sandra Guy wrote for the *Chicago Sun-Times* (September 15, 2005), "If Lampert is serious about making Sears the retailer it should have become 30 years ago, he has a funny way of showing it, the skeptical analysts say." She added, "Lampert's latest moves signal his high energy and confidence, despite the nay-sayers."

Lampert's tenure at Sears has been controversial. He "runs Sears like a hedge fund portfolio, with dozens of autonomous businesses competing for his attention and money," Mina Kimes wrote in the July 11, 2013 *Businessweek*. "An outspoken advocate of free-market economics and fan of the novelist Ayn Rand, he created the model because he expected the invisible hand of the market to drive better results. If the company's leaders were told to act selfishly, he argued, they would run their divisions in a rational manner, boosting overall performance."

Lampert became a multimillionaire in his early 20s, and by his late 20s, he co-owned the Texas Rangers baseball team with George W. Bush, the future governor of Texas and president of the United States. Despite such success, for years Lampert lived in rented apartments and drove a beat-up car; when his mother complained about the dilapidated state of her own seven-year-old automobile, Lampert responded by advising her to take better care of it. In contrast to his earlier frugality, Lampert now drives a sports car and owns a $20 million mansion in a gated community in Greenwich, Connecticut. He and his wife, Kinga Lampert, have two children.

Lampert blogs at "Eddie Lampert's Blog": http://eddielampert.com/.

Further Reading:

Associated Press Mar. 28, 2005
Businessweek July 11, 2013
Chicago Sun-Times Sep. 15, 2005
Chicago Tribune Mar. 28, 2005
HFN Sept. 20, 2004
New York Times Nov. 18, 2004; Sep. 9, 2005
Washington Post Sept. 10, 1995
WWD June 8, 2005

Lazarus, Rochelle

Former CEO, Ogilvy & Mather

Born: 1947; New York City

In the opinion of Shelly Lazarus, the chief executive officer (CEO) emeritus of the advertising agency Ogilvy & Mather Worldwide, "All the affirmative action in the world will not help women become top officers of a company." She made this observation to Stuart Elliott of the *New York Times* (February 19, 1997) only months after the former CEO, Charlotte Beers, named Lazarus as her successor at the agency, which was the sixth-largest in the world and counted IBM, American Express, Mattel, and Ford among its clients. The transition, which took place on January 1, 1997, marked the first time one woman had succeeded another as head of a major agency.

Education and Early Career

Shelly Lazarus was born in New York City on September 1, 1947, to Lewis L. and Sylvia Ruth Braff. Lazarus knows the exact moment when her ascent in the world of advertising began: It happened in 1967, during her senior year at Smith College, which is in Northampton, Massachusetts. Known then as Shelly Braff, she was engaged to a medical student named George M. Lazarus. "I wanted to get married," she told Elliott, "and someone had to work for us to get married." Out of curiosity, she joined a classmate in attending a career conference in Manhattan given by the Advertising Women of New York. "I had never been interested in advertising before, but I just fell. They told you why they made commercials the way they did, what little buttons to push. I loved the art and science of it."

After graduating from Smith in 1968, she interned at General Foods Corporation before going on to earn an M.B.A. in 1970 from New York City's Columbia University, where she was one of four women in her class. In the same year, she wed George Lazarus. Her first job was as an assistant product manager for Clairol. However, within a year she had made the move to Ogilvy & Mather to work on the Lever Brothers account. In 1974, by which time she was the only female account supervisor in the company (and was seven months pregnant, to boot), she left New York for Dayton, Ohio, with her husband, who had to fulfill a commitment to serve in the Air Force. She told Alison Fahey of *Advertising Age* (February 5, 1990) that the two years she spent in Dayton, where she worked as a department-store buyer, "were not happy ones."

Later Career

After Lazarus and her family returned to New York City in 1976, she went back to work at Ogilvy & Mather Worldwide as an account supervisor for Avon, the Ralston Purina Company, and the Campbell Soup Company. In 1977 she was made management supervisor on the Clairol account. In 1980 she was assigned to work on the American Express Company account. Her management of that key account over a seven-year period demonstrated her superlative ability to keep clients satisfied. "She never takes you for granted," Anne Fudge, president of the Maxwell House Coffee Company, told Elliott. "She's always working it, calling to see how it's going, to see how you're doing." The good working relationship Lazarus established with Abby Kohnstamm, an executive at American Express, would prove extremely valuable a few years later.

In the meantime, Lazarus had been promoted in 1987 to general manager of Ogilvy & Mather's direct marketing branch, which was seen as the least exciting aspect of the agency's business. "I didn't care," she told Patricia Sellers of *Fortune* (August 5, 1996). "I wanted to run something." By 1989 she was doing just that, as president of Ogilvy & Mather Direct. In 1991 she moved back to the advertising side of the company, when she was appointed to head its flagship New York office, and in February 1994 she was made president of all North American operations.

During the early 1990s, Lazarus made two deals that established her as chief- executive material. By 1992, American Express's mainstream charge-card advertising was being handled by another agency, Chiat/Day. Lazarus was able to use her previous good relations with American Express—and Abby Kohnstamm in particular—to lure the charge-card advertising account away from Chiat/Day and bring it back to Ogilvy & Mather. Then in 1994, after Kohnstamm had moved to an executive position at IBM, Lazarus negotiated the consolidation of all of IBM's advertising, which would then be handled exclusively by Ogilvy & Mather. (The computer giant's advertising accounts, together worth between $400 and $500 million in annual billings, had previously been split up between 40 different agencies.) In January 1997, Lazarus estimated that billing for IBM was close to $750 million.

The more flamboyant Charlotte Beers, 11 years older than Lazarus, had often been referred to as the most powerful woman in advertising, a title she had earned even before she arrived at Ogilvy & Mather from the Chicago agency Tatham RCSG, which she had headed for 10 years. At Tatham, Beers had been in charge of 750 people. When she was hired by Ogilvy & Mather in 1992 to oversee the company's 8,000 employees and 270 offices around the world, many observers felt the choice was a gamble. Beers made it pay off, reviving the company and, with Lazarus's help, winning back lost accounts. In 1996, when Beers announced she was stepping down as chief executive, the selection of Shelly Lazarus to succeed her was roundly praised by those familiar with her long tenure at Ogilvy & Mather. Beers had described Lazarus as a "natural leader" to Sally Goll Beatty of the *Wall Street Journal* (December 11, 1995). "The facts are, she's had the stature and momentum for some time."

"In a way, Shelly paved the way for me," Beers told Stuart Elliott (September 9, 1996) on the day of the announcement. The January transfer of office coincided with the 25th anniversary of Lazarus's employment at the agency.

"I had never been interested in advertising before, but I just fell. They told you why they made commercials the way they did, what little buttons to push. I loved the art and science of it."

Her career experience at all levels of the advertising business had given Shelly Lazarus perspective available to almost no other woman. In 1995, women accounted for 56 percent of workers in the advertising industry as a whole, but for only 17 percent of industry executives earning a salary of $200,000 or more. However, Lazarus did not see the dearth of female ad executives as the result of oppression—at least not anymore. She told Stuart Elliott, "Women have won their freedom, so a lot of working mothers are exiting the work force at more senior levels. . . .But that limits the pool of women to get to be senior executives and gives the perception there's still a glass ceiling."

Lazarus, a mother of three, didn't neglect her family for her career. "If there's a school play, or I have to take my daughter to camp, I don't go to the client meeting," she told Elliott. "And I don't think I've found anyone who doesn't respect that." She told Elliott that her agency "has always been a meritocracy, and I have never actually felt my femaleness. . . .It was almost irrelevant." Yet she did cite a particular advantage of being one of the few women in an industry that designs its messages for a primarily female audience of consumers. "I added value because I had the [same] hormones going through my blood as the people we were selling to. I could say 'As a woman . . .'"

Her beliefs about women's possibilities in the workplace were based on a bottom-line pragmatism other women sometimes found disturbing. She did not allow anyone working part-time or flex-time at Ogilvy & Mather to become a senior partner, a stance that upset many working mothers, who were far more likely to need flexible scheduling. Lazarus felt the issue was very simple. "Just because you're a woman with a child, you can't be allowed lower standards of performance," she told Patricia Sellers for her *Fortune* piece, entitled "Women, Sex and Power." Most of the powerful women profiled in Sellers's article shared Lazarus's distrust of affirmative-action policies. "I'm going to make a rash statement," Lazarus told Elliott. "There's an inverse relationship between the number of special programs a company has and how accepting it is of people who are different."

Shelly Lazarus—now Ogilvy & Mather's chairman emeritus—was profiled in 2013 by Christopher Zara for the *International Business Times*. To her, the very nature of advertising has been completely transformed. "When I started it was basically print, outdoor, television and radio. For most packaged goods companies, you could do two television commercials and three print ads a year and you were done. The big decisions were whether you were going to run on primetime, or daytime or late night, and which of the women's magazines were you going to run the print ads in. And then," she concluded, somewhat tongue in cheek, "we could all go to lunch." Some aspects of the industry, though, remain a constant. "The trick," Lazarus continued, "is to figure out how to make sure that you're meeting the needs and expectations of all different target audiences you have."

She told Kim Foltz of the *New York Times* (November 17, 1991) that there was a time when advertisers promoted the ideal of the superwoman, who "created the unrealistic expectation that women could do everything. . . .With any luck we've seen the last of her." However, those who knew Lazarus might say that a "superwoman" is exactly what the CEO, wife, and mother had become. Lazarus insisted it wasn't true. "Someone once described me as a swan," she told Sellers. "I look smooth going across the lake, but underneath, I'm paddling like crazy."

Further Reading:

Advertising Age Feb. 5, 1990; May 27, 1991; Sept. 9, 1996

Fortune Aug. 5, 1996

International Business Times Jun. 27, 2013

New York Jun. 13, 1994

New York Times Nov. 17, 1991; Sept. 9, 1996; Feb. 19, 1997

Wall Street Journal Dec. 11, 1995; Sept. 9, 1996

Lyne, Susan

Media executive

Born: 1950; Boston, Massachusetts

Reviewing the long career of Susan Lyne, one might be forgiven for thinking that her résumé belongs to several different people. Over the past three-plus decades, her leadership style has been in demand, regardless of the industry in which she works.

Early Life and Education

The oldest of five children in an Irish Catholic family—one son and four daughters—Susan Markham Lyne was born on April 30, 1950 in Boston, Massachusetts, to Eugene and Ruth Lyne. Her father was a lawyer and entrepreneur and the family was raised in comfortable circumstances. After graduating from high school, Lyne attended— in succession— art school, George Washington University, and the University of California at Berkeley, leaving each without graduating. (Lyne still does not hold a college degree.) In a conversation with Jennifer Reingold for the *CNN Money* Web site (October 3, 2011), Lyne suggested that her dropping out did not reflect a lack of seriousness or ambition but, rather, the revolutionary spirit of the times. "I never really thought twice about leaving school," she said. "It was a moment when we felt we were going to change history." In Berkley in the late 1960s, she lived in a house run by associates of the leftist activist Tom Hayden, a co-founder of Students for a Democratic Society. Lyne herself did not fully take part in the scene; she made silk-screen art and found work at the Blue Fairyland preschool, helping with candle-making. It was then that she met Jane Fonda, whose daughter attended the preschool. (Fonda later married Hayden.)

Later Career

In 1975 Lyne moved to San Francisco, across the bay from Berkeley. That year she became an associate editor at *City* magazine, where she discovered her talent as an editor. "I could write a piece and it would be fine," Lyne told Jennifer Reingold, "but I could assign a piece and it would be brilliant. I could make another person's work that much better by the questions I asked." In 1976 she joined the *New Times*, a San Francisco–based bi-weekly publication, where she worked as the West Coast editor. During her time there she got an interview with Bill and Emily Harris, imprisoned members of the Symbionese Liberation Army (SLA), a radical group that between 1973 and 1975 committed a series of bank robberies and various violent acts. The group gained notoriety when its members kidnapped the newspaper heiress Patty Hearst, who ultimately joined the SLA for a period of time and participated in several bank robberies. A detail from the interview that Lyne conducted, cited in court by the prosecutor in the Hearst case, helped lead to Hearst's conviction.

Lyne left the *New Times* in 1978 and moved to New York City. That year she became the managing editor of the *Village Voice*, owned at the time by the media mogul Rupert Murdoch. Next Lyne joined IPC Films, a film-production company founded by Jane Fonda and Bruce Gilbert. In her capacity as vice president in charge of creative development, Lyne looked for stories and articles that could be made into films. In 1984 Lyne married George Crile III, a reporter and producer with the long-running CBS news magazine *60 Minutes*. The following year she left IPC Films. She had become impatient with how long movies took to develop; at the same time, the new popularity of the videocassette recorder (VCR) convinced her of the importance of film in people's lives. Around that time she approached Rupert Murdoch with the idea of publishing a quality magazine focusing on the film world, with her as editor. Murdoch agreed and *Premiere* launched in 1987, quickly becoming very popular with the general public.

"One of the things I do more of is to make sure I can carve out a certain period of time every week to step back and think about the big picture."

Lyne served as the magazine's editor for nine years. On several occasions during that time, Joe Roth, president of the Walt Disney Co., tried to recruit her. In January 1996 Disney announced that Lyne would be its executive vice president for acquisitions and development of intellectual material and new opportunities—a newly created post. Writing for the *New York Times* (January 3, 1996), Deirdre Carmody paraphrased Roth as saying that Lyne "would be the most senior creative person in the motion picture group in New York and would be looking for opportunities to acquire screen plays and stage plays, as well as dealing with agents and publishers about books that might be made into films." Discussing his decision to hire Lyne, Roth told Reingold, "In my 40 years in the business, I've rarely asked anyone [out of the business] to come in. But she had great business skills and great people skills and great taste." Two years later Lyne was promoted to executive vice-president in charge of movies and miniseries for the ABC television network, which Disney owned. In that capacity she oversaw the airing of such biographical films as *The Three Stooges*, *The Audrey Hepburn Story*, *Anne Frank: The Whole Story*, and the Emmy Award–winning *Life with Judy Garland: Me and My Shadows*; she also launched the six-part miniseries *Rose Red*, written by the novelist Stephen King, the premiere of which was watched in 20 million households.

In January 2002, as ABC was experiencing declining prime-time ratings, the company announced that Lyne would replace its creative executive, Stu Bloomberg, making her president of ABC's entertainment division. Lyne thus took on the biggest challenge of her wide-ranging career up to that time. By then ABC had had four presidents of entertainment in five years (including Lyne), and the network lagged behind NBC and CBS in the ratings. By May 2002 Lyne and her team had looked over 110 scripts and screened 29 pilots. From those she chose eight series for the coming TV season, including *Legally Blonde*, based on the hit movie. Meanwhile, ABC finished the present season without a show among TV's 25 top-rated programs. Making matters worse, ABC was in last place among the major networks in winning viewers between the ages of 18 and 49, a highly sought-after demographic.

Then, early that summer, Lyne inadvertently caused some minor controversy by proclaiming that ABC's main goal was not to create innovative shows but to provide good entertainment. In explaining her comments, Lyne said to Michael Freeman for *Electronic Media* (September 9, 2002), "I was really speaking more to the fact that all of us in the business—critics and executives alike—can get into a tunnel-like mentality because [of] all of the material we have to review for TV. We can sometimes miss the fact [that] an engaging show is an engaging show, even if it does not break any new ground. We are going to do great programming at this network, but I don't measure the quality of a show or the value of a show by whether it is different than anything that has been done before." In January 2003, after the ratings collapse of *Who Wants to Be a Millionaire*, ABC announced that it would air five reality-TV shows, including *Extreme Makeover*, about people undergoing plastic surgery. By the end of that year, ABC's ratings had improved and the network was attracting more viewers between the ages of 18 and 49. Lyne also developed such shows as the drama *Lost* and the drama-comedy *Desperate Housewives*, set to air in the TV season starting in the fall of 2004. Prior to that, however, in April of that year, Lyne was fired from ABC—as were several other executives in the network's entertainment division. As recently as a week before the firing, Lyne had been assured that she was going to keep her job. (*Desperate Housewives*, a ratings hit, went on to win six Emmy Awards for its first season.)

In a conversation with Adam Bryant for the *New York Times* (October 3, 2009), Lyne called the firing a "defining moment" for her. "I was totally shocked," she said. "But it was also one of those moments where I couldn't hide. There was no, 'She's leaving to explore other opportunities,' or all the niceties of job changes in the corporate world. And the fact that it was as public and as sudden actually turned out to be liberating, because I didn't have to make things up or try to put a nicer face on it." She added, "And it gave me an ability to really look honestly at my tenure there, and to think really clearly about what I wanted to do next. And I had never in my life taken time off. So I had gone from one job to another, always because someone offered me a job. But I had never been able to direct my own career. It was the first time in my life I was able to do that. So what I thought was the worst thing that could have happened to me actually turned out to be a real opportunity."

As she had done before, Lyne moved on to an entirely new venue. In 2004 she joined the board of directors of Martha Stewart Living Omnimedia (MSLO), the publishing, broadcasting, and merchandising company founded and owned—via a majority of shares—by the home-enhancement icon Martha Stewart. In October 2004 Stewart was sent to a minimum-security prison for five months for conspiracy, obstruction of justice, and two counts of making false statements in a case that originated with allegations of insider trading. In November 2004 Lyne was appointed president and CEO of MSLO. That year the company had lost $60 million, so Lyne had a hard road ahead of her. Lyne made trips to the prison in West Virginia where Stewart was held; because Stewart was legally forbidden to discuss company business in detail, "I could report in to her on what we had done, but I couldn't ask her opinion about something, or get her desires going forward," Lyne told Laura Rich for the *New York Times* (April 24, 2005). "It had to be far more general than a typical business conversation. But we talked a lot about how and why she formed the company and how she looked at the brand, and the things that she loved about the magazines, and just her whole point of view on why this was important. I just got a very clear sense of what drove her and what was important to her." As the head of the company, Lyne "cut costs and boosted morale," according to Reingold, "both inside MSLO and with advertisers." By the end of 2006, she could proclaim that MSLO was gaining momentum. That year *Crain's New York Business* (September 16, 2007) declared Lyne to be one of the "most powerful women in New York." (In April 2005 Stewart had returned to the company, but she was still not legally permitted to be involved in it full time.)

In the summer of 2008 Lyne stepped down from her post as president and CEO of MSLO. A few months later she took on the job of CEO at Gilt Groupe, an online startup that sells high-end luxury goods at a discount. The timing of her arrival, with regard to the global economy, was less than propitious: Lyne started her new job in September 2008, which coincided with the beginning of the worldwide financial crisis. Another hurdle was her lack of familiarity with the world of Internet startups. But as before, Lyne unselfconsciously asked about everything she did not understand. By the end of 2010, the company had made around $400 million in revenue, and in September of that year she was made chairman.

In 2013 Susan Lyne left Gilt Groupe and joined AOL as CEO of its Brand Group. On September 2, 2014, Kara Swisher reported for the Web site *Re/code* that Lyne was "stepping down from that role to run a venture fund inside" AOL that would be "aimed at women-led digital startups." "This has always been in the back of my head and has been my passion," Lyne was quoted as saying. "Women are such an important part of the Internet and need to be represented better in funding."

Lyne's husband died of pancreatic cancer in May 2006. During his illness she continued to work full time, although, as Reingold reported, Lyne "suffered along with her husband." She told Reingold that she "needed a thread to the future, something that would connect me to life after George. Work was an antidote to the sadness. I can't tell you it was the right decision, but it felt like salvation at the time."

In her interview with Adam Bryant, Lyne talked about her leadership style: "My biggest challenge as a manager overall has always been moving from the nice to the 'This is what we're going to do.' And I still always like to get input, listen to what people have to say. But it's really clear that the decision has to be made at some point, and I'm a whole lot more comfortable with that now than I was 25 years ago." Later in the interview Lyne added: "One of the things I do more of is to make sure I can carve out a certain period of time every week to step back and think about the big picture. I think early in my career I was constantly looking at what was coming next week, next month, but rarely carving out time to really think about the future. It's useful on so many levels, not just because it does give you long-term focus, but because it forces you to reassess all those short-term decisions, too. I need time alone, quiet time alone, to do my job well."

Further Reading:

CNN Money Oct. 3, 2011

Electronic Media Sept. 9, 2002

New York Times Jan. 3, 1996; Apr. 24, 2005; Oct. 3, 2009

Re/code Sept. 2, 2014

McAndrews, Brian

CEO, Pandora radio; Advertising executive

Born. 1959

Brian McAndrews made waves in the world of high-tech business in 2007, when he left the online advertising firm aQuantive (once known as Avenue A), for a position as senior vice president of Microsoft's Advertiser and Publisher Solutions Group. In his new post McAndrews was named the top executive on *Advertising Age*'s 2008 "Digital A-List," but despite such praise, he remained at Microsoft for only a short time, leaving the company in early 2009. After a stint as a venture partner at Madrona Venture Group, McAndrews assumed the helm of Pandora Media in 2013.

Education and Early Career

Brian Patrick McAndrews was born in 1959. He was always savvy about business; when he was just 11, he started a lawn-mowing business in his Westport, Connecticut neighborhood. He made fliers with his own slogan ("A professional job without the professional price") and charged $10 to $15 per lawn.

McAndrews attended Harvard University in Cambridge, Massachusetts, where he lettered in track and field and graduated in 1980. In 1984 he earned an MBA from California's Stanford University Graduate School of Business.

Later Career

From 1984 to 1989 McAndrews was a product manager for General Mills and in 1990 he began working as the director of marketing for the broadcasting company ABC in Los Angeles. In early 1993 he was made vice president of current programming, and two years later he moved up to executive vice president of production for the ABC TV Network Group, which entailed supervision of all the company's in-house production units as well as its production partnerships with such firms as DreamWorks.

In March 1998 McAndrews moved to New York City to become executive vice president and general manager of ABC Sports. The following year he quit his position with ABC and joined Avenue A, an Internet marketing firm based in Seattle, Washington. He became president and chief executive officer and took the company public in 2000. When the company struggled to make a profit, McAndrews divided it into two separate divisions in 2001: Avenue A, which operated online media planning and buying services, and Atlas, which provided technology tools and services to advertisers. (One example of such a tool was a program McAndrews marketed that could track whether or not a user clicked on an ad, whether or not he or she goes on to visit the advertiser's Web site, and whether or not a purchase is ultimately made.) McAndrews' clients soon included such major corporations as Nike, Starbucks, Lancome, and HBO.

The company's name changed in 2003 to aQuantive, and the following year it acquired the Web design shop Razorfish and launched Drive Performance Media (DRIVEpm), a network that bought and sold online ad inventory. In all, McAndrews guided the company through more than a dozen acquisitions.

In August 2007 Microsoft Corp. acquired aQuantive for $6 billion. McAndrews was named senior vice president of Microsoft's new Advertiser and Publisher Solutions Group, which encompassed all three of aQuantive's business units (Avenue A/Razorfish, which had become the world's largest interactive advertising firm, Atlas, and DRIVEpm). The news of his appointment was widely touted. "Microsoft has used its might, clout and smarts to take on any number of products and services—the browser, the operating system, the portable music player, to name just three—with varying degrees of success," Louise Story wrote for the *New York Times* (September 26, 2007). "Now, Microsoft is taking solid aim at a business that is arguably outside its core competence: advertising. And it is deliberately facing off against a specialist, Google. The general in charge of part of Microsoft's assault [is] Brian McAndrews." Story explained, "Mr. McAndrews has a long-term strategy that boils down to divorcing online advertising from Internet searches. The two have been viewed as a couple, because so many people use portals and search engines as their home base on the Web, but Mr. McAndrews says that model shortchanges advertisers and Web publishers. Mr. McAndrews's proposed system, called 'conversion attribution,' would track all of the online places where consumers see ads and give advertisers a fuller picture of the various ways that consumers reach them. Tracking is important, because the site that gets credit for prompting a user's visit is the one that gets paid for it."

"I share Pandora's longstanding belief that musicians have to be compensated fairly, but the existing system has been put together piecemeal and does not serve anyone well."

In January 2009 McAndrews left Microsoft and in 2013 became the CEO of Pandora, the Internet streaming service that has 76 million listeners. The news was greeted with great enthusiasm in the financial community, but, as Ari Levy and Andy Fixmer wrote in *Businessweek* (March 13, 2014), "Pandora continues to struggle with the same obstacles it's been dealing with for years. It remains enmeshed in a protracted battle with the music industry over royalty payments, and it's not yet profitable. On March 6 [2014] the company, which makes its money from ad sales and ad-free subscriptions, reported its slowest-ever increase in monthly listener hours."

The changing nature of media makes McAndrews' challenges all the more intense. "Pandora was an early leader in Internet music streaming," Adam Lashinsky wrote in the November 11, 2014 *Fortune*, "and deployed unique technology that guessed a listener's musical tastes. Its revenue this year will top $900 million. But music streaming has become a crowded market: iHeartRadio… and Apple's iTunes Radio compete on ad-supported music. A number of services including Spotify, Apple's Beats Music, and Amazon offer on-demand subscriptions. Services like Rdio offer both." There has also been widespread criticism among musicians over Pandora's less-than-spectacular royalty payments. "I share Pandora's longstanding belief that musicians have to be compensated fairly, but the existing system has been put together piecemeal and does not serve anyone well," McAndrews said, as per an article written by Ben Sisario in the *New York Times* (September 11, 2013).

Sisario continued: "Mr. McAndrews' corporate biography has already been tailored for digital music. His playlists, according to Pandora, 'reflect his love for Elton John, Billy Joel, the Rolling Stones and Bruce Springsteen,' as well as younger acts like Bruno Mars and Rihanna."

Further Reading:

Advertising Age Nov. 5, 2001; Mar. 17, 2008

American Executive Feb. 1, 2005

Businessweek Mar. 13, 2014

Fortune Nov. 11, 2014

New York Times Sep. 26, 2007; Sept. 11, 2013

McCann, Renetta

Advertising executive

Born: 1956; Chicago, Illinois

Before Renetta McCann was named the 2002 Adwoman of the Year by the Women's Advertising Club of Chicago, the 24-year ad-industry veteran had been nominated for the award several times earlier without a win. Indeed, McCann had taken to calling herself "the Susan Lucci of the Women's Advertising Club of Chicago"—a reference to the soap-opera actress who became famous for her 19 consecutive, fruitless Daytime Emmy nominations. "One look at me and you can only imagine the boundaries I've had to negotiate, the challenges I've had to traverse," McCann said during her acceptance speech, as quoted by Sonia Alleyne for *Black Enterprise* (September 2002). Knowing that audience members would assume that she was speaking of obstacles familiar to African-American women in the business world, she delivered her punch line: "Such are the trials of being a short person." McCann likes to defy expectations.

Education and Early Career

The eldest of five children, Renetta E. McCann was born in Chicago, Illinois, in 1956. According to Matthew Jones in *diversityinbusiness.com* (September 2004), her mother was a teacher and earned two master's degrees. In 1978 McCann graduated from Northwestern University, in Evanston, Illinois, with a degree in communication studies. She wanted to work in the advertising industry, but as she told Laurie Freeman for *Advertising Age* (February 15, 1999), "I knew, coming out of school, that I needed skills and more training." Shortly after she completed college, she was accepted into a training program at Leo Burnett Worldwide Inc., a top advertising agency based in Chicago that created marketing campaigns for such companies as McDonald's and Kellogg's. "I felt confident that Burnett had the program to teach me the next set of things I knew I needed to know," McCann continued to Freeman. She began as an assistant in Burnett's media department, which was responsible for placing clients' advertisements in newspapers and magazines, on radio, and on television. She became a media supervisor in 1982.

Later Career

McCann has credited much of her success to her mentor at Burnett, Chuck Quarnstrom, who was serving as a vice president when she began her career. "Mentoring is very personal and Chuck trained a lot of people who are now media directors," she said to Freeman. "I don't think he treated me any different than other trainees, but he set a great example professionally—and the way I operate today is very much the way Chuck would do things." "He instilled . . . things such as listening to clients," she told Jennifer Derryberry for *Advertising Age's Business Marketing* (August 1, 1995), "turning over rocks and stones to find answers, and the beauty of doing good work."

In 1986 the professional development organization Design and Art Direction (D&AD) recognized McCann by awarding her its prestigious Black Pencil, which honors people in advertising who produce groundbreaking work or redefine the field. She was the first Black Pencil honoree from a media department. That same year Leo Burnett promoted her to assistant media director. By 1988 she had been named vice president, and one year later she became media director. McCann subsequently took the lead in pitching for business from several high-profile clients, winning virtually all, including Sony's Consumer Electronics in 1991; Fruit of the Loom in 1992; Disney World in 1994; and Johnnie Walker whiskey in 1995. In 1997, as the media department increasingly took control of the company's advertising campaigns' strategies, Burnett spun it off into a separate company, Starcom Media Services, which would also track market trends. McCann, who had accepted a promotion to senior vice president at Leo Burnett Worldwide in 1995, was appointed managing director of Starcom North America in 1999; in 2000 she took over as CEO.

"As a woman of color, the rules of how I play the game are different. . . . My clients want to know how my presence will enhance their bottom line. And, in somewhat of a Pavlovian manner, I have developed a style that works with clients as well as works internally with employees."

In a single year (2000) McCann attracted more than $700 million worth of new business, with such iconic American brands as Hallmark, Polaroid, McDonald's, and Sara Lee. For years her workforce of 600 in the U.S. and Canada—half of whom were hired under her watch—had the lowest employee-turnover rate in advertising, indicating her remarkable ability to inspire loyalty in a notoriously volatile industry. "I developed my personal brand over time," she explained to Charmon Parker Williams for *BlackMBA Magazine* (Fall 2004). "As a woman of color, the rules of how I play the game are different. . . . My clients want to know how my presence will enhance their bottom line. And, in somewhat of a Pavlovian manner, I have developed a style that works with clients as well as works internally with employees."

Through a series of mergers and acquisitions, Starcom became part of the Starcom MediaVest Group, which in turn joined forces with other U.S. advertising and media properties to form the media group Bcom3. In 2002 the global-communications conglomerate Publicis Groupe purchased Bcom3, placing Starcom under its aegis. Throughout this period McCann maintained her title and Starcom flourished, even as the media industry grappled with reduced advertising and cuts in spending, first because of the bursting of the late-1990s dot-com stock-market bubble, and then because of the terrorist attacks of September 11, 2001. Key to McCann's success was her reputation as a strategist and media thinker, which led Disney to hand over responsibility for its corporate brand management to Starcom North America. "We were able to take the clues that they gave us and put it into a story that was coherent for them as a company," McCann told Alleyne. "Everybody talks about the Disney account as if it is one thing, but we picked up 16 pieces of business [with Disney]."

In August 2004 McCann was again promoted, this time to CEO of the Americas for SMG. In his announcement of McCann's promotion, SMG Worldwide CEO Jack Klues said, as quoted by Aaron Baar in *Adweek* (August 3, 2004), "Renetta has consistently demonstrated a keen ability to run an effective organization while aggressively stewarding her clients' brands and championing innovation and results in consumer contact."

"This was probably a little bit of an overdue announcement," Jack Klues said, regarding McCann's advancement, according to *Media Daily News* (August 4, 2004). "In terms of recognition for Renetta, it's more external recognition because she's always been a trusted advisor to me, and certainly a big contributor to the SMG board at large." McCann's job encompassed oversight of SMG's four principal units: Starcom, Media-

Vest, StarLink, and GM Planworks, the last of which developed media strategies for General Motors. Collectively, SMG controlled nearly $13 billion in ad dollars spent in the U.S., Canada, and Latin America—16 percent of the total expended on advertising in the Western Hemisphere—making SMG the largest media buyer in the Americas.

A highly sought-after speaker at advertising and media-industry conferences, McCann served as chair of the American Association for Advertising Agencies' Media Policy Committee; as a member of the advisory board of Northwestern University's Media Management Center; as a member of the American Advertising Federation's Business Practices Leadership Council; and as a board member of the Audit Bureau of Circulations and of Chicago United, a coalition of senior executives who advocate for racial diversity among business leaders. Her trophy collection includes several Effies, presented by the New York American Marketing Association to the creators of each year's most effective advertising campaigns, and Cannes Lions, awarded annually at the International Advertising Festival. McCann was given the Black Expo President's Award in 2000. The following year she was named a "Media Maven" by *Advertising Age*. In 2002 *Ebony* included her among "57 Most Intriguing Blacks," and *Black Enterprise* chose her as "Corporate Executive of the Year." In 2003 *Essence* listed her among "50 Women Who Are Changing the World," and the Women's Leadership Exchange presented her with its Compass Award, for her contributions in changing perceptions of women as leaders. Her other honors include a *BusinessWeek* Media Strategies Award and the *Chicago Magazine* Association's Vanguard Award.

In 2012 McCann returned to Leo Burnett. As Lewis Lazare reported in the *Chicago Business Journal* (September 11, 2012), "McCann is rejoining Burnett as chief talent officer, a post that will give her a role in determining what kind of talent across all departments joins Burnett…" In 2014 the American Advertising Federation named McCann the year's "Industry Influential for her tireless effort in championing multiculturalism in the advertising world, and promoting opportunities in the industry for a diverse range of candidates."

Further Reading:

Advertising Age Feb. 15, 1999

Advertising Age's Business Marketing Aug. 1995

Adweek Aug. 3, 2004

American Advertising Federation Web site

Black Enterprise Sept. 2002

BlackMBA Magazine Fall 2004

Chicago Business Journal Sept. 11, 2012

diversityinbusiness.com Sep. 2004

Meyrowitz, Carol M.

Executive officer, TJX Companies

Born: 1954, New York City

As the chief executive officer (CEO) and president of the TJX Companies, Carol Meyrowitz oversees more than 160,000 employees and 2,850 off-price retail stores—stores that charge significantly less for high-quality brand-name apparel and home merchandise than most other retail outlets. In September 2011 TJX owned 963 T. J. Maxx, 875 Marshalls, and 366 HomeGoods stores in the U.S.; 213 Winners, 82 HomeSense, five Marshalls, and three StyleSense stores in Canada; and 322 T. K. Maxx and 24 HomeSense stores in four European nations (England, Ireland, Germany, and Poland), making it the largest off-price retailer for clothing and home products in the world. Except for one 10-month period, when she served as an independent adviser for TJX, Meyrowitz has been a TJX employee since 1983, when she was hired as a buyer for one of its chains; she was named president of TJX in October 2005 and CEO in January 2007.

Education and Early Career

The daughter of Sidney Meyrowitz and Helen (Schoenberger) Meyrowitz, Carol M. Meyrowitz was born in New York City on February 28, 1954. Her late father was a furrier who owned his own business. Her mother is an accomplished artist; she has exhibited widely, and her work is in the permanent collections of several museums. Meyrowitz's older brother, Andrew, is a real-estate broker and developer. No readily available print or Internet publications mention Meyrowitz's childhood, the schools she attended (although she is a graduate of New Jersey's Rider University), or her activities until 1983, the year she began her career with TJX (then known as the Zayre Corp.).

Her first job was buyer for Hit or Miss, a chain that carried off-price women's-specialty apparel.

Later Career

Based in Framingham, Massachusetts, TJX grew out of the New England Trading Co., a wholesale women's-undergarment supplier founded in 1919 in Boston by two brothers, Max and Morris Feldberg, who had immigrated to the U.S. from Russia. Ten years later the Feldbergs moved into retail sales with a store that sold women's hosiery—the first of the Bell Hosiery Shops. In 1956 Max's son, Stanley Feldberg, and Sumner Feldberg, Morris's son, opened a discount department store called Zayre; it too expanded into a chain and the company went public in 1962. In 1969 the Zayre Corp. purchased Hit or Miss.

In 1976—spurred by the burgeoning successes of such chains as Wal-Mart—the Feldbergs hired a Marshalls executive, Bernard "Ben" Cammarata, to launch a new line of off-price stores selling upscale apparel and home products. Thus was born T. J. Maxx, which began with two stores in 1977; by 1994, when Howard Rudnitsky profiled Cammarata for *Forbes* (January 31, 1994), there were 514 T. J. Maxx outlets in the U.S. Zayre introduced the catalogue retailer Chadwick's of Boston in 1983, BJ's Wholesale Club in 1984, and HomeClub (a big-box store specializing in materials for building contractors and do-it-yourself homeowners) in 1986. In 1988, spurred by shrinking profits, the Zayre Corp. sold its 392 Zayre discount stores to Ames Department Stores for $800 million and became the TJX Companies, the umbrella for T. J. Maxx, Hit or Miss, Chadwick's, HomeClub, and BJ's. (TJX spun off HomeClub in 1989 and BJ's in 1997; neither is now associated with TJX.) In 1991 TJX purchased the Winners chain in Canada. The year 1992 marked the debut of the HomeGoods chain, and 1994 that of T. K. Maxx in England.

In 1995 TJX acquired Marshalls, whose motto was "Never pay full price for fabulous" and which was then the nation's second-largest off-price retail chain; the Marmaxx Group came into being soon afterward. The next year TJX sold Chadwick's and in 1998 it launched A. J. Wright, an off-price chain whose merchandise was less costly than that sold at T. J. Maxx or Marshalls. Winners introduced HomeSense, a chain similar to HomeGoods. TJX bought the Bob's Stores chain in 2003.

Meyrowitz started to rise through the ranks early on: From 1987 to 1989 she served as Hit or Miss's vice president and merchandising manager. (In 1995 TJX closed 69 Hit or Miss stores and sold the chain's 399 remaining stores because of "problems in the women's discount apparel industry," in the words of a *New York Times* [August 16, 1995] reporter, which had led to plummeting sales.)

In 1989 Meyrowitz was promoted to vice president and senior merchandise manager of Chadwick's of Boston. In 1990 she became Chadwick's general merchandise manager. From 1991 to 1996 she served as the chain's senior vice president of merchandising. Meyrowitz then became Chadwick's executive vice president of merchandising, a position she held until 1999, when she became the senior vice president of merchandising for the Marmaxx Group, the umbrella for the TJX brands Marshalls and T.J. Maxx. (TJX sold Chadwick's in 1996.)

Meyrowitz's next Marmaxx titles were executive vice president of merchandising (2000–01) and president. Concurrently, in 2001 she took on the position of executive vice president of TJX. In 2003, according to Wolfgang Saxon's obituary of Stanley Feldberg for the *New York Times* (May 16, 2004), TJX's annual revenue equaled about $12 billion and its workforce totaled about 100,000 employees. In 2004 Meyrowitz served as TJX's senior executive vice president.

At the beginning of 2005, Meyrowitz left TJX to seek "new opportunities and challenges," as she put it, according to Jessica Pallay in the *Harrisonburg* (Virginia) *Daily News Record* (November 15, 2004). Ernie Herrman, who had been the Marmaxx Group's chief operating officer, was named TJX's president. For 10 months in 2005, Meyrowitz served as an adviser to the TJX Companies and a consultant for Berkshire Partners, a Boston-based private-equity firm (not connected with Berkshire Hathaway, Warren Buffett's company).

"Given the challenging times, we believe our results speak to our ability to hold our own in tough business cycles."

In October 2005 Meyrowitz returned to TJX to assume the post of president. (Herrman was given the titles of senior executive vice president and group president.) "In Carol, we have an extremely creative merchant with great strategic vision, leadership ability, and operational experience, as well as extensive off-price expertise and knowledge of TJX," Ben Cammarata, TJX's CEO at that time, was quoted as saying in *Business Wire* (October 6, 2005). In 2006 Meyrowitz joined Cammarata as one of TJX's two directors. (TJX also has a half-dozen independent directors, who are not TJX employees.) "Carol has been responsible for some of [TJX's] most successful initiatives," Cammarata was quoted as saying in an article for *just-style* (September 8, 2006). "She is a visionary leader and great generator of ideas."

In 2007 Meyrowitz succeeded Cammarata as CEO. (He retained the position of chairman of the board.) At around that time a widespread security breach of the company's computer system occurred, giving hackers access to the credit and debit cards of TJX customers who had bought merchandise at company stores. The company announced that the stolen information affected millions of customers who made purchases at TJX stores between May 2006 and January 2007; TJX later revealed that people who had bought merchandise at any TJX store from January 2003 to June 2004 were also at risk due to suspected computer hacking in 2005. According to a December 31, 2007 *Chain Store Age* article, Meyrowitz handled the crisis in an exemplary fashion. "If there were an award for grace under pressure, Carol Meyrowitz . . . would deserve it. The fact that the largest payment-card data breach to date occurred on her watch may always be a chapter in her memoirs, but it is not the whole story. What's more telling is how Meyrowitz confronted the crisis, assumed control of security risks within her company, and encouraged cooperative action between banks, payment-card companies and merchants industrywide."

In 2008 TJX sold the Bob's Stores chain to two private-equity firms. Because of the worldwide recession and "unfavorable exchange rates," as an Associated Press (AP) writer put it (November 12, 2008), TJX's profits declined by 6 percent that year. "Given the challenging times, we believe our results speak to our ability to hold our own in tough business cycles," Meyrowitz said, according to AP. "We are extremely focused on buying right and running with leaner-than-usual inventory levels, which has led to faster inventory turns and strong merchandise margins."

In 2009 Meyrowitz signed a new contract with TJX that guaranteed an annual base salary of at least $1.47 million. That same year Meyrowitz earned $17.4 million in total compensation. In 2007 and 2009 TJX opened T. K. Maxx stores in Germany and Poland, respectively. In 2010 the company announced plans to open more than 1,000 new stores and to introduce "smaller concept" stores. That year TJX shut 71 of its A. J. Wright stores and converted 91 others to T. J. Maxx, Marshalls, or HomeGoods outlets, and closed two distribution centers; in the process 4,400 employees were laid off. In a company press release (December 10, 2010), Meyrowitz stated, "While I believe this move makes us a much stronger company and will benefit TJX in both the near-term and long-term, it was not an easy decision as many positions will be eliminated and it will be difficult for our affected associates. As a company, however, it will allow us to focus our financial and managerial resources on our highest return businesses, all of which have significant growth opportunities, as well as to significantly improve the economic prospects of our business." Meyrowitz's words were quoted in nearly 700 online publications, ranging from *CNN Money* and *Daily Finance* to the *Forest Park* (Illinois) *Review*, which reported that the A. J. Wright store in the Forest Park Mall was scheduled to close at the end of February 2011.

Meyrowitz's total compensation in 2010 was $23.1 million and included $1.6 million in salary. In February 2011 she signed a new employment contract with TJX, according to which she would continue to serve as CEO for the next two years and would remain a director. "The re-signing is clearly an endorsement of the accomplishments and the good work that she and the organization have done under her regime," Michael Tesler, a partner with the consulting firm Retail Concepts, told Thomas Grillo for the *Boston Herald* (February 2, 2011). In fiscal year 2011 Meyrowitz received more than $23 million in total compensation, and TJX's net sales grew by 8 percent. In *Retail Merchandiser* (June 1, 2011), Meyrowitz was quoted as saying that in 2010 "our bottom line grew substantially." "This speaks to the extraordinary flexibility of our off-price business model . . . " she said. "We are running our business with lean, fast-turning inventories, which, in 2010, again led to even stronger merchandise margins. This, combined with our continued cost reduction initiatives, helped drive large increases in profitability."

"Meyrowitz's leadership has sustained consumer confidence in her company," *Chain Store Age* (December 31, 2007) declared. In addition, the article continued, she "has reinvigorated TJX's merchandise offerings with more fashion-forward goods, and tested designer departments. The results of her efforts, and her steadfastness, are seen in the chain's performance. At a time when many retailers are struggling, TJX remains on the upswing." Marianne Wilson and Connie Robbins Gentry, writing in the December 17, 2010 *Chain Store Age*, lauded Meyrowitz—"the leader of the largest off-price retail organization in the United States"—as having proven herself "to be totally in sync with her customers and their needs."

In 2010 TJX ranked 119th on the *Fortune* 500 list, with revenues of $21.9 billion, 8 percent more than in 2009. *Fortune* has listed Meyrowitz herself among the world's 50 most powerful women in business.

The TJX Foundation, which the Feldman family set up in 1966 (as the Zayre Foundation), aided about 2,000 nonprofit organizations in the U.S., Canada, and Europe in 2010. According to its Web site, the foundation "focuses its charitable giving on programs that provide basic-need services to disadvantaged women, children and families in communities where we do business." In 2004 Meyrowitz won the Woman of the Year Award from the Needlers Foundation, which, like the TJX Foundation, contributes money to various charities. The award came with a cash prize of more than $700,000, which Meyrowitz contributed to the Joslin Diabetes Center. Meyrowitz is a member of the center's board of overseers. She has also served on the boards of directors of Amscan Holdings Inc., the Yankee Candle Co., Staples Inc., and Party City Holdings.

Meyrowitz is married to John deBairos, who owns a real-estate firm. They have two adult daughters, Ariel and Danielle. In her spare time Meyrowitz enjoys traveling, working out, and reading.

Further Reading:

Boston Globe Apr. 30, 2010

Boston Herald Feb. 2, 2011

Chain Store Age Dec. 31, 2007; Dec. 17, 2010

Harrisonburg (Virginia) *Daily News Record* Nov. 15, 2004

just-style Sept. 8, 2006

TJX.com

USA Today Dec. 30, 2009

Moreno, Arturo

Owner, Los Angeles Angels baseball team

Born: 1946; Tucson, Arizona

Although he came to national attention in the 1980s for his entrepreneurial savvy in developing a billboard business in Phoenix, Arizona, Moreno made history in 2003 when he became the first Hispanic majority owner of a major sports franchise in the United States, purchasing Major League Baseball's Angels.

Education and Early Career

Arturo "Arte" Moreno was born in August 1946 in Tucson, Arizona. He is the oldest of eleven children, a fourth-generation American, and the son of a newspaper publisher. Moreno's grandfather started a successful weekly Spanish-language newspaper for Tucson's sprawling Latino population. Moreno worked in the newspaper's office during high school, developing an exemplary work ethic while discovering the importance of his Mexican heritage.

After graduating from high school in 1965, Moreno enlisted in the U.S. Army even as the turmoil over American involvement in the Vietnam War escalated. His two-year stint included a tour of duty in Vietnam, where he experienced fierce combat around Da Nang—an experience that would shape his conservative political beliefs and his unwavering patriotism. He returned to Arizona, committed to a business career. With the help of the G.I. Bill, Moreno enrolled in the University of Arizona, graduating with a degree in marketing in 1973. Throughout his university time, Moreno worked selling shoes, learning firsthand how to appeal to customers.

After graduation, recognizing the potential of billboard advertising given the open expanses around the Phoenix area, Moreno joined Eller Outdoor Advertising Company in the sales division. He struggled initially in the small but highly competitive billboard industry, but his charisma and ability to easily relate to customers quickly established him as a force in the Phoenix business community.

"I owe it to the fans to give them hope. I'm not trying to tell you we're doing everything right all of the time, but it's not because we're not trying."

After seven years learning the business, making key contacts, and networking with advertising firms across the country, Moreno joined Outdoor Systems in 1984, at the time a midsized marketing firm worth about $500,000. He quickly rose within the corporate structure and within three years became the company's chief executive officer (CEO). Under his direction, Outdoor Systems grew exponentially. By the mid-1990s the company was worth an estimated $90 million and Moreno had become a nationally recognized entrepreneur, profiled in news magazines.

Later Career

In 1996, Outdoor Systems' stock went public, and Moreno became one of the richest entrepreneurs in America. By 1999, however, Moreno was growing restless in the billboard industry, which was facing competition from the growing cable-television and Internet advertising markets. Moreno always had been interested in sports (an alumni benefactor of the University of Arizona, he was a proud supporter of its athletic programs), particularly baseball. He had coached his sons' Little League baseball teams for ten years. From 1985 to 1992, Moreno was one of 17 partners (including actor Bill Murray) who owned the Salt Lake City Trappers, a successful minor-league baseball franchise. Moreno loved the intimate atmosphere of the ballpark—he relished time he spent with the fans and devised innovative marketing techniques to attract fans to games. Helped by the team's winning records, Moreno developed his own sense of baseball marketing. It was a remarkable run: The partnership purchased the team for a paltry $150,000 and sold it in 1992 for $1.5 million.

In a bold move, Moreno sold Outdoor Systems to Infinity Broadcasting in 1999 for $8.3 billion. After testing a few projects—including a used-car franchise and a golf course—Moreno was determined to buy a Major League Baseball (MLB) team. He already had purchased a 5-percent stake in the Phoenix Suns of the National Basketball Association. In 2000, he became a minority shareholder (5.3 percent) in the Arizona Diamondbacks of the National League and was part of its World Series championship over the Yankees in 2001. In one of the few missteps in Moreno's career, he attempted to purchase the team outright and assume the role of managing general partner, but was outmaneuvered by a consortium of the team's partners. Although he made a second attempt, in the end Moreno was bought out.

Moreno did not have to wait long for another opportunity. In 2002, he showed interest in acquiring the Anaheim Angels, then owned by Disney. The franchise had just won its first World Series but lacked an identity and had only a slender share of the highly competitive sports market in the Los Angeles area. In the spring of 2003, Moreno made his offer: $180 million for a team that at the time had a market value of $250 million. The club was struggling; despite its championship, the franchise attracted only 2.3 million people in annual attendance (14,000 season ticket holders) and generated a thin $100 million in revenue. MLB owners quickly approved the sale, and on May 15, Moreno became the first Hispanic majority owner of a major league franchise in American professional sports history.

Moreno immediately made his mark on the Angels operations. Attendance in the first year of his tenure leaped by more than a million. By 2009, annual attendance exceeded 3.5 million. From 2004 to 2009, the Angels won the highly competitive American League Western Division. By 2009, the franchise was valued at $500 million. In 2006, Moreno negotiated a lucrative exclusive contract with Fox Sports Network to televise all the Angels home games, a deal responsible for generating on average $500 million each year.

However, despite such success, Moreno faced a firestorm of criticism in 2005 when he moved to change the franchise name to the Los Angeles Angels of Anaheim in an attempt to broaden the team's appeal to the lucrative Los Angeles market. Some saw the move as a bid to reach the large Latino population in Los Angeles; Moreno insisted that he was entirely motivated by economics. Although Moreno faced a lawsuit from Anaheim city officials and a backlash of criticism from residents who had long regarded their baseball team as distinct from Los Angeles, Moreno prevailed.

Moreno brought to the Angels franchise his business acumen and charisma. Determined to fill seats after taking control of a franchise that had just won a World Series but had one of the lowest attendance records in Major League Baseball, Arte Moreno initiated a number of risky price cuts for tickets (most notably for children under age 12); revamped the souvenir and concession operations (in addition to cutting beer prices, he approved the $44 family special: four tickets, four drinks, and four hot dogs for $44); and approved ticket-incentive packages for families. All of these moves, some observers speculated, were geared to attract lower-income Latino fans in the Los Angeles area. That argument extended as well to Moreno's bold player personnel moves. In his first year, he made headlines when he invested more than $140 million to bring four superstar free agents to the Angels: pitchers Bartolo Colon and Kelvim Escobar and outfielders Vladimir Guerrero and Jose Guillen. That the new players were all Latino ignited further controversy—but fans responded. Moreno himself dismissed insinuations that his moves were racially motivated, claiming he had simply acquired the best talent in positions the team needed. The team's success on the field and in the stands amply proved his point.

Ultra-competitive, he shaped a business plan centered on two simple goals: Fill the seats and win games. He did both. During home games, he would often leave the owner's box to mingle among fans. That populist style, which endeared him to the Angels' fan base, was further enhanced when he turned down more than $3 million in potential yearly revenue when he opted to name the team's new stadium Angels Stadium instead of securing a corporate sponsorship. The mix of business savvy and unaffected populism defined Moreno's signature success. And he has to maintain his equilibrium in the face of the Angels' sometimes less-than-stellar seasons. "I owe it to the fans to give them hope," he was quoted by Bob Nightengale in *USA Today* (June 24, 2013). "I'm not trying to tell you we're doing everything right all of the time, but it's not because we're not trying.""

Further Reading:

Angels Essentials, 2007

Great American Billboards, 2007

Moneyball, 2004

Playing America's Game, 2007

USA Today, June 24, 2013

Sammons, Mary

Former CEO, Rite-Aid

Born: 1946; Portland, Oregon

Mary Sammons, the former chairman and chief executive officer (CEO) of the drugstore chain Rite Aid, has been widely credited with leading the once-struggling company back to profitability.

Education and Early Career

The daughter of Lee W. and Ann (Cherry) Jackson, Sammons was born on October 12, 1946 in Portland, Oregon. In 1970 she earned a B.A. in French and a teaching certificate from Oregon's Marylhurst College.

After graduating, Sammons worked as a substitute teacher, and in 1973 she answered an ad for management trainees placed by the Portland-based retail chain Fred Meyer. She was hired as a buyer in 1975, and over the next several years she worked her way up through the company's ranks, becoming the chief executive officer and president in 1999. During her time at Fred Meyer, Sammons introduced a number of changes to the store's marketing strategies, sponsored new merchandising systems, and created initiatives to improve customer service and employee morale, all of which helped to improve the store's image and bottom line.

Later Career

Later in 1999, Fred Meyer was bought out by the Kroger chain, and Sammons followed her boss, Robert Miller, to Rite Aid—the nation's number-three drugstore chain, after CVS and Walgreens. When Sammons was hired to be the president and chief operating officer of the chain, she became the highest-ranking woman executive in mass retailing. (Miller had been hired as the company's new chairman and CEO.) At that time the company was dealing with an accounting scandal that resulted in CEO Martin L. Grass, the son of Rite Aid's founder, being sent to prison for eight years. Because of his mismanagement, Rite Aid was in deep debt, its suppliers were not being paid, store shelves were empty, customers were defecting in droves, and employee morale was at an all-time low.

Working under Miller, Sammons introduced a number of measures to improve the company. She started by instituting a program for employees—called RAPTAR—which stood for Recognition, Appreciation, Praise, Treat Associates Respectfully—aimed at improving company culture and morale. Among other initiatives, she oversaw the redesign of many of the stores, making the profitable pharmacy counter a focal point, and partnered with outside firms to open walk-in clinics at some Rite Aid locations.

"If your people don't feel valued and important, then it's hard for them to take care of the customers. It was clear that our people knew the kinds of things they need to do. We just need to make it possible for them to do it. And that helped set the stage for what we saw as the foundation that we needed."

Sammons became the CEO of Rite Aid in June 2003. That year she was named *Retail Merchandiser*'s Retail Executive of the Year for orchestrating the company's impressive turnaround. (She was the first figure from the drugstore business ever to be named to the title.) "One of the principles that has guided Sammons since she became president and CEO of the company," Maria Pikalova wrote in the online publication *Good2Work* (September 3, 2007), "is that a retailer's most important resource is its people. 'If your people don't feel valued and important, then it's hard for them to take care of the customers,' says Sammons. 'It was clear that our people knew the kinds of things they need to do. We just need to make it possible for them to do it. And that helped set the stage for what we saw as the foundation that we needed. So we went through a number of meetings to come to agreement on our core values as a company. We believe that's where we needed to start.'"

In 2007, the year Rite Aid acquired rival chains Brooks and Eckerd, Sammons became company chairman. In an April 2010 interview with *Leaders* magazine, Sammons was quoted as saying that she was "pretty persistent about what I think needs to happen, am willing to go the extra distance to make things happen, and will remain focused until we get what we want accomplished; that I practice what I ask others to do—work hard and get results, have the courage to take risks, and be optimistic we can achieve what we set out to achieve. But I don't believe I can do it all myself, so I empower members of my team to do what they need to accomplish to reach the overall goal."

Sammons was featured regularly on lists of the most powerful women in the business world, including those compiled by the editors of *Fortune* and *Forbes*. She and her husband, Nickolas F. Sammons, have been married since 1967; they have one son, Peter. Mary Sammons served as Rite Aid CEO until 2010.

Further Reading:

Chain Drug Review Apr. 26, 2004

Drug Store News July 17, 2006; Sep. 8, 2008

Forbes Aug. 30, 2007

Good2Work Sept. 3, 2007

Leaders Apr. 2010

Retail Merchandiser Feb. 1, 2004

Sen, Laura J.

President and CEO, BJ's Wholesale Club

Born: 1956

Since 2009 Laura J. Sen has been the chief executive officer (CEO) of BJ's Wholesale Club, which sells a wide variety of household items at discounted prices to customers who each pay an annual membership fee to shop at one of the company's almost 200 locations. Although smaller than such competitors as Sam's Club (which is owned by Wal-Mart) and Costco, BJ's has earned a spot on the *Fortune* 500, with reported annual profits of $95 million. Sen, one of the few female CEOs of a *Fortune* 500 firm, has been widely praised for her management style; she spends at least 20 percent of her time walking the aisles of BJ's clubs, talking to employees and shoppers. She told Catherine Elton for the *Boston Globe* (January 9, 2011): "I say to the team members [employees], 'If you had a magic wand, what would you do?' And then I pause and say, 'Because I have a magic wand.'" "That is why she is so successful," Burt Flickinger III, a retail consultant, told Elton. "Most of her competitors tend to spend their time behind their desks in corporate headquarters or spend excessive time with Wall Street analysts, bankers, or investors. Laura is fully focused on the front lines."

Education and Early Career

Laura J. Sen was born on July 7, 1956 and raised with her two siblings in Wakefield, Massachusetts. Her mother, an Irish-American, and father, a Chinese-American, met while working for the Massachusetts Department of Transportation, she as a secretary and he as an engineer. Although her ethnic background made her somewhat unusual in her middle-class suburban neighborhood, Sen was a popular figure at Wakefield High School, where she was a cheerleader and competed in field hockey, gymnastics, and track.

After graduating from high school, Sen studied French at Boston College. Although she was proficient in working with numbers, she had little interest in business courses, finding them inconsistent with the liberal political views she then held. Sen spent her junior year in Paris, initially sharing an apartment with an elderly French woman who died soon after the start of the semester. Unwilling to return home, Sen set about finding new lodgings; she quickly found work as an au pair for a wealthy family. "I had never been around people who owned jets and skied in Gstaad and had clothing custom-made. It opened my eyes," Sen told Amy Zipkin for the *New York Times* (April 25, 2009).

Sen earned a B.A. in romance languages in 1978. She married her college sweetheart, Michael Egan, a fledgling microbiologist who later became the head of a biotechnology firm. Sen herself became an executive trainee with the New England–based department-store chain Jordan Marsh. Unhappy working in the firm's handbag department, where she had been assigned, she left after a year to join the Zayre Corp., a retail conglomerate based in Framingham, Massachusetts. Hired as a gofer, as she told Zipkin, within a few years Sen had been placed in charge of inventory management for the company's toy division. (During her tenure in that post, the wildly successful Cabbage Patch and E.T. dolls were introduced, sparking buying frenzies that posed particular challenges for the inventory system.)

Later Career

Sen was promoted several times during her decade at Zayre and held titles including stationery buyer and children's-apparel buyer. She was serving as the divisional merchandise manager of lingerie when the corporation dissolved. She explained the complex machinations to Zipkin: "Zayre Discount Stores was sold to Ames Department Stores in 1989. BJ's and HomeBase, another former Zayre unit, [had been] spun off to form Waban Inc. One of my mentors was at BJ's and asked me to join it. But while the breakup was going on, we weren't allowed to transfer from one subsidiary to another. Management wanted to keep the talent intact to facilitate the transfer to Ames. Meanwhile, I got an offer from another chain. The mentor convinced Zayre's management that because I was going to leave anyway, they might as well make an exception and let me go to BJ's."

"I didn't have a blueprint. I made it up as I went along."

BJ's was started in 1984 and named in honor of a daughter (Barbara Jean) of one of the founders. It was still a relatively small concern when Sen joined. "I put together processes and systems for logistics, distribution and inventory control," she explained to Zipkin. "I didn't have a blueprint. I made it up as I went along. I designed cross-dock buildings to receive truckloads of merchandise and ship it on pallets to the stores." By 1994 Sen had been promoted to senior vice president of general merchandise.

In 1997 Waban dissolved, and BJ's and HomeBase each went public in separate offerings. From January 1997 to February 2003, Sen, who remained with BJ's, served as executive vice president of merchandise and logistics. In mid-2002 Sen had been a strong candidate for the post of CEO; she was passed over, however, in favor of Michael Wedge, then the executive vice president of club operations, who ascended to the top spot in September of that year. Sen admitted to Zipkin, "I tried working with [Wedge] but my impression was that our management styles were very different." After six months she was asked to leave the company. Rather than feeling angered or dismayed, she looked forward to spending more time with her family. "My daughter was 15 and my son was 13," she told Elton. "I thought, 'This is my big chance to be a mom.' I've never been home being a mom. But all they needed at that point was money and a ride."

Sen instead threw her energies into her own retail-consulting firm, advising such companies as Kroger, Harris Teeter, Meijer, and Fred Mayer on business development, merchandising, and logistics. She also became involved with several Boston-area nonprofit groups, relishing the chance to play a hands-on role in their operations. She became a member of the board at the Pine Street Inn, a local homeless shelter where she regularly served dinner and organized special events. She also completed a rigorous training program in order to volunteer as a tutor in Boston's Chinatown district, and when she joined the board of the Boston Ballet, she began taking classes at the group's studios.

In late 2006 Wedge, who had presided during a period of disappointing sales and slow growth, left BJ's. Herb Zarkin, a longtime BJ's executive, took over as CEO. Thinking that Zarkin might be able to use her consulting services, Sen met him for lunch at a steakhouse in Framingham. Instead of hiring her as a consultant, Zarkin insisted she rejoin the company, telling her that he would not leave the restaurant until she agreed. Surprised, but happy, she did so. "The next day I called her," Zarkin recalled to Elton, "and I said, 'You know, Laura, we never talked about titles, stock options, or salaries.' And she said, 'Herb, I trust you.

Whatever you do I know will be the right thing.' She isn't driven by money or the title, she is driven by doing her job, coming up with new ideas, making sure we give back to the community. She is driven by all the right things." "It takes awhile to understand the club industry," he later told Christina Veiders for *Supermarket News* (February 18, 2008), "and her knowledge is a blessing for us. Laura is not a stranger. We don't have to do a dance for a long period of time in order to understand each other."

Sen told Elton that "other than the days my two children were born and the day I got married," the day she returned to BJ's as an executive vice president, in January 2007, "was one of the most amazing days of my life." In January 2008 Sen was promoted to president and chief operating officer (COO), which placed her in charge of day-to-day operations. "Expertise and logistics and merchandising is viewed as a big asset when it comes to the club warehouse business, where efficient delivery of goods to the sales floor at the lowest possible cost is critical," Veiders wrote, explaining Sen's ascension. "The core business hasn't changed since I started in 1989," Sen told Veiders. "It is just a matter of how we execute against that. We have a team not just at the executive level but throughout the organization that has a very deep background. They know how to do this."

Sen made an immediate practice of walking around stores and asking employees of all ranks for their suggestions. She found, as she later told Jenn Abelson for the *Boston Globe* (February 8, 2009), that "the merchandise had grown so much that it was difficult for members to find what they wanted. We had strayed from wholesale club fundamentals—value, merchandise excitement, and efficiency." Sen and Zarkin devised a plan to rid the club of slow-selling items, including private-label products of questionable quality, and to stabilize relationships with the company's vendors. By the third fiscal quarter of 2008, BJ's was reporting a large increase in net income that represented a strong turnaround from the lag in sales under Wedge.

Sen took over as CEO when Zarkin stepped down in February 2009. While her career was thriving, her private life was taking a devastating turn. Her husband of almost three decades was battling melanoma, and during the last weeks of his life, Sen moved into his hospital room. "When Michael was dying, Laura was starting to develop some public notoriety as a female CEO," Ann Carter, a personal friend and fellow businesswoman, told Elton. "You couldn't help but feel the irony of Laura finally getting her due, but knowing she would trade it all for some kind of miracle where Michael was concerned." Egan died in April 2009. Sen returned to work a few weeks later, and in August of that year, she and BJ's donated $100,000 to the Beth Israel Deaconess Medical Center for the creation of the Michael Egan Memorial Research Laboratory.

Sen's grief did not seem to affect her job performance, and she remained a visible force in the business world. In 2010 she was named to the *Forbes* list of the 100 most powerful women in the world (at number 82), and during the first quarter of 2011 the net income of BJ's rose 19 percent, to $33.7 million, while sales rose 10 percent, to $2.77 billion. Most analysts credited the good overall performance to the company's focus on everyday food items and gasoline, rather than big-ticket electronics or other luxury items.

On June 29, 2011 BJ's reached a $2.8 billion buyout agreement with the private-equity firms Leonard Green & Partners and CVC Capital Partners. "BJ's will benefit from the continued execution of our business plan and the significant retail expertise of our new partners at LGP and CVC, as well as from continued investments in our clubs, our people, and technology, and the future of our business," Sen declared in a statement, as quoted by Abelson in the *Boston Globe* (June 30, 2011). Abelson reported that the move would allow BJ's to expand beyond its core markets in the Northeast and Southeast without having to worry about quarterly profits.

Sen has one daughter, Kathryn, and one son, Sean.

Further Reading:

Boston Globe Feb. 8, 2009; Jan. 9, 2011, June 30, 2011

Boston Herald Dec. 13, 2008

Forbes Oct. 13, 2010

New York Times Apr. 25, 2009

Supermarket News Feb. 18, 2008; Nov. 24, 2008

Sinegal, James D.

Former president and CEO, Costco

Born: 1936; Pittsburgh, Pennsylvania

When Costco was founded in 1983, it represented a new kind of discount store, based on the "warehouse model" pioneered by James Sinegal's mentor, Price Club founder Sol Price. Costco, which in the beginning mostly sold groceries in bulk, now sells items ranging from big-screen television sets to grandfather clocks to designer clothes. Often praised as the "anti-Wal-Mart," Costco is known for valuing its customers and employees above its profit margin, which—though shareholders' occasional grumbling might suggest the opposite—has remained healthy.

Education and Early Career

James D. Sinegal was born on January 1, 1936 in Pittsburgh, Pennsylvania. His father was a coal miner and steelworker until he broke his back; afterward he started a small business. Sinegal has cited the less-than-privileged circumstances of his childhood as a major factor in the way he ran his business, as they inspired his efforts to give employees fair salaries and benefits. In 1951, when Sinegal was 15, the family moved to San Diego, California, where Sinegal graduated from high school in 1953. He then enrolled at San Diego Junior College (now San Diego City College), from which he received an associate's degree in 1955. That year he began attending San Diego State University as a premedical student.

In 1954, while he was still at San Diego Junior College, Sinegal took a part-time job with FedMart, a discount department store that had been opened that same year by Sol Price, who would later be known as the pioneer of the warehouse-store retail model. Price—who had graduated from San Diego State University—became a mentor to Sinegal, who was often referred to by the media as Price's "surrogate son." Starting in an entry-level position at Fed-Mart and working his way up, Sinegal eventually became the company's executive vice president of merchandising and operations.

Later Career

Sinegal implemented a similar policy of internal promotion at Costco. "If somebody came to us and said he just got a master's in business at Harvard, we would say fine, would you like to start pushing carts?" he explained to Nina Shapiro for *Seattle Weekly* (December 15, 2004). "That's how I started in this business--tying mattresses on tops of cars." Price's influence on Sinegal's later vision for Costco was significant in other ways as well. Posted on Sinegal's office bulletin board was a memo from Price, dated August 8, 1967; according to Shapiro, it read, "Although we are all interested in margin, it must never be done at the expense of our philosophy."

In 1975 FedMart was sold to the German retail operation Hugo Mann, and Price was ousted from the company. The following year, Price opened Price Club—the first warehouse club, with an annual membership fee of $25. Sinegal followed his mentor to Price Club, where he became executive vice president by the end of the decade. Originally conceived as a discount office-supply store for small businesses, Price Club almost failed in its first few years before deciding to expand its offerings and attract a wider customer base. In 1977 the company had one warehouse with annual sales of $13 million; in 1982 it had ten warehouses with annual sales of $366 million. Concurrently, Sinegal also briefly held positions as vice president of merchandising for Builders Emporium, a chain of home-improvement stores, and as president of his own company, Sinegal/Chamberlin & Associates, a wholesale food distributor.

In 1983 the entrepreneur Jeff Brotman recruited Sinegal to be his partner in a new warehouse-club venture. Brotman and Sinegal opened the first Costco in a warehouse in Seattle, Washington, purposely targeting urban shoppers. That same year Sam Walton, the founder of Wal-Mart, opened the first Sam's Club, which was also a warehouse operation inspired by Price's example and which was Costco's biggest rival. But while Sam's Club boasted the distinct advantage of Wal-Mart's buying power, its affiliation with the megastore has made it difficult for Sam's Club to craft a distinct identity. "The biggest thing with Sam's was that it didn't have a free hand to compete with Wal-Mart," Price told *Fortune* magazine's John Helyar (November 24, 2003). "There was this fundamental thing where they didn't want to kill Wal-Mart." Price explained to Helyar that the other shortcoming of Sam's Club was that it did not pursue the "higher class" of customer to whom Costco catered. To keep its discerning shoppers happy and stay one step ahead of Sam's Club, Costco continually introduced new offerings. In 1986 Costco began selling fresh meat and produce; Sam's Club began selling fresh groceries three years later. In 1995 Costco added gas pumps to many of its locations, adding to its ability to provide "one-stop shopping"; Sam's Club followed suit in 1997. Also in 1995 Costco started its own line of clothes, Kirkland Signature; Sam's Club introduced its own line, Member's Mark, in 1998. "Pity poor Wal-Mart…" Helyar wrote. "In this one niche, it's run up against a company that shows you can't discount some old business verities: The nimble first mover can outrun the powerful colossus; the innovator can stay a jump ahead of the imitator; the quality of leadership can trump the quantity of resources."

The one rough patch in the company's history came in 1993, when Costco bought Price Club, creating the company PriceCostco Inc. As Helyar wrote, "what appeared to be a harmonic convergence of protege and mentor instead became a troubled marriage," as Sinegal and Price's son, Robert, had difficulty in sharing leadership duties. Eight months after the merger, Costco created a separate company called Price Enterprises, led by Robert Price, which eventually evolved into PriceSmart and now operates warehouse clubs overseas. In 1997 Sinegal's company restored the name Costco Wholesale Corp. Still, there were no hard feelings between mentor and protege. "Jim has done a pretty damned remarkable job," Sol Price told Helyar. "He puts a great emphasis on quality and has moved into the food business and other new lines. We [the Prices] were very good at creating, but Jim was very good at developing."

By having each Costco outlet stock, for example, a $14.99 seven-pound chocolate cake a couple of aisles away from a $300 cashmere coat or a $3,000 plasma-screen television, Sinegal created stores where people did not come just for everyday items. "Our customers don't drive 15 miles to save on a jar of peanut butter," he told Helyar. "They come for the treasure hunt." Markups of products at Costco were capped at 14 percent, except for its premium Kirkland brand, which was capped at 15 percent; Wal-Mart's markup was closer to 20 percent, while department stores could increase items' prices by up to 50 percent. Costco also gave blanket permission for returns on all items except computers--a customer did not need a receipt, there were no questions asked, and there was no time limit. "I'm a big admirer of Wal-Mart, but I admire Costco more," Charles Munger, Warren Buffett's business partner at Berkshire Hathaway and a Costco board member, told Julie Schmit in *USA Today* (September 24, 2004). "Virtually none of the sins of modern capitalism are at Costco." The company was widely lauded for its employee benefits, highly unusual in an industry known for paying minimum wage and offering minimal health-care coverage. Costco workers reportedly earned the best salary in the retail industry. The vast majority of employees were eligible for health-care benefits, for which they paid only a small percentage of the cost. While those policies stemmed partly from a generous company philosophy, they were also effective for Costco's bottom line. Happier employees, Sinegal claimed, were more productive employees. "Paying good wages is not in opposition to good productivity," he told Nanette Byrnes for *Business Week* (September 23, 2002). "If you hire good people, give them good jobs, and pay them good wages, generally something good is going to happen." For Costco, good wages led to low employee turnover. Satisfying employees might also lead to minimal "shrinkage"— retail lingo for employee theft; at Costco, as Helyar reported, the rate of such activity was 13 percent of the industry average.

"Retail is detail. Show me a big-picture guy, and I'll show you a guy who's out of the picture."

Not everyone, however, agreed that such treatment of workers was good for the bottom line. The Deutsche Bank analyst Bill Dreher told Stanley Holmes and Wendy Zellner for *Business Week* (April 12, 2004), "At Costco, it's better to be an employee or a customer than a shareholder." Many shareholders contended that if Costco were to lower wages and raise health-care prices to meet the industry averages, the company would be even more profitable—and that its stock price would go even higher. But Sinegal rejected that view. "We think when you take care of your customer and your employees, your shareholders are going to be rewarded in the long run," he told Helyar. "And I'm one of them [the shareholders]; I care about the stock price. But we're not going to do something for the sake of one quarter that's going to destroy the fabric of our company and what we stand for." Costco stock reached a then-all-time high in March 2000, at $60 a share, setting off a wave of speculation about whether the company could keep up its high stock value. "Costco is still unique, the best in its class," the PaineWebber analyst Jeffrey Edelman wrote, arguing that the stock was a safe investment, as quoted in the business journal *MMR* (June 26, 2000). "It sets the standards for the industry, continues to gain market share and has significant expansion opportunities."

It was precisely that expansion, however, that later brought the stock prices down. In the years after 2000, the company opened a larger number of stores than in the past, and more of them in new markets—a more expensive proposition than expanding where there were already outlets. Because Costco did not advertise in ways other than direct mail, building a new store's ideal customer base and reaching peak profit potential might take as long as five years—which made the expansion efforts between 2000 and 2003 a good long-term investment, but not one that pleased shareholders in the short-term. In May 2003 Costco shares were trading at approximately $35 each. By July 2007 the company had slightly surpassed 2000 levels, hitting a high of $60.31 per share. Again, analysts disagreed about whether the company's stock-market success would be sustainable. "I'm not disputing that Costco is a great company," the HSBC analyst Mark Husson told Nat Worden for the finance Web site *TheStreet.com* (March 14, 2006). "I just think the stock has gotten too expensive considering the risks that it's facing." But Husson was one of only two analysts (out of 24 on Wall Street) who held a negative rating on the stock. The Morningstar analyst Anthony Chukumba told Worden that he expected even more growth from Costco. "Costco's stock is starting to get pricey, but I think it definitely deserves a premium over Wal-Mart since it's one of the few retailers out there that competes head-on with them and, quite frankly, beats the pants off them. They're incredible merchants. Their customer service is pretty much the best out there in all of retail. They treat their employees better. They pay them more. Their benefits are better, and the company still has room to grow both at home and abroad." "We've been a growth company since our inception," Sinegal told Worden. Still, he added that he was reluctant to make any concrete statements about the future. "The way we view things at the moment, we think it's possible that we could double the size of our company in the next 10 years, but that's obviously easier to say than to do," Sinegal said. "That plan could be altered by a lot of different things. We can't account for floods, wars, depressions and everything else that could happen."

Sinegal regularly turned down raises and occasionally even bonuses in an effort to keep his salary within the same realm as that of the company's lowest-paid employee. Admittedly, with an annual salary of $411,688 in 2006, plus 2.4 million shares of Costco stock, worth about $1.3 billion, Sinegal was no pauper. But in an era in which CEOs' salaries are typically in the millions of dollars, Sinegal's take-home pay seemed modest, especially for the CEO of a company as successful as Costco. (In June 2007 Ellen Simon reported for the Associated Press reported that Sinegal was the lowest-paid CEO among the 368 examined by the Securities and Exchange Commission that year.) Costco, which had $101 million in annual sales in 1984, ended the 2006 fiscal year with sales totaling $58.96 billion. Employing around 118,800 workers and boasting profits of $1.1 billion in 2006, Costco was one of the largest companies in the U.S. Still, in a 2005 presentation for local business leaders in Bend, Oregon, Sinegal said about Costco, as reported by Chuck Chiang for the *Bulletin* (November 18, 2005), "We like to think of ourselves as a small company that's hands-on." "Retail is detail," he told Julie Schmit. "Show me a big-picture guy, and I'll show you a guy who's out of the picture." That devotion to every aspect of his business led Sinegal to win numerous accolades for his management prowess; he was named one of *Business Week*'s best managers of 2002 and one of *Time*'s top 100 "People Who Shape Our World" in 2006. "Sinegal manages to be demanding without being intimidating," John Helyar wrote. Helyar also wrote, "He's got energy that leaves people half his age floundering in his wake." And yet, Helyar continued, even as Sinegal headed one of the only large retailers that managed to compete successfully with the mega-conglomerate superstores, "he seems more like a twinkle-eyed grandfather (which he is, eight times over) than a killer retailer." For his part, Sinegal saw the key to Costco's success as being simple. "This is not a tricky business," he explained to Mark Veverka for *Barron's* (May 12, 2003). "We just try to sell high-quality merchandise at a cost lower than everybody else."

The company's enormous success is predicated, perhaps paradoxically, on a particularly bare-bones business strategy. A typical Costco store has no signs marking the aisles and no shopping bags in the checkout lines. The stores rely primarily on natural light (to save on electricity). Other than direct-mail campaigns, the chain does not advertise. No salespeople walk the floors, except in the stores' electronics sections. Unlike such superstores as Wal-Mart or Kmart, which can carry more than 100,000 products, a Costco outlet stocks approximately 4,000 items at any given time, both in an effort to offer only products of greatest value to customers and to defray shipping and stocking costs for the company. "Costco's business plan is elegantly simple—and simply elegant," Veverka wrote of what is known in the industry as the "Costco site-maximization strategy." But what has truly distinguished Costco from its rivals is its focus on an elegantly simple customer base. Warehouse operations, such as Costco and its rivals Sam's Club and BJ's, are open only to members; annual membership fees for Costco range from $45 to $100, depending on added perks. And while the discounted prices and bulk quantities they offer might indicate otherwise, warehouse clubs actually attract the largest proportion of affluent shoppers of all U.S. retail channels—according to A. C.

Nielsen, about 54 percent of the stores' traffic. The retail consultant Michael Silverstein described the typical Costco shopper to Helyar as one who wants to "trade up" to top-of-the-line brand names when it comes to luxury goods such as watches and golf clubs but seeks to "trade down" to discounted basic goods such as paper towels and detergent. Costco, more than Sam's Club or BJ's, fulfills those desires. In 2003 Costco was the country's biggest seller of both fine wines ($600 million worth) and rotisserie chickens (55,000 per day). In 2002 the chain sold approximately 60,000 carats of diamonds and 45 million hot dogs. "It's the ultimate concept in trading up and trading down," Silverstein told Helyar. "It's a brilliant innovation for the new luxury."

In 2006 Sinegal was a recipient of the American Association of Community College's outstanding alumni award for his success at Costco and his philanthropic work. Sinegal has also been actively involved in Democratic Party politics.

At the end of 2011, James Sinegal, well into his seventies, stepped down from Costco's helm.

Further Reading:

Barron's May 12, 2003

Bulletin Nov. 18, 2005

Business Week Sept. 23, 2002; Apr. 12, 2004

Fortune Nov. 24, 2003

MMR Jun. 26, 2000

Seattle Weekly Dec. 15, 2004

TheStreet.com Mar. 14, 2006

USA Today Sep. 24, 2004

Storch, Gerald L.

Former chairman and CEO, Toys "R" Us

Born: 1956

Gerald L. Storch assumed the post of chairman of the board and chief executive officer of Toys "R" Us on February 7, 2006, four months after he abruptly left his post as vice chairman of the Target Corp. Despite fierce competition from Wal-Mart and Target and the decline in toy sales in recent years (partly because of the growing popularity of electronic games), Storch has said that to a large extent the troubles besetting Toys "R" Us were self-inflicted. "In every segment of retail, there are dedicated specialty retailers that are succeeding against Wal-Mart and Target," he told Michael Barbaro for the *New York Times* (November 19, 2006). "The model is out there." Storch, Michael Barbaro observed, "is clearly more comfortable crunching numbers and fine-tuning store operations than he is around toys." But, he also wrote, "such analytical steeliness may be just the medicine that Toys 'R' Us needs to survive."

Education and Early Career

Gerald L. Storch was born on October 31, 1956 and grew up in Jacksonville, Florida. Easily accessible sources contain no information about his parents, childhood, or any other aspect of his personal life aside from his higher education. Storch attended Harvard University, in Cambridge, Masschusetts, where he was editor in chief of a short-lived campus magazine called *Harvard Response*. He earned a B.A. with honors in 1977 and then enrolled in Harvard's dual-degree graduate program in law and business. He received an M.B.A. with honors in 1981 and a J.D. magna cum laude in 1982. In the latter year he joined the Boston office of McKinsey & Co., a New York City–based management-consulting firm, where he specialized in retail-sector matters and consumer and financial services. Storch later worked in other branches and became a partner of the firm during his 12 years with McKinsey.

Later Career

In 1993 Storch joined the Dayton-Hudson Corp., in Minneapolis, Minnesota, with the title of senior vice president of strategic planning. The fourth-largest retailer in the U.S. at that time, Dayton-Hudson owned 834 general-merchandise retail stores in 33 states, including two discount chains—Target and Mervyn's—and the more upscale chains Dayton's, Hudson's, and Marshall Field's. Among Storch's priorities was the revival of the nearly 300 Mervyn's stores, many of which were struggling to remain competitive with such rivals as Kohl's, Sears, JC Penney, and Montgomery Ward (the last of which closed its doors in 2001 and now sells only through its catalogs and the Internet). In a failed marketing campaign undertaken before his arrival, Mervyn's had tried to promote trendier clothing labels at the expense of traditional brands. Storch steered Mervyn's back to "more middle-of-the-road approaches" to fashion, as Sally Apgar and Kristin Tillotson reported in the *Minneapolis Star Tribune* (July 20, 1995), focusing on such clothing labels as Levi's, Lee, and Dockers and on well-known home-appliance brands. "Our customers want things that are fun and cool but not too crazy," Storch told Apgar for the *Star Tribune* (July 23, 1995). "We had gone too far before. The customer voted." He added that less familiar private labels "are still a key strategic advantage that will positively differentiate us from the competition." But over the next few years, Storch's remedial actions produced mediocre results.

In 1996, prompted by the success of Target stores, which in 1995 had accounted for two-thirds of Dayton-Hudson's revenues, Storch and Robert J. "Bob" Ulrich, who had become Dayton-Hudson's chairman and chief executive officer in 1994, launched what they termed the Targetization of all the firm's stores. Until then each Dayton-Hudson chain had operated its business independently. As Apgar wrote for the *Star Tribune* (March 1, 1993), "It was unheard of for a [Hudson's, Dayton's, or Marshall Field's] department store buyer who'd been to New York City on a buying trip to share his or her fashion list with a buyer at Target . . . or Mervyn's. . . . But now hip tips are swapped along with negotiating points to use on certain manufacturers." Storch told Apgar, "If some of the excitement level at Target is transferred to the other operating companies, that's great. If some of the urgency transfers, that's great. If some of the culture transfers, that's great." He also said, "More and more American corporations are coming to the same conclusion that you simply can't afford to operate in a Balkanized fashion. That's why we believe in the power of one." (Like "Targetization," "power of one" became a Dayton-Hudson mantra.)

Also in 1996 Dayton-Hudson began offering a Target credit card to attract more customers. "We viewed this from the beginning as much more important [than] a branding matter," Storch told a reporter for MMR (Mass Market Retailers, December 14, 1998). "We viewed it as part of a loyalty program as well." Kenneth B. Woodrow, then Dayton-Hudson's president, told the MMR writer that the card gave the company "a platform from which to communicate with a guest [that is, customer] on a one-to-one basis that we've never had before. We know who that guest is for the first time, and we know what she's buying. We can wrap services around the card that we can't offer in the stores themselves, so it gives us a way to intensify our relationship with the guest." At the end of 1997, Dayton-Hudson reported $751 million in profits, a 62 percent increase from the previous year. By the end of the next year, 11 million cards were in the hands of consumers.

In 1999 Storch became president of credit and new business at Dayton-Hudson. In that position he oversaw the development and expansion of SuperTargets, combination grocery stores-discount superstores that contained Starbucks cafes and offered Archer Farms (Target's label) foods. "We're working to convey the atmosphere of an upscale grocer . . ." Storch told Jim McCartney for the *Saint Paul* (Minnesota) *Pioneer Press* (October 6, 1999). "We want to bring fashion to food." In 2001 Storch was promoted to vice chairman of what had been renamed the Target Corp. His responsibilities included financial services and new businesses for the Target, Mervyn's, and Marshall Field's stores. In an interview with for MMR (March 19, 2001), he reiterated his belief that Target's success lay in enhancing its brand, which "stands for being cool and hip and hot, and for providing value as well." "We had three strategic choices," he told a writer for *The Economist* (May 3, 2001). "To specialise, to become the low-cost producer or to differentiate ourselves. . . . Target chose differentiation—by repositioning itself as a branded designer chain, but priced for the masses."

Among other initiatives that Storch directed, Target introduced a program called Take Charge of Education, whereby 1 percent of the sum that enrollees spent in credit-card purchases was donated to schools that program participants chose from a list compiled by Target. Target also joined with Visa to launch the Target Visa card nationwide. In late 2001 Storch and Jeff Bezos, the CEO of Amazon, signed a five-year contract that called for Amazon to integrate Target.com product offerings and order fulfillment with its own; in exchange, Target agreed to pay Amazon an annual service fee and share a fixed portion of the profits that accrued from Web transactions. Target's alliance with Amazon was another way "to reach an addition[al] stream of customers on the Internet," according to Storch, as quoted by the *Alameda* (California) *Times-Star* (November 6, 2001). By the end of 2002, Target posted overall sales of nearly $40 billion; in 2003 the amount was $43.9 billion. At that point Target surpassed Kmart to become the second-biggest discount retailer in the U.S., behind Wal-Mart. The knowledge that the figure of $43.9 billion was precisely the amount that Wal-Mart had amassed in sales in 1992 led Storch to tell Julie Schlosser for CNNMoney.com (October 18, 2004), "This is uncanny. You could say, 'We're ten years behind.' Or you could say, 'Wow, we're the same size as the world's largest company was ten years ago!'" According to Schlosser, Target may have had "only a fifth of the sales and profits of Wal-Mart but [it] reels them in with ten times the panache." Schlosser also wrote that, by offering affordable clothing by such couture designers as Isaac Mizrahi and Mossimo Giannulli, Target had emerged as "the king of cheap chic." In 2003, according to the *New York Times* (October 5, 2005), Storch's earnings amounted to $1.8 million, with bonuses and options constituting 45 percent. In 2004, according to the same *Times* article, the total was $2.17 million.

"Toys 'R' Us had fallen into the pattern of being a follower, not a leader. Instead of buying product that is hot, we need to make products hot. We need to be like a fashion house."

One day in October 2005, Storch suddenly handed in his resignation, for reasons that neither he nor Target publicly revealed. The following February Toys "R" Us announced the appointment of Storch as the company's new chairman and CEO. Founded by Charles Lazarus, Toys "R" Us began in 1948 as a Washington, D.C., store called Children's Bargain Town, which sold furniture for babies and children. In response to public requests, Lazarus added toys to his stock, and in the late 1950s, he redesigned his store as a supermarket in which customers could pick out items themselves. His second store opened with the name Toys "R" Us (with a backward R—a stylistic choice that drew criticism from parents and teachers). The company went public in 1978. With the opening of its first Babies "R" Us store in 1996, the firm separated most of its items for infants (ranging from pacifiers, nursing bottles, and onesies to strollers and cribs) from products for older children. Because the average buyer of baby merchandise shops for such goods considerably more often than the average person shops for toys, impulse purchases of toys (for older children in tow, for example) in the Toys "R" Us stores began to drop significantly. Toys "R" Us branches grew shabby, and marketing efforts, such as the placement of circulars in newspapers, grew lackadaisical, further eroding customer interest. Competition from Wal-Mart and Target compounded the problem of steadily shrinking sales. In July 2005 Toys "R" Us was sold and the company reverted to private ownership. John H. Eyler Jr. handed in his resignation, and Richard L. Markee, the head of Babies "R" Us, took over as interim CEO. In January 2006 Toys "R" Us closed dozens of its stores and cut 3,000 jobs, reducing its work force by 11 percent of the total.

When Storch assumed the top spot at Toys "R" Us in February 2006, according to Michael Barbaro, "he found an undisciplined company that he believed blamed others for its problems rather than facing its own mistakes. He also found a corporate culture wedded to impulsive strategic forays rather than hard data." Storch told Barbaro, "Toys 'R' Us had fallen into the pattern of being a follower, not a leader. Instead of buying product that is hot, we need to make products hot. We need to be like a fashion house." Determined to end what he has termed "victim thinking," Storch adopted the slogan "Playing to win" and ordered the words affixed to employees' ID badges. He dismissed more than half of the company's senior executives, replacing some of them with people recruited from Best Buy and Home Depot, and created a new position, director of trends, to make sure that Toys "R" Us became aware of all the latest crazes early on. He impressed upon store managers the importance of having knowledgeable salespeople on staff. "When a customer comes in our store, our people can tell them what's a great toy for a 10-year-old boy for their birthday, because all we do is toys," he explained to Jeffrey Gold for the Associated Press, as reported in the Canadian Press (July 3, 2006). "When you go to a large, multi-product discount chain, you'll be lucky to find someone who can point you to the toy department, or will even take you there, much less answer specific questions." Storch also instituted monthly conference calls that were mandatory for selected managers—including some from branches in the 33 countries overseas in which Toys "R" Us had stores. He ordered renovations of the dowdiest stores, increased signage at all locations, and demanded more aggressive marketing campaigns, including the publication of better-designed, more-attractive advertising supplements. He has also placed some Babies "R" Us and Toys "R" Us branches under one roof. In time for the 2006 Christmas season, he negotiated contracts for 70 exclusive products, among them the Thomas Ultimate Train Set, the Lego Star Wars X-Wing Fighter, and the Girlfriendz line of Bratz dolls.

"It is not only the future of Toys 'R' Us that is at stake here," Michael Barbaro warned. "Major toy makers say that their profitability depends on its survival. If Toys 'R' Us fails, everyone from industry conglomerates like Hasbro and Mattel to scrappy innovative upstarts like Wild Planet and Zizzle say they will be at the mercy of the penny-pinching merchants at Wal-Mart and Target." "The reality," Neil B. Friedman, the president of Mattel Brands, told Barbaro, "is that it's not healthy for this industry to not have a healthy Toys 'R' Us."

Storch left Toys "R" Us in 2013. He now heads Storch Advisors, a consulting firm.

Further Reading:

Alameda (California) *Times-Star* Nov. 6, 2001

Bloomberg.co.uk Dec. 29, 2006

 Business Wire Mar. 1, 1993; Feb. 7, 2006

CNNMoney.com Oct. 18, 2004

Current Biography, 2007

The Economist May 3, 2001

Minneapolis Star Tribune Mar. 1, 1993; Jul. 20, 1995; Jul. 23, 1995; Mar. 12, 1996, Jun. 20, 2001

New York Post Nov. 6, 2006

New York Times Nov. 19, 2006

Saint Paul Pioneer Press Oct. 6, 1999

Storch Advisors Web site

Toys "R" Us Web site

Thomas-Graham, Pamela

Corporate executive; writer

Born: 1963; Detroit, Michigan

It's hard to imagine anyone more conversant with the rigors of succeeding in traditionally white male bastions than Pamela Thomas-Graham. She holds three Harvard degrees and in 1995 became the first black woman to be made a partner at McKinsey & Co., the world's largest management consulting firm. She later emerged as NBC's highest-ranking black executive when she was appointed president and CEO of CNBC.com, the online companion to the network's financial cable channel, in 1999. Subsequent positions included a leadership role at the fashion firm Liz Claiborne; currently she is an executive at the financial behemoth Credit Suisse. In her scarce spare time, she writes a popular series of mystery novels featuring Nikki Chase, a black female Harvard economics professor turned amateur sleuth.

Education and Early Career

Thomas-Graham was born in Detroit, Michigan, on June 24, 1963. "My family emphasized that it was important to achieve," she told Amy Oringel in an interview posted in the business section of the Oxygen Network Web site. "My mother always worked and I was proud of her for that. So from a very early age, my image was of a woman who had her own very real place in the world." After attending Lutheran High School West in Detroit, she was admitted to Radcliffe College (now part of Harvard University). Although initially she found the prestigious school intimidating, she obtained her undergraduate degree in economics there, graduating magna cum laude and winning election to Phi Beta Kappa. She also earned the Captain Jonathan Fay Prize—the highest honor bestowed by Harvard-Radcliffe for the graduating female student with the greatest promise. As an undergraduate she took part in an occasional theater production, but did little extracurricular or creative writing, except for a short stint on a campus arts paper.

Thomas-Graham was admitted to both the Harvard Law School and the Harvard Business School, earning both a J.D. and an M.B.A. She was an editor of the *Harvard Law Review* and spent her summers gaining a wide variety of job experience: working for Bain & Co., a management-consulting firm; in the corporate-finance division of Goldman Sachs in New York City; and at Sullivan & Worcester, a Boston law firm. After graduating in 1989, she joined McKinsey & Co., the world's largest management- consulting firm. "I found the things I liked about law I could do in consulting," she told Tonia Shakespeare for *Black Enterprise* (October 1996), explaining that the stimulating environment and corporate culture at McKinsey, a privately held concern, were similar to those at a law firm. She elaborated further on the similarities: "[Consultants] give people business advice in the same way lawyers give legal advice." But she bemoaned the fact that many young people weren't aware of the possibilities in the field, saying, "Consulting is not an industry many people understand. As a result, most do not look at it as a career opportunity. Some don't even know it exists."

Later Career

Thomas-Graham routinely worked 16 hours a day at McKinsey, advising her clients, which were for the most part *Fortune* 500 companies. After studying a client's business practices and financial data, Thomas-Graham was often able to formulate strategies that, when implemented, would add several million dollars to the company's bottom line. In December 1995 she was made the first black female partner at McKinsey. (Of the firm's 600 partners, only 34 others were female, and only two others were black.) At the age of 32, she was also one of McKinsey's youngest partners. Although she was one of the leaders of the media and entertainment division, she was frequently mistaken for a clerical worker by clients who had never encountered a black female executive. She explained to Oringel, "As a woman of color in business, you're instantly more visible, and the reality is more people will be judging you. Several times, clients have assumed that I was the partner's secretary—not the partner. But I always try to conduct myself positively and set an example." Thomas-Graham experienced racism outside of the business world as well, telling Donna Greene for the *New York Times* (July 18, 1999), "I have been followed through stores on Madison Avenue because people assume that I as a young black woman couldn't have the income to be shopping there. I've never had a violent confrontation, but I've had many instances of feeling diminished and demeaned because of people's attitudes toward me as a black woman."

Despite the pressures of an 80-hour work week and the strain of maintaining a positive attitude in the face of both subtle and overt racism, Thomas-Graham excelled at McKinsey—and found the time to write as well. "I wanted to do something that's more creative than what I do in my day job," she told Marilyn Mc-Craven for *Emerge* (September 1999). "I wanted to use a different part of my brain." She decided to write a mystery novel because she had always enjoyed the genre. "I particularly love reading mysteries about women written by women," she told a reporter for the Barnes & Noble Web site, "so I'm a big fan of Sue Grafton, Sara Paretsky, and Valerie Wilson Wesley, and I really liked the idea of having a smart feminist detective who is an amateur living her life but gets drawn into some interesting intrigue." Her first effort, *A Darker Shade of Crimson*, was published by Simon & Schuster in 1998. Set in Cambridge, Massachusetts, the story involves the murder of the Harvard Law School's first black female dean of students. Critics often point out the similarities between Thomas-Graham and her fictional amateur detective, Nikki Chase, since both are successful, Harvard-educated black women. But while Thomas-Graham has pursued a career in the business world, Chase has remained in academia, teaching economics and sitting on university committees when she is not sleuthing. Like Thomas-Graham, Chase is often judged first by her race, rather than her accomplishments. Unlike her creator, Chase is single, and between hunting for clues, she deals with the issue of interracial dating—which, as Thomas-Graham has pointed out in interviews, is a common occurrence at Harvard, where the majority of available males are white. *A Darker Shade of Crimson* was named "page-turner of the week" by *People* magazine in April 1998.

"As a woman of color in business, you're instantly more visible, and the reality is more people will be judging you....But I always try to conduct myself positively and set an example."

In 1997, on the strength of the manuscript for her first book, Simon & Schuster signed Thomas-Graham to a three-book contract, with each book to be set at a different Ivy League college. The second novel, *Blue Blood* (1999), brought back Nikki Chase—this time to solve the murder of a white law professor at Yale. *Orange Crushed* (2004) was set at Princeton. In answer to those who say that as a black author she should write in a genre better suited to socially relevant themes, Thomas-Graham told Ronald Roach for *Black Issues in Higher Education* (May 14, 1998), "The murder mystery format, while entertaining, lends itself to one that can serve as a forum for social and political comment." She elaborated on that point in her interview with Marilyn McCraven, saying, "There are a lot of ways to promulgate a serious message. At the moment, this is my best method and it seems to be working." After she began writing she continued to work at McKinsey & Co., telling Alex Kuczynski for the *New York Times* (May 2, 1999) that she had new advice for her media clients as a result of her sideline: "I'm much more in favor of large author advances now," she joked.

Despite her continued success at McKinsey, Thomas-Graham accepted a position at CNBC.com, which began as an Internet division of the financial television channel owned by NBC. "It was always my intention to head up a company," she explained to Amy Oringel, "and the decision was an easy one. [At NBC] I am part of a wonderful institution, but operating in an entrepreneurial environment where I can implement my own working style." Appointed president and CEO of the division in September 1999, she was charged with transforming CNBC.com from what was essentially a high-tech promotional tool for the cable channel into a full-service financial Web site, able to compete with CNNfn, Yahoo! Finance, and the host of other interactive financial sites already on the Web. In addition to financial news and commentary, the site featured fund-screening options and a portfolio tracker that could be personalized by each viewer. "What we're trying to do with this is to capture the essence of the CNBC brand, but really enrich it and make it more personal and more focused on tools and utility," she explained to Kenneth Li in a cover-story interview for *Industry Standard* (October 15, 1999).

In 2005 Thomas-Graham took on a new role, that of group president at Liz Claiborne. The hitherto-unfamiliar world of the fashion industry didn't faze her in the least. "This business is twice the size of CNBC and lets me work with a portfolio of brands rather than a single brand," she said, as reported by Diane Brady in *BusinessWeek* (October 9, 2005). "I'm a Harvard MBA. Having a bigger P&L [profit and loss statement] and more complexity appeals to me."

Pamela Thomas-Graham was named one of *Ms.* magazine's women of the year for 2003. Thomas-Graham is currently a high-placed executive for the financial giant Credit Suisse. According to the Credit Suisse Web site, Thomas-Graham is "responsible for designing and developing market segment strategies to attract and grow client relationships in key communities, including women, African-Americans and the LGBT community."

Pamela Thomas-Graham is married to Lawrence Otis Graham, a Princeton-educated attorney and author who is perhaps best known for his 12th book, *Member of the Club: Reflections on Life in a Racially Polarized World*, which includes an account of what he observed while posing as a busboy at an all-white Connecticut country club. Discussing their relationship, Thomas-Graham told Donna Greene, "Lawrence was highly successful when I met him and I had achieved quite a lot before I met him. Clearly, I think that the two of us combined are even more than the two of us separate." She continued, "But the reason I married him is he is incredibly supportive of my professional goals and I of his. We draw strength from each other."

Further Reading:

Barnes & Noble Web Site

Black Enterprise Oct. 1996

Black Issues in Higher Education May 14, 1998

BusinessWeek Oct. 9, 2005

Crain's New York Business May 15–21, 2000

Emerge Sept. 1999

Fortune Aug. 4, 1997

ndustry Standard Oct. 15, 1999

New York Times May 2, 1999

New York Times (Westchester section) Jul. 18, 1999

Oxygen Network Web site

Selected Books:

A Darker Shade of Crimson, 1998

Blue Blood, 1999

Orange Crushed, 2004

Welch, John F.

Former CEO, General Electric (GE); business consultant; writer

Born. 1935, Salem, Massachusetts

John "Jack" Welch Jr. is arguably one of the most admired and respected managers in business history. Welch is best known for his 20-year reign as head of the General Electric (GE) Company. While more than 100,000 employees were laid off during his tenure, which lasted from 1981 to 2001, Welch's no-nonsense approach to management helped transform GE into one of the largest and most profitable businesses in the world. Since stepping down from his post, Welch has penned several best-selling books and worked as a business consultant.

Education and Early Career

John Francis Welch Jr. was born in Salem, Massachusetts, on November 19, 1935, the only child of an Irish-American couple. His father, John Sr., a conductor on the Boston & Maine Railroad, was 42 years old when his son was born, and his mother, the former Grace Andrews, was 38. Although his father was often away from home, traveling along the New England coast, Welch has recalled that his family was "close-knit" and that his parents provided him with "tremendous support systems," especially his proud, strong-willed mother. "I was an Irish altar boy who went to Mass every morning because my mother sat in the front row," he told one interviewer. Grace Welch was always on hand to cheer her son on the playing fields and to infuse him with ambition and self-confidence. Although Welch suffered from a serious stammer in childhood, she assured him that he did not have a speech impediment by explaining that his brain worked so fast that his mouth could not keep up with it.

Welch's fierce determination exhibited itself early in childhood. One friend, Samuel E. Zoll, who became a judge in Massachusetts, remembers him as "a nice, regular guy, but always very competitive, relentless, and argumentative." He remembers the time when Welch gave him a dressing down on the basketball court for failing to stop a much bigger opponent from scoring. At Salem High School, where Welch was captain of the golf and hockey teams and a baseball pitcher, the school magazine recorded as his favorite saying the question: "We're still pals?" He graduated in 1953 in the top 10 percent of his class.

Welch went on to the University of Massachusetts at Amherst, where he studied chemical engineering, made the dean's list for four straight years, and played intramural hockey and golf. After obtaining his B.S. with honors in 1957, Welch won a graduate fellowship in chemical engineering at the University of Illinois, where he received his M.S. in 1958 and his Ph.D. in 1960. The subject of his doctoral dissertation was condensation in nuclear-reactor steam systems.

Later Career

In 1960 Welch went to work for GE in the company's engineered-materials plant in Pittsfield, Massachusetts. He plunged into what he has described as "the whole game of tying markets to technology," and by 1962 he had moved a new heat-resistant plastic called Noryl out of the laboratory and into production in a plant whose construction he supervised. He then masterminded an all-out marketing campaign that made Noryl a popular material for use in auto-body parts, computer casings, and appliances, and his success with it established GE as a major plastics manufacturer ahead of such competitors as the Du Pont Company. Eventually, Welch supervised the building of Noryl plants in Europe and Japan, where he "was literally a one-man engineering operation," according to one GE associate, who added, "If things weren't moving fast enough, he moved them." When the housewares division refused to use a tough new plastic that GE had developed for electric can openers, for example, Welch sold it to competitors, after which GE also began to use the plastic.

It was because of that type of aggressive behavior that Welch developed a reputation for abrasiveness, but the successful results he achieved at GE overrode any objections to his style. In 1968 he was named general manager of GE's worldwide plastics business. Within three years he turned that once-marginal division into a $400 million-a-year cornerstone of the company, and his responsibilities were increased to include management of the metallurgical and chemical divisions. In 1972, at the age of 36, he became one of the youngest vice presidents in GE's history.

In 1973 Welch was promoted to vice president and chief executive of the components and materials group. In 1977 he was made a senior vice president in charge of consumer goods and services, a division that he greatly strengthened during his tenure. Pouring resources into GE's growing multibillion-dollar financial services unit, the General Electric Credit Corporation, he made it the core of a financial services "empire within the GE empire," as Peter Petre wrote for *Fortune* (July 7, 1986). Petre further noted: "Savvy and fast-moving, GE Credit has scored again and again by pouncing into developing financial markets like tax-sheltered equipment leasing, exploiting them fast, and moving on as competition heats up or laws change."

Welch also helped to move the company into more innovative business planning. "Everything he's touched at GE he's left in super shape," said one admiring Wall Street analyst. In 1979 he became vice chair of GE, and on April 1, 1981 he took over as its chair, the surprise winner of a six-way contest to succeed the retiring Reginald H. Jones.

The company that Welch inherited in 1981 was the nation's 10th largest industrial concern, with sales of $25 billion—about 1 percent of the gross national product—and earnings of $1.5 billion. Half of its sales came from so-called smokestack manufacturing plants that produced everything from lightbulbs and locomotives to toaster ovens and turbines. The other half came from high-technology products, such as aircraft engines, space-age plastics, nuclear weapons, nuclear-energy and nuclear-medical systems, and from an expanding business in services, the fastest-growing sector of the American economy. The anchor of the services colossus was GE Credit, which not only leased products and made venture-capital deals, but also acted as a giant tax shelter, allowing GE to avoid paying any federal income taxes between 1981 and 1983, on total earnings of $5.5 billion.

One of the first problems that Welch had to address in settling into what he has called "the all-time job" was the fact that although it was rated the nation's best-managed company, GE's enormous size and diversity led many on Wall Street to dismiss it as a slow-growth behemoth that could do no better than "lumber along," approximating the growth of the economy. The result of such assessments was that GE stock "slept through the decade" of the 1970s, according to a reporter for *Fortune* (January 25, 1982).

Welch had no intention of trying to manage that lumbering giant. Such a company would have trouble surviving, much less prospering, in the Darwinian struggle he foresaw for American business throughout the 1980s and whose prelude he saw in the recession that gripped the American economy in 1981, which was then the worst economic downturn since the Great Depression. At a meeting with security analysts, Welch asserted that "in this slower growth environment, the winners will be those who insist on being number one or number two in every business they are in," and he added that because of intensifying domestic and especially foreign competition, "the managements and companies in the eighties that hang on to losers for whatever reason won't be around in 1990."

The "losers" at GE were to be found for the most part among the company's older, slow-growing manufacturing concerns, although a few of those older businesses—such as lighting, major appliances, and electric motors—were highly profitable. The "winners," including the profitable manufacturing concerns, were a group of 16 of GE's almost 40 businesses that accounted for some 90 percent of the company's sales and earnings. Welch organized his 16 winners into three groups, or "circles": the profitable core of manufacturing concerns and groups of businesses in the two areas in which he believed GE's future lay—namely, services and high technology. He put managers of the remaining businesses on notice that they faced sale or shutdown if they failed to become the first or second outfits in their fields. Over the next five years, Welch closed 73 GE plants and facilities and sold 232 businesses and product lines for $5.9 billion.

Welch's sales and shutdowns slashed GE's employment by 132,000 jobs, more than a quarter of its workforce, and they reportedly impaired morale among many of the company's 300,000 remaining employees, especially those in the slow-growth manufacturing businesses. Although GE's annual report for 1986 stressed that "the strength of our balance sheet allowed us to [cut jobs] in ways that were fair and compassionate to those involved" and that "lengthy notification periods, equitable severance packages, retraining and placement centers were used whenever business realities caused us to close a plant or exit a business," it was at this time that Welch was dubbed "Neutron Jack," a nickname that offended him. "Nuking somebody means you kill him," he told Peter Petre. "We start a renewal process. . . . People who have been removed for not performing may be angry, but not one will say he wasn't treated with dignity. . . . We can look ourselves in the mirror every morning and say we did what we could."

"...[T]he managements and companies in the eighties that hang on to losers for whatever reason won't be around in 1990."

Welch also responded to reports about his aggressive management style. One of them, written by Steven Flax for *Fortune* (August 6, 1984), observed that "according to former employees, Welch conducts meetings so aggressively that people tremble. He attacks almost physically with his intellect—criticizing, demeaning, ridiculing, humiliating." "Jack will chase you around the room, throwing arguments and objections at you," one former GE executive said, as quoted in *BusinessWeek* (June 30, 1986), of his ordeal in trying to win Welch's approval for a project. "Then you fight back until he lets you do what you want—and it's clear you'll do everything you can to make it work." In his interview with Peter Petre, Welch insisted, "I got a raw deal with all those things about tough guy Jack—fear, intimidation, guns and sticks and whips and chains. If you're mean you don't belong at General Electric." On another occasion he explained, "The job of the enterprise is to provide an exciting atmosphere that's open and fair, where people have the resources to go out and win. The job of the people is to take advantage of this playing field and put out 110 percent."

If many subordinates were intimidated by such ground rules, some reveled in the new authority and independence that Welch gave them. By eliminating whole layers of GE management, Welch quickened the pace of decision-making and encouraged an entrepreneurial attitude of "ownership" and risk-taking among the managers who remained. "We have to get people to trust that they can take a swing and [for the right reasons] not succeed," he told Howard Banks for *Forbes* (March 26, 1984). "In big corporations the tendency is not to reward the good try." Welch practiced what he preached. On one occasion, when a $20-million project was dropped because of a change in the market, he promoted the manager and gave him a bonus.

Most of Welch's spending in the early 1980s was aimed at GE's core businesses. He poured $14 billion into factory automation and other capital improvements, using the bulk of those funds to update dozens of GE's aging manufacturing plants across the country. In an attempt to create a new business and position the company to dominate what he saw as an emerging "megamarket," he authorized a $500-million investment in the development of factory-automation equipment to sell to other companies, but the market failed to develop as GE had anticipated, and the company suffered a $120-million loss. "We picked the right market, but we couldn't have executed [the strategy] much worse," Welch told Petre. He sharply reduced GE's forecast for 1990 sales from $5 billion to the $1 billion that he had originally predicted.

Despite that setback, GE, under Welch's stewardship, increased its earnings by a healthy 54 percent between 1981 and 1985. When sales went up by only 13 percent during the same period, Welch argued that the problem was more apparent than real, since it was the result of getting rid of businesses whose high sales and low earnings made them only marginally profitable. But critics maintained that more substantial proof of his success would not come until he could show substantial revenue growth.

One way to spark such growth, Welch realized, would be by making a major acquisition. By mid-1985, GE had $3.2 billion in cash on hand earmarked for that purpose and had compiled a shopping list of some 3,000 companies as potential acquisitions. Its only large purchase, however, had been the $1.1-billion acquisition of the Employers Reinsurance Company in 1984. On Wall Street, where corporate takeovers had become commonplace, financial analysts were surprised at the absence of a big move by GE. "What are they going to do with that money?" one analyst asked. Welch's answer came in December 1985, with GE's $6.4-billion acquisition of RCA, another giant electronics company. It was the largest merger in business history outside of the oil industry. Writing for the *New York Times Magazine* (September 20, 1987), L. J. Davis asserted that it was made possible only because of "the Reagan administration's tolerant attitude toward corporate mergers that in years past would have drawn antitrust prosecution."

The merger was a "friendly" acquisition that Welch, who avoided hostile takeovers, had first proposed in an informal meeting with RCA chairman Thornton Bradshaw. It neatly fulfilled Welch's major goals in making a huge acquisition. It provided the "positive earnings contribution" he had wished for by boosting GE's sales from $30 billion a year to $40 billion. It also gave GE a broader base in the services and technology industries, thus insuring the company against what Welch saw as an ongoing "deindustrialization" of America. RCA's military-electronics division, for instance, when added to GE's own defense businesses, raised the company from fourth to third among the nation's Pentagon contractors, and RCA's "crown jewel," the top-rated National Broadcasting Company, promised to become "a fabulous money machine" for GE, according to L. J. Davis.

The full impact of the merger became evident when it catapulted GE from 10th to sixth place on *Fortune*'s list of the 500 biggest industrial companies in the United States. Welch touted the merger as good not only for GE and RCA but good for America. Its real significance, he asserted, lay in the fact that his merger had created a business colossus strong enough to take on the Japanese and other foreign rivals. Some observers dismissed his logic as "flag waving." One critic, Bruce Nussbaum, complained in *BusinessWeek* (December 30, 1985) that far from increasing GE's competitiveness, the merger would make the company "a Born-in-the-USA conglomerate with a declining exposure to foreign competition and a major presence in relatively cozy markets." Nussbaum observed, "The Pentagon isn't about to award B-1 bombers to Mitsubishi, and the Federal Communications Commission is prohibited by law from licensing Hitachi to run NBC's broadcast stations."

Despite such criticisms, investors applauded the RCA acquisition, which added 14 cents a share to GE's earnings for 1986. Welch received further accolades for purchasing 80 percent of Kidder, Peabody & Company, a Wall Street brokerage firm, for $600 million. That brought the number of businesses, large and small, that GE had purchased during Welch's chairmanship to 338 and their total cost to $11.1 billion.

The newly restructured GE's earnings for 1986 were $2.49 billion, up more than 6 percent from the previous year and its stock, which had split two shares for one in June 1983, did so again in May 1987. By then, within just over six years since Welch became chairman, the value of the stock had more than tripled, bettering the Dow Jones Industrial Average and the Standard & Poor's index of 400 industrial stocks by about 40 percent. In the same six years, GE rose from 10th to third among American corporations in the total market value of its stock, more than $50 billion.

As the object of adulation—sometimes even amounting to veneration—among many in the business community, Welch easily weathered a number of scandals in which GE was involved during the mid-1980s. "The most gut-wrenching" of the scandals, Welch told Peter Petre, came to a head in May 1985, when GE pleaded guilty to defrauding the Air Force of $800,000 five years earlier in work on a Minuteman missile project. Besides returning the money, GE paid a fine of $1.04 million for the false billing, and the entire company was banned from bidding on government work for a brief time. Another scandal arose in February 1987, when officials at GE's new subsidiary—Kidder, Peabody, & Co.—were threatened with prosecution on charges of criminal insider trading. Weeks later federal prosecutors decided against an indictment after GE ousted the brokerage firm's top management and oversaw a $25.3 million settlement with the Securities and Exchange Commission. GE's prompt actions led the U.S. Attorney General to praise the company as a "responsible corporate citizen." New troubles arose in September 1987, when several of GE's top executives were ordered into court in a civil lawsuit brought by three Ohio utility companies. The three firms accused GE of fraud and racketeering in selling them a nuclear reactor with an allegedly faulty design.

Such problems did little to shake the confidence in GE or in Welch that was displayed by many Wall Street analysts, and double-digit growth was predicted for the company. Such confidence was inspired in part by the fact that within six months of the RCA acquisition, which required $5.4 billion in loans, Welch had "whipped [GE's] balance sheet back into shape," as James R. Norman reported for *BusinessWeek* (March 16, 1987). He did so by selling $1.7 billion worth of RCA's assets, by selling GE's consumer-electronics operation along with RCA's, and by using the sales and outright dismissals to trim his combined staffs to the size of GE's alone in 1985.

Those actions and Welch's combative management style resulted in a "disastrous" morale problem for many at RCA, according to one insider, but the cuts and sales also brought Welch a staggering new cash hoard of $2.8 billion. Under Welch's innovative leadership, GE continued to see unprecedented growth and expansion throughout the 1990s, and in 1999 the editors of *Fortune* magazine named him the "Manager of the Century." By the start of the new millennium, the company was earning nearly $130 billion in annual revenues, a five-fold increase from 1980. Its market value was estimated to be $410 billion at the time of Welch's retirement in 2001. Despite his unquestionable accomplishments, Welch's generous retirement plan, which included a reported annual compensation of $8 million, drew heavy criticism in some quarters.

In 2001 Welch, who had been succeeded at GE by Jeffrey Immelt, published the memoir *Jack: Straight from the Gut*, which reached number one on the *New York Times* best-seller list. Welch had received a record-breaking $7.1 million book advance from Warner Books to write the volume. Welch and his third wife, Suzy, then co-authored the 2005 international best-seller *Winning*, a treatise on the intricacies of business management, and its 2006 companion volume, *Winning: The Answers*. They also wrote a widely read weekly column, "The Welch Way," which appeared in *BusinessWeek* from 2005 to 2009 as well as in dozens of major newspapers around the world.

In 2009 Welch, who spent a large portion of his time lecturing all over the world, launched the Jack Welch Management Institute, which offered graduate business degrees in collaboration with Chancellor University in Cleveland, Ohio. Welch is the father of four children (Katherine, John, Anne, and Mark). He has been married to his third wife, the former Suzy Wetlaufer, since 2004. The two met when Wetlaufer interviewed Welch while working as an editor for the *Harvard Business Review*. (His first marriage, to Carolyn B. Osburn, the mother of his children, lasted from 1959 to 1987. His second, to Jane Beasley, lasted from 1989 to 2003. Those two unions ended in divorce.)

Further Reading:

BusinessWeek Dec. 30, 1985; Mar. 16, 1987; June 30, 1987; Dec. 14, 1997

Forbes Mar. 26, 1984

Fortune July 7, 1986; Jan. 5, 1987

New York Times Dec. 28, 1980

New York Times Magazine Sept. 20, 1987

Wall Street Journal Aug. 20, 2010

Washington Post Aug. 27, 2010

Selected Books:

Jack: Straight from the Gut, 2001 (with John A. Byrne)

Winning, 2005 (with Suzy Welch)

Winning: The Answers, 2006 (with Suzy Welch)

Wexner, Leslie H.

Chairman and CEO, L Brands; philanthropist

Born. 1937, Dayton, Ohio

"I'm a super specialist, I know only the women's apparel business..." Leslie Wexner, helmsman of The Limited and Victoria's Secret, has said. "But I bet I know more about women's apparel than anyone in the country." A dynamic, visionary businessman who has made specialty retailing his specialty, Wexner is one of most successful retailers in the United States.

Education and Early Career

"My idea was that the easiest business to go into is the business you're in—and there's room for more than one competitor," Wexner told Penny Gill, who profiled him for *Stores* (January 1993), the magazine of the National Retail Federation. In Wexner's case, that business was the rag trade, for he was born into a family of clothing merchants. His father, Harry Wexner, emigrated from Russia to the United States when he was thirteen, and by the time Leslie was born—on September 8, 1937, in Dayton, Ohio—he was working as a manager of a chain of budget clothing stores. Leslie Wexner has credited his father with teaching him the importance of hard work and attention to detail. From his mother, Bella (Cabakoff) Wexner, a department-store buyer, he learned that anything is possible.

In 1951, after a series of moves, the Wexners settled in Columbus, Ohio, where Harry and Bella opened a women's clothing store. They named the store Leslie's, after their son. At first Leslie didn't aspire to a career in retailing. His earliest ambition was to become an architect. As he grew older, at least partly as a result of pressure from his father, he became more interested in running his own business, and after entering Ohio State University, he majored in business administration.

After graduating with honors from Ohio State in 1959, Wexner entered law school, but he dropped out two years later. He began helping his parents run the family business, though at the time that line of work had little attraction for him. "I actually had in mind that I wanted to learn the real-estate business, and thought I would get a job with a local real-estate broker or developer," he told Penny Gill. "Even after I had started working full time in my parents' stores and had quit looking for another job, I still didn't intend to make retailing my career—every day was going to be my last day, and I was going to do something else. But opportunity did not knock." So Wexner began looking for ways to create his own opportunities.

Later Career

At the time, Leslie's was a moderately successful operation that sold all types of women's clothing. Leslie Wexner thought the store would be more profitable if it sold only sportswear, because the few stores that had adopted this approach had proved especially popular among women. "Although I didn't understand fashion, I understood that [sportswear] was what all my female friends wore," he recalled to Penny Gill. After trying, unsuccessfully, to talk his father into stocking just sportswear, Leslie decided to strike out on his own. With a $5,000 loan from his aunt, he opened his own sportswear store in a suburban shopping center in 1963. "Literally the day the store opened I didn't have a name for it," he told Penny Gill, "and finally I said maybe we should call it 'The Limited' because we're limited to only selling sportswear."

Wexner worked long hours to make his store a success—a habit that has continued throughout his life—often arriving at work at 7:00 a.m. and leaving around midnight. He washed the store windows himself, and he did his bookkeeping on his day off. But Wexner thrived on the hard work; indeed, he didn't view it as something distasteful at all. "If you want to torture me, take my work away," he told William H. Meyers in an interview for the *New York Times Magazine* (June 8, 1986).

Before long, it was clear that Wexner's retailing strategy was a winning formula. In its first year, The Limited's sales were $160,000. By the end of the second year, Wexner had opened two more stores. In 1965 Milton Petrie, the founder and chairman of a giant chain of women's clothing stores, stopped by The Limited while visiting his own stores in Columbus. Petrie was so impressed with the operation that he offered to buy 49.5 percent of it. He also offered Wexner a top job in his organization, with a salary of $75,000. Wexner declined. "Those numbers were like the GNP to me, but I still said no," he told William Meyers. "I wanted to run my own business."

Although no deal was consummated by the two men, Wexner came away from his meeting with Petrie with many new ideas about how to build a multi-store business. "I had never known anyone who ran a very large business, and at that time, in my wildest dreams I probably couldn't have imagined a business being more than five or ten stores in my lifetime," Wexner told Penny Gill. "And here I met a person who had about seventy stores. So I was looking at him and saying, 'What man has done, man can do'—and thinking maybe I could do close to that in my lifetime." Wexner has credited Petrie with helping him to overcome his "shop-keeper's mentality" and to think like an entrepreneur.

Throughout the 1960s The Limited continued to grow, with Wexner opening one store after another. Inevitably, there came a time when he began to look for ways to expand his business beyond Ohio, and, once again, a serendipitous meeting with an older, successful businessman provided him with ideas that helped him attain his goals. That man was Alfred A. Taubman, a real-estate developer who specialized in shopping centers and malls. Taubman taught Wexner the importance of attractive store design and of finding the right location for his stores. The two men also began working together: Taubman provided Wexner with prime space in his malls, and Wexner became an important tenant, renting large blocks of space as his empire grew. Wexner once likened his relationship with Taubman, which has endured over the years, to that which exists between "father and son."

In 1969, with five stores in his chain, Wexner decided to raise money for future expansion by taking the company public. To do so, he enlisted the help of an old school friend, who eventually raised $345,000 by selling company stock at $7.25 a share. Wexner gave stock to his parents, who were working for him by that time, and to his sister. (His father served as chairman of the board until his death, and his mother has worked as the secretary of the company.) The money that was raised by the stock sale was enough to launch Wexner on a course of rapid expansion during the 1970s. By 1976 he had opened one hundred stores.

While The Limited was expanding, its customers were growing older. Many of the teenage baby boomers whose penchant for sportswear had inspired the first store were now hard at work climbing corporate ladders. They still wanted comfortable clothes at reasonable prices, but they now also wanted clothing that was of a higher quality and that reflected their new level of sophistication. One of the strategies Wexner came up with to respond to these new consumer demands was to sign on several top designers, such as Krizia, to produce exclusive collections for his company.

Wexner's ability to keep abreast of—and meet—the evolving needs of his customers enabled him to stay one step ahead of the competition. "Leslie senses what consumer lifestyles are and what consumer desires will be years ahead—he just senses it," Howard Gross, the president of The Limited Stores, told Penny Gill. "He claims he's not a merchant/marketing genius, he just works hard at it. But his merchant skills are just phenomenal." Equally important, Wexner has a keen understanding of the mind of the consumer. "You have to understand that no one has to buy anything," he told Caroline Mayer of the *Washington Post* (March 31, 1985). "On a utility basis, everybody has enough clothing in their closets to last them one hundred years. So the issue in retailing is to create a demand to stimulate people to buy."

But conceiving designs that will create consumer demand is only a part of running a chain of clothing stores. Producing those designs and bringing them to market as quickly as possible is another, equally important, part of the business. With a view to speeding up production, in 1978 Wexner purchased Mast Industries, a global supplier that works closely with more than one hundred producers all over the world and that owns many factories in Asia. "Mast is The Limited's trump card," the president of a competing chain of clothing stores told William Meyers. "It's light-years ahead in terms of understanding how to get things done in the Far East." Mast's employees found the fabrics, placed garment manufacturers under contract to cut the fabric and created the garments, and oversaw the shipping of the completed garments to Ohio—all in a matter of weeks.

Wexner, along with other specialty retailers, has drawn the ire of American textile manufacturers for contracting with suppliers in the Far East. The arrangement, his critics argue, squeezes the American firms out of the market and thus precipitates the loss of American jobs. Wexner has responded to the charge by claiming that the large American textile mills have not been able to provide him with merchandise in the quantities he required. He has challenged American companies to become more flexible in meeting the needs of specialty stores.

In 1978, in addition to purchasing Mast Industries, Wexner set up a computer network to link all of the stores in the chain and built a huge, automated distribution center in Columbus, Ohio. Once again, his aim was to get his merchandise into his stores as quickly as possible. In a building capable of housing 30 football fields, hundreds of employees sorted, tagged, and packed the millions of garments shipped in from the Far East each year. The clothing moved from employee to employee via computerized conveyor racks. It took, on average, only forty-eight hours for a garment to move into the distribution center and out to a store—a process that could take up to several weeks in a less-automated warehouse. The distribution system that Wexner developed and refined also enabled The Limited to ship new designs to each of its stores every few weeks, rather than every season, as was the practice among traditional retailers. "In this business you can't be patient," Wexner told William Meyers. "You've got to get your stuff to the customer first if you want to be successful."

To finance the purchase of Mast Industries and the opening of new stores, The Limited borrowed heavily. At first the company managed its debt easily, but in the late 1970s sales dropped off, and Wexner was forced to temporarily put his expansion plans on hold. Wexner has since admitted that he probably tried to do too much too fast during the 1970s. But by the early 1980s, thanks to a resurgence in sales, The Limited's debt had been substantially reduced and Wexner was ready to begin a new wave of expansion.

Wexner's business strategy in the 1980s was to launch and buy clothing chains that specialized in women's apparel, but that served slightly different markets. By this time The Limited was catering to women looking for business attire. Thinking that there was a market for livelier, funkier designs, Wexner began his expansion drive by launching Express in 1980. The new chain's stores displayed trendy, affordable styles for the young-at-heart. "We have never really defined Express in terms of chronological age," Michael A. Weiss, the president of Express, told investors, as quoted in the 1992 annual report. "We've always defined ourselves in terms of attitudinal age." In the late 1980s and early 1990s, Wexner ventured into several other niche markets with the establishment of The Limited Too, which sold girls' sportswear, Structure, which represented Wexner's first foray into menswear, Cacique, which sold lingerie, and Bath & Body Works, specializing in toiletries.

"You have to understand that no one has to buy anything. On a utility basis, everybody has enough clothing in their closets to last them one hundred years. So the issue in retailing is to create a demand to stimulate people to buy."

Wexner began acquiring existing specialty stores in 1982, when he purchased Victoria's Secret, which sold lingerie, and Lane Bryant, which specialized in conservative and—in the opinion of some—unstylish clothing for large and tall women. Under Wexner's direction both stores took on new images. The revitalized Victoria's Secret stores featured silk and lace lingerie sensuously displayed on padded hangers, and the stores themselves were decorated with Victorian furnishings: changes that helped make the chain synonymous with genteel sexiness. And Lane Bryant quickly became known for selling stylish, contemporary designs. Wexner's other acquisitions during the 1980s were Lerner New York, which sold women's clothing at affordable prices, Henri Bendel, a high-fashion specialty store, Abercrombie & Fitch, which specialized in classic yet hip menswear, and Penhaligon's, which sold fragrances. Two of the new companies drew Wexner into the business of catalogue sales: Victoria's Secret and Lane Bryant spawned Victoria's Secret catalogue and Brylane catalogues, respectively.

During his interview with Penny Gill, Wexner explained why he decided to embark on a campaign of launching and buying companies and talked about the success of the program: "All our acquisitions, except Mast, were failures when we acquired them....[We] purposely picked businesses that were losers but that we thought we could turn around, because there was more value in them—that is, we could get paid for our work rather than paying somebody else for theirs. I don't think there has ever been a retail business that has as consistent a record of picking niches of retailing and either remerchandising [them] or starting a business to hit niches the way we've done it. I'm very proud of that fact."

Wexner's other strategies to enhance sales included building superstores that boasted three times more floor space—and thus merchandise—than that which was found in the original Limited outlets. He also grouped different specialty stores together in the same malls so that he could negotiate lower rents and get better locations—the kinds of benefits department stores enjoyed. And in 1987 Wexner decided to decentralize The Limited. He divided it into smaller operating companies, each with its own president. Wexner remained at the helm as chairman. He has said he considers this step a milestone in his career. Decentralization, he told Penny Gill, "allows each business on a cost-effective basis to be self-sufficient, which means it can move faster and with greater agility, and it has more control over its destiny."

The recessionary 1990s flattened the growth curve somewhat at The Limited, but Wexner's faith in his original merchandising premise wasn't shaken—the notion that specialty retailing was the wave of the future. "I do believe in the fundamental assumption that the fewer things you do, the likelier you are to do them well," he told Penny Gill. "I think specialty retailing is as valid, and perhaps more valid, than twenty years ago. In a world that's changing faster... it becomes increasingly difficult to be knowledgeable and/or competitive if you have a broad-based business."

According to his colleagues, Wexner is an intense, energetic, and demanding man who expects loyalty, hard work, and dedication from his employees. His executives have praised him for his ability to nurture talent, and they have described him as a good mentor. "He has incredibly high standards and insists on excellence," Cheryl Turpin, the president of Lane Bryant, told Penny Gill. "He perceives no limits to what people can do and doesn't give up on his standards or vary in his implementation of them. At the same time, though, he is always straightforward and honest, and very supportive."

More than 90 percent of The Limited's employees (called "associates" by Wexner) were shareholders; the fact that his people had a stake in the company contributed to its success, Wexner believes. "I thought it would be significant for the people working in the business to have a piece of the action," he told Penny Gill. "It's not that I saw the future. I just liked the idea of the fairness of the people working in the enterprise being able to invest in it. But looking back, it was a pretty good idea, because it has not only been fair...but also it has been tremendous as an enabling factor in the success of the business. It creates a harmony of interest among the people in the distribution centers, financial people, store managers, salespeople, all across the business. And that people side of the business is something I'm very proud of."

Wexner is also proud of his philanthropic activities, resolving to use his wealth to make a difference in the world during his lifetime. With that goal in mind, he and his mother established the Wexner Foundation, which supports many educational, cultural, and civic programs. Always interested in fostering leadership, he also donated $2 million to a graduate study program at Harvard University. He was a national vice-chairman and international co-chairman of the United Jewish Appeal, and he supports other Jewish philanthropic organizations.

Wexner has tried to improve the quality of life in Columbus by helping to finance the construction of the Wexner Center for the Visual Arts at Ohio State University and the Wexner Research Center at Children's Hospital and by donating his time and money to a variety of local charities and civic and cultural organizations. He has also lent his support to his alma mater, Ohio State University, and he served on its board of trustees.

Leslie Wexner married Abigail S. Koppel, a New York attorney, in 1993. An art enthusiast, Wexner collects contemporary works of art and is a trustee of two art museums, the Whitney Museum of American Art in New York City and the Columbus Art Museum in Ohio.

Wexner was recently designated the wealthiest single individual in the state of Ohio, with an estimated net worth of $5.8 billion.

Further Reading:

New York Times Mar. 31, 1985

New York Times Magazine June 8, 1986

New York Aug. 5, 1985

Newsweek Dec. 30, 1985

Stores Jan. 1993

Washington Post Mar. 31, 1985

WCPO.com Aug. 1, 2014

Who's Who in America, 1992–93

Woertz, Patricia A.

CEO, Archer Daniels Midland Co.

Born: 1953; Pittsburgh, Pennsylvania

On May 1, 2006 Patricia A. Woertz succeeded G. Allen Andreas to become the eighth chief executive officer (CEO) in the 104-year history of the Illinois-based Archer Daniels Midland Co. (ADM), one of the world's largest agricultural processors and producers of biofuels. Woertz, who has a distinguished record of penetrating the so-called glass ceiling for female advancement in corporate America, has downplayed her reputation as a trailblazer, despite her appointment as ADM's first-ever female CEO.

Education and Early Career

Patricia A. Woertz was born on March 17, 1953 in Pittsburgh, Pennsylvania, one of the two children of Chuck Woertz, the CEO of a large home-construction and development company in western Pennsylvania, and Vi Woertz, a school librarian. As a child Woertz spent summers taking unusual field trips with her family—which included her brother, Chuck Jr.—visiting corporate offices and touring manufacturing plants. "My mother felt we'd be earning a living during our entire adult lives, and therefore believed we should spend summers in learning activities," Woertz said, as quoted by Ameet Sachdev and Mark Skertic for the *Chicago Tribune* (April 30, 2006). "Consequently, I got to see a plate glass factory in Pittsburgh, a U.S. Steel plant and how Heinz made ketchup." The Woertz family also made trips to local oil refineries and to the headquarters of Mellon Bank (now called the Mellon Financial Corp.). Woertz took a liking to the industrial environments that she visited. "Definitely there was a seed of inspiration sown there. I've always enjoyed seeing how things are made," she told Jon Birger for *Fortune* (October 16, 2006).

Woertz enrolled at Penn State University in State College, Pennsylvania, where she earned a B.S. in accounting in 1974. That year she took her first job, as a certified public accountant for the Pittsburgh office of the global accounting firm Ernst & Young. Woertz was one of only two women in the class of 200 first-year recruits at the company. After a three-year stint at Ernst & Young, which counted the Houston-based Gulf Oil Corp. as one of its clients, Woertz, lured by the opportunity to work in the global-energy industry, joined Gulf Oil in 1977.

Later Career

Gulf, which had been embroiled in a political scandal in the mid-1970s involving illegal contributions to the reelection campaign of President Richard M. Nixon, took measures to revamp its internal auditing department. "Gulf was cleaning house, and I saw opportunities in the energy field," Woertz said to Michael Kinsman for the *San Diego Union-Tribune* (June 4, 2006). At Gulf, Woertz had responsibilities in the areas of oil refining, marketing, strategic planning, and finance. In the early 1980s Gulf Oil resisted a corporate takeover from the chairman of Mesa Petroleum, T. Boone Pickens, who was known to "frighten a firm by first investing in it and then proclaiming that he could run the corporation, which invariably dwarfs Mesa in size, better than its current officers," as John Greenwald wrote for *Time* (March 4, 1985). Though Pickens's bid to take over Gulf Oil failed, the company succumbed in 1984 to a $13.4 billion merger with the Standard Oil Co. of California (Socal), one of the largest global-energy companies in the world. The merger, the largest corporate consolidation in history up to that time, raised concerns over potential antitrust violations at the Federal Trade Commission, which required Socal (known after the buyout as the Chevron Corp.) to sell off thousands of its holdings, including pipelines and gas stations. Woertz was assigned the task of overseeing the divestitures as well as reducing the overall debt. "It was a kind of turning point in my career," she told Jon Birger. "I learned about M&A [mergers and acquisitions] and how to value assets and work with investment bankers."

In 1987 Woertz, who was by then married with three young children, moved with her family to the Chevron headquarters in San Francisco. There, she became the manager of strategic planning, overseeing the information-technology, refining, and marketing divisions. "I looked for and took the opportunities I could," she told Michael Kinsman. "The oil business was global and that gave me lots of opportunities." Her career advancement sometimes came at the expense of her family life. Noted for her intense work ethic, Woertz admitted to Susan Berfield for *BusinessWeek* (May 14, 2006) that "some people expressed surprise I had kids." Kenneth Derr, the CEO of the Chevron Corp. from 1989 to 1999, recalled the combination of focus and ambition Woertz demonstrated early in her career. "She told me she wanted to be chairman," Derr said to Jon Birger. He added, however, "Some people spend more time worrying about the next job than doing the one they've got. That wasn't Pat."

She credited her husband, a logistics consultant (whom she later divorced) for putting her career ahead of his own. "At one point, we sort of said to each other, 'Gee, somebody's career is going to have to take priority,'" Woertz said to Jon Birger. In 1993 Woertz was appointed president of Chevron Canada Ltd., a refining and marketing subsidiary, located in Vancouver, British Columbia. Entrusted with overseeing 430 employees, a Canadian-based refinery, 230 service stations, and annual revenues of $500 million, Woertz became the first female president of a Chevron subsidiary and the highest-ranking female executive in the company's 95-year history. "There is not a job I've held in my career that was held by a woman before me," Woertz said in a 2000 interview, as quoted by Sachdev and Skertic. In 1996 Woertz became president of Chevron International Oil and vice president of Chevron U.S.A. Products, assuming responsibility for the supply and distribution of the firm's petroleum products worldwide. She became president of Chevron U.S.A. Products in 1998.

"I hope people will judge me by my performance . . . Obviously, I'm a woman, but I also am an executive [who] has developed skills through the years just like any other executive, male or female."

In 2001 Woertz's career benefited from another historic corporate merger, this time Chevron's buyout of the American oil company Texaco Inc. The merger, which was valued at $35.2 billion, made the new ChevronTexaco the third-largest oil and gas producer in the United States. Woertz became executive vice president for global downstream, "which is essentially almost everything that happens to oil once we get it out of the ground," Woertz explained in a speech she delivered for the Women in Leadership Conference at the Haas School of Business at the University of California at Berkeley (October 26, 2002). As the highest-ranking female in the oil industry, Woertz managed business operations that spanned six continents, including the running of more than 20 oil refineries and the marketing of the Chevron, Texaco, and Caltex brands at more than 25,000 retail outlets. She attributed her rise in leadership circles in part to her having served as president of both Chevron Canada and Chevron International Oil, which honed her global-business acumen. "These assignments exposed me to different cultures and provided experience in the quite different dynamics of running international operations," she told the Haas audience. "They prepared me, as much as anything could, for expanding my responsibilities in 2001 from refining and marketing operations in one country only—the United States—to the responsibility I have today for operations in over 180 countries throughout the world."

In early 2002, not long after ChevronTexaco's formation, its downstream division suffered a setback, due to lower refining margins—resulting from sinking gas prices in a weak U.S. economy—as well as to operational inefficiencies; downstream revenues plummeted from $1.1 billion to only $43 million. For her part, Woertz cut $500 million in costs, beginning in 2003, by restructuring her upper-management team, reducing operating expenses, and negotiating favorable oil deals for her refineries. Her strategy "underscores the shadow side of creativity," she explained in a speech given in 2005 at the University of Pennsylvania's Wharton Business School, as quoted by Jon Birger. "Nothing is created without something being destroyed." Woertz also began to analyze the geographical regions that consistently saw the highest returns on investment, identifying Asia, Latin America, and the west coast of North America in particular as locations that rewarded the company's focus. "We asked what areas we would be investing in. We also found out which areas would be less likely to attract new capital. Europe was identified as an area that is non-strategic. Now we are studying these areas to see what our new ideas could be," she told Lucinda Kennedy for the *London Sunday Times* (August 22, 2004). Thanks to Woertz's efforts, ChevronTexaco's profit margin from international assets rose from 5 percent to 10 percent by the end of 2003.

In February 2006, after nearly three decades of service at Chevron, Woertz left the company, in part to seek a CEO position elsewhere. (As Jon Birger noted, the current Chevron CEO, David J. O'Reilly, at age 60, was "presumably several years from retirement.") Woertz's decision, one of the bolder moves in the modern corporate arena, was met with great enthusiasm by the executive search committee at the Decatur, Illinois–based Archer Daniels Midland Co., which had been scouting candidates to fill its top executive spot. Dubbed "the alpha male of agribusiness" by Susan Berfield, ADM is one of the world's largest processors of oilseeds and corn for the food industry. G. Allen Andreas had served as its CEO since 1997 and as chairman since 1999; his uncle and predecessor, Dwayne O. Andreas, had led the company's growth from a $450 million business in the early 1970s to a firm with revenues of $14 billion. G. Allen Andreas retained the chairmanship while Woertz took on the CEO post, which for a time made ADM the largest publicly traded company run by a woman. ADM's choice of Woertz, rather than a successor groomed within the company, came as a shock to many familiar with ADM's history. "By God, if you only knew the culture there," a former ADM manager told Jon Birger. "Bringing an outsider, a woman no less, into a company that's a bastion of lifers and good ol' boys—I can't tell you how huge a change that is." Andreas saw Woertz's selection as a sensible one. "We were looking for skills to manage the business. She's capable, knowledgeable, and had strong ethics," he told Susan Diesenhouse and Michael Oneal in the *Chicago Tribune* (April 29, 2006). Leonard Teitelbaum, an analyst with the financial firm Merrill Lynch & Co., suspected that for ADM, "it would be easier to teach an energy executive the agricultural side of the business, than an agricultural executive the energy side," as he put it, according to Sachdev and Skertic. Diesenhouse and Oneal framed

Woertz's appointment differently: "She's a woman, she hails from Big Oil and she's not a member of the Andreas family. For all three reasons, [Woertz] is a trailblazer." On April 28, 2006 ADM officially named Woertz as CEO, the eighth in the company's 104-year-history. With her appointment Woertz became just the 10th woman ever to head a *Fortune* 500 company. "She understands how to get the product from the processing plant to the consumer's gas tank," the analyst Gregory Warren of Morningstar Inc. said to Diesenhouse and Oneal. "ADM is betting the future on energy products."

Woertz herself continued to downplay her gender, preferring to highlight her corporate track record. "I'm fairly certain that Archer Daniels Midland didn't hire me because I'm a woman. I think my background and my performance mean more," she told Michael Kinsman. I hope people will judge me by my performance . . . Obviously, I'm a woman, but I also am an executive [who] has developed skills through the years just like any other executive, male or female."

Woertz's tenure began during a favorable period in ADM's history. From 2003 to 2005 the company saw an impressive 17 percent revenue growth and amassed $35.9 billion in total revenue, while developing a reputation as "one of Wall Street's hottest alternative-energy plays," in Birger's words. "Because the company is in good shape, the pressure is more intense on her than if she was inheriting a mess," the executive coach Debra Benton pointed out to Del Jones for *USA Today* (April 28, 2006). "If she does well, at least for a while, people will say she inherited it. If she fails, they'll say women don't have the right stuff." "This isn't a turnaround situation, it's about growing for the future," Woertz said to the Associated Press, as quoted by Jones. She explained to Birger, "My objectives in my first 100 days have been to listen and learn and build trust. I've met with over 4,000 employees, been to 32 ADM locations. I want to get to a lot of people early on and find out what we do very well and where we can improve." From the outset Woertz touted the company's historically profitable food and feed businesses, which have included corn and oilseed processing, while strengthening ADM's commitment to renewable energy sources (or biofuels), such as ethanol, made from crops including corn and sugarcane. With hefty tariffs on fuel imports; with rapid strides in molecular science making it possible to create ethanol from sources other than corn kernels and sugarcane; and with ethanol's value soaring in the energy market, due in large part to federal subsidies (refiners of the substance receive a 51-cent federal tax credit for every gallon of gasoline into which ethanol is blended), some experts forecast a "transformation from a petroleum-based economy to a carbohydrate-based economy," as Mark Emalfarb, a biotechnology executive, told Diesenhouse and Oneal. Consequently, Woertz has positioned ADM at the forefront of the energy as well as the agricultural processing industry. In one notable move, Woertz instructed ADM's Washington, D.C. office to register as a political lobbyist, hoping to generate increased governmental support for ethanol production and usage. Woertz has urged ADM's research and development divisions to shift their investments from strictly corn-based ethanol to cellulosic ethanol, produced from grasses and agricultural waste; she has also outlined plans to allocate large portions of the company's $3 billion capital-improvement budget for the construction of a dozen new production plants worldwide, including locations in Cedar Rapids, Iowa, and Columbus, Nebraska. "I come from an industry that understands margins can be the jaws of life or the jaws of death," she said to Birger. "Any industry building capacity as rapidly as the ethanol industry has to ask itself whether margins are going to fluctuate. ADM's strength is we're building these big plants that are very cost-competitive."

Judy Olian, the former dean of the Smeal College of Business at Penn State University, commented on Woertz's management style, as quoted by Sachdev and Skertic: "Pat is a straight-shooter. She doesn't like to waste time on things that people should have been prepared with. She expects you to have done your homework. She expects people to have in-depth knowledge of what they're responsible for. And she does her share of it. She asks questions and expects polished answers." Woertz serves on the boards of the American Petroleum Institute, the California Chamber of Commerce, the University of San Diego, and the Smeal College of Business. She graduated from the International Executive Development Program at New York City's Columbia University in 1994, and received the Alumni Fellow Award from the Smeal College of Business in 2002. *Fortune* magazine ranked Woertz fourth on its list of the 50 Most Powerful Women in Business in 2006.

Further Reading:

BusinessWeek May 14, 2006

Chicago Tribune Apr. 29, 2006; Apr. 30, 2006

Forbes Oct. 19, 2006

Fortune Oct. 16, 2006

London Sunday Times Aug. 22, 2004

San Diego Union-Tribune Jun. 4, 2006

USA Today April 28, 2006

Zander, Edward J.

Former president and CEO, Sun Microsystems

Born: 1947; Brooklyn, New York

When Edward J. Zander joined Sun Microsystems, Inc. in 1987, the company was known primarily for manufacturing computer workstations for engineers. Zander, who helped develop and market Sun's widely used Solaris program, had been instrumental in transforming the firm into one of the world's foremost producers of the high-powered computer systems, high-speed microprocessors, and sophisticated software packages that drove the Internet. "Unless you're a CIO [chief information officer] or a Webmaster, you probably aren't aware of how much you rely on Sun," David Kirkpatrick wrote for *Fortune* (April 17, 2000). "But every time you buy a stock on E*Trade, an old crock on eBay, or a book on Amazon, Sun is in the background."

Education and Early Career

Edward J. Zander was born in the New York City borough of Brooklyn in 1947. His father was a Jewish immigrant from Poland who dreamed of becoming a lawyer, but became a furrier instead in order to support his ailing parents; he rose at five o'clock in the morning six days a week to go to work in Manhattan. His mother came to the United States from Greece, after her entire family was killed by Turks in 1922. As a child Zander lived in a tight-knit Brooklyn neighborhood; he was a fan of the Brooklyn Dodgers and enjoyed family trips to Coney Island. He has described Brooklyn in that era as "the best place on earth." When Zander was 12, his father moved the family to Commack, New York, in the heart of Long Island, where the Zanders bought their first home. The move was difficult for Zander, who became more introverted in Commack. He made few friends in the town, and, although loath to discuss it with journalists, he reportedly had to deal with several painful instances of anti-Semitism there. As a teen, Zander had a variety of jobs, including delivering newspapers and flipping hamburgers for Buddy Burger. After graduating from high school, he attended Rensselaer Polytechnic Institute in Troy, New York, where he received a bachelor's degree in electrical engineering. He soon received his MBA from Boston University, met his future wife, Mona, and got a job as an engineer at Data General Corp. By his own estimation, Zander did not do well as an engineer. He persuaded a superior at Data General to give him a chance in the marketing department instead. Zander excelled in the new position, turning several poorly designed products into high-selling merchandise. "It was like a light went off," he told Peter Burrows for *Business Week* (December 13, 1999). "Until then, I didn't know I had a creative side." Zander worked at Data General for nine years, in various senior marketing positions, before being hired by Apollo Computer in 1982 as vice president of marketing. The workstation industry was just beginning to emerge at that time, and Zander developed a successful marketing strategy for Apollo's workstation products.

Later Career

In 1987 Zander was hired by Sun Microsystems, then largely a manufacturer of workstations for engineers, as vice president of corporate marketing. In that position he was in charge of developing worldwide marketing, product, and merchandising strategies for Sun's hardware and software products and technologies. Made president of SunSoft—the company's software subsidiary— in 1991, Zander was influential in leading the development of the

Solaris operating system, which became one of the most widely used software packages among Internet companies hosting Web sites or conducting e-commerce. In 1995 Zander made a move to the presidency of another subsidiary, Sun Microsystems Computer Co. (SMCC). In this capacity he oversaw all aspects of Sun's multibillion-dollar network computing-systems business. The year was an important one for the firm: In 1995 Sun introduced Java technology, the industry's first universal software platform. Java allowed developers to write a single application that would run on any computer system, and machines equipped with Java could communicate with each other, even if one was made by IBM and the other by Apple. (In another landmark event that year, *Toy Story*, Disney's first all-computer-generated animated feature, was made, using more than 100 Sun computer systems.)

In January 1998 Zander was promoted to chief operating officer (COO) of Sun, giving him responsibility for the company's seven product divisions, including research and development, engineering, sales, service, support, manufacturing, and marketing. As the new COO, Zander had discussions with CEO Scott McNealy on ways to change the course of the company's business. "I told him we've got to stand for something," Zander recalled to Burrows, referring to Sun's lack of a focused marketing platform. Zander came up with Sun's slogan about "dot comming the world," which became part of the company's advertising campaign. In addition, he coined the phrase, "We're the dot in dot com," also used in Sun advertising. "All of a sudden, everyone understood what Sun was all about—my mother, my customers, and 30,00 employees," he explained to Burrows.

In April 1999 Zander was made president of Sun Microsystems, Inc., in addition to COO. (McNealy retained the titles of CEO and chairman.) There was some speculation in the industry that McNealy engineered the promotion to keep Zander, who was frequently being wooed by other companies, at Sun. He reportedly relished hands-on problem solving, and launching an overhaul of the company. Zander told Burrows, "I want Sun to be the IBM of the Internet age." Toward this end, he assigned task forces to rethink how operations were performed at Sun. One change at the firm was that all of Sun's new computers would be manufactured so that any problems that occurred in them could be diagnosed and fixed remotely. Zander also instructed his sales staff to concentrate on enterprises that provided hosting services for Web sites, as that industry rapidly expanded.

"All of a sudden, everyone understood what Sun was all about—my mother, my customers, and 30,00 employees."

The company was listed as number 150 on the *Fortune* 500 list for the year 2000, and during the fiscal year that ended on June 30, 1999, it posted almost $12 billion in revenues. Sun's stock rose dramatically, bringing the firm's market capitalization up to $170 billion. Analyst John B. Jones of Salomon Smith Barney told Peter Burrows, "I don't know how Sun could be doing any better, and I give Ed 80 percent of the credit."

Friends of his nicknamed the hard-working Zander "Fast Eddie" for his high energy, competitiveness, and wisecracking humor. Well-spoken and sharply dressed, Zander was noted in the industry for his drive and solidity. Each morning at eight o'clock he had a conference call with salespeople to see if any major customers were having problems with their equipment. Zander was said to listen with fairness to both clients and employees. "If you cross him, you're going to get a fight," Dave Herter, a friend and former co-worker, told Burrows. "But if it's just a case of not meeting your numbers, he doesn't say 'you screwed up.' He says, 'How are we going to fix this?'"

Zander's legacy in the technology sector is secure; sadly, his subsequent, post-Sun career is more controversial. His tenure as CEO of Motorola from 2004 to 2007 was widely seen as disastrous. Subsequently, according to a report in *Fierce Wireless* (June 18, 2013), Zander has "largely kept out of the public eye since then. However, he is [a] board member of several companies."

Further Reading:

Business Week Dec. 13, 1999

Fierce Wireless Jun. 18, 2013

Fortune Apr. 17, 2000

Sun Microsystems Web site

Appendixes

Historical Biographies

Mildred Custin

Retail fashion executive

Mildred Custin developed the chain of 12 Bonwit Teller women's specialty outlets into bellwethers of fashion in the late 1960s.

Areas of Achievement: Fashion, business

Born: January 25, 1906; Manchester, New Hampshire

Died: 1997; Palm Springs, Florida

Early Life

Mildred Custin was born in 1906 in New Hampshire and raised in Boston, Massachusetts, where she graduated from Simmons College. Custin began her career in Boston, as a gift buyer for the now-defunct Shepard's department store and then at R. H. White's department stores. In 1935 she began work at the iconic Philadelphia department store John Wanamaker, where she rose from gift buyer to merchandise manager.

Life's Work

In 1958 Mildred Custin became president of the three Bonwit Teller stores in Philadelphia, which were at that time independent of Bonwit Teller stores in nine other cities. She turned the drab Philadelphia stores into showcases that reflected her fine taste in selecting high-style garments and accessories and her creative genius in promoting them.

When Genesco, Inc. acquired the Philadelphia stores in 1963, she became a director of the 721 Corporation, the Genesco subsidiary controlling the Bonwit Teller chain. In 1965 she moved to New York City as president of the chain and later became chairwoman. Custin transformed the decor of the flagship store, filling it with boutiques, and subsequently attracting a who's-who of international haute couture. She promoted a host of trendy new designers (Calvin Klein among them) and daringly introduced a men's haberdashery, where Bill Blass offered his first men's creations. "It was a daring move at the time to try to sell men's wear in what had been strictly a women's specialty store," Anne-Marie Schiro wrote in the *New York Times*. "Ms. Custin offered her customers Cardin's neo-Edwardian silhouette, then considered radical, the first Bill Blass men's wear, Hermes ties from Paris and Turnbull & Asser shirts from London. At Christmas time, men were catered to with special shopping evenings."

Custin retired as chairwoman of Bonwit Teller in 1970 and subsequently ran a retail- and fashion-consulting business until 1990. She died at her home in Palm Springs, Florida in 1997.

Significance

Mildred Custin was an innovative and major force in the history of fashion retailing, who "never lacked daring," as Schiro wrote. "She believed that women were better than men at the fashion business. 'We are more inclined than they are to take risks…' she said. 'All women who have reached the top in fashion did it by risking their necks. If I saw something I liked, I'd fill the store with it. I trusted my judgment.'"

Further Reading:

Current Biography, 1967, 1997

New York Times Apr. 1, 1997

John Diebold

Communications pioneer

John Diebold was a management consultant and computer pioneer

---

Areas of Achievement: Management consulting, communications

Born: June 8, 1926; Weehawken, New Jersey

Died: December 26, 2005, Bedford Hills, New York

Early Life

John Diebold, serving in the U.S. Merchant Marine in the waning years of World War II, kept thinking, as he later recalled, "If we can build tools and . . . have automatic firing control [in anti-aircraft systems], why can't we have an automatic factory?" He pursued that line of inquiry—the application of electronic computers to factory mechanisms—in earning his M.B.A. in 1951 at Harvard University and then carried that application on to wider usage. In his book *Automation: The Advent of the Automatic Factory* (1952), he tried, as he said, "to tell people, particularly managers, that something so significant was brewing that it would change everything, that technologies such as computers and automation would transform the way we do business." Following a stint as a junior consultant with a Chicago management-consultant firm, he launched the Diebold Group in 1954.

Life's Work

From an office in the Diebold family home in Weehawken, New Jersey, the consulting firm expanded nationally over the following several years and internationally beginning in 1958. By the end of the following decade, Diebold was directing the activities of offices in 13 cities on five continents, persuading corporations, governments, banks, hospitals, and other entities to automate their data processing and other procedures, store their records electronically, and install interoffice computer networks, and he offered them help in doing so. In the United States alone his clients included scores of major corporations, such as Boeing, Xerox, IBM, and AT&T, as well as numerous smaller entities and the municipal governments of New York City and Chicago. Diebold published some dozen books, including *Man and the Computer: Technology as an Agent of Social Change* (1969) and *Making the Future Work: Unleashing Our Powers of Innovation for the Decades Ahead* (1984). Diebold died at his home in Bedford Hills, New York in 2005.

Significance

John Diebold was an "evangelist of the future. In 1952, at a time when computers weighed five tons, his book *Automation* described how programmable devices could change the day-to-day operations of all kinds of businesses." (Jennifer Bayot, *New York Times*).

Diebold was a visionary pioneer in the modern revolution in communications technology and the adviser to myriad industrial, business, and other clients worldwide in the automating of their procedures. He founded the Diebold

Institute for Public Policy Studies. While his firm had no connection with Diebold Inc., the maker of ATMs, he was apprising banks of the benefits of a national system of electronic funds transfer years before interstate ATM networks became a reality.

Further Reading

Current Biography, 1967, 2006

New York Times Dec. 27, 2005

Selected Books

Automation: The Advent of the Automatic Factory, 1952

Making the Future Work: Unleashing Our Powers of Innovation for the Decades   Ahead, 1984

The Innovators: The Discoveries, Inventions, and Breakthroughs of Our Time, 1990

Edward Albert Filene

Merchant and reformer

Edward Filene, the head of Filene's department store, was not simply an innovative retailer. Staunchly progressive, he was a pioneer in the development of credit unions and was a strong supporter of Franklin Roosevelt's New Deal.

Areas of Achievement: Retail, social reform

Born: September 3, 1860; Salem, Massachusetts

Died: September 26, 1937; Paris, France

Early Life

Edward Filene was born in Salem, Massachusetts in 1860, the second son and second of five children of William Filene and Clara (Ballin) Filene. Both parents were natives of Germany. His father, a liberal who left Prussia in 1848, had been a merchant tailor in Boston and later owned a retail store in Salem. Soon after Edward's birth the family moved to Lynn, Massachusetts, then to New York City in 1863. Financial reverses there brought them back to Lynn seven years later. In 1881 the elder Filene opened a retail store in Boston. Edward Filene was educated in the public schools of Lynn, except for an unhappy year and a half at a German military academy also attended by two of his brothers. Partly because of his limp—the result of a childhood accident—and recurring eczema during his adolescence, Filene was a shy youth and remained socially awkward for life.

Edward Filene's failure to attend Harvard, which had accepted him as a student, was partly attributable to his eczema, as he himself said, but also the result of his father's declining health, which forced Edward and his younger brother Lincoln to assume greater responsibilities in the family business. Determination to overcome these disappointments, combined with restless ambition, a philosophical temperament, and the political idealism inherited from his father, led Edward Filene to carve out a niche for himself as an innovative leader in both business and civic affairs.

Life's Work

At the Filene store each brother took up duties best suited to his personality. Lincoln handled daily operations and human relations, while Edward, as president, developed ideas and policy. By 1891, when their father turned over the business to them, William Filene's Sons had become a leading Boston department store, and soon it became one of the most profitable in America. Both as merchant and as social thinker, Edward Filene believed in raising profits and the general living standard through mass distribution of goods made possible by such devices as chain-store efficiency and installment buying. One of the marketing techniques he developed to achieve these ends was the bargain basement, where slow-moving goods received progressive price cuts for every day they remained unsold.

Filene was an early advocate of medical and unemployment insurance, employee credit unions, minimum wages, and generally high wages, which would benefit not only the employees but also the business through greater employee efficiency. The resulting prosperity, he believed, was the best way to insure peace, both domestic and international. As another means of attaining efficiency and industrial harmony, Filene advocated sharing both decision-making and profits with employees. His most cherished project was a profit-sharing plan that included limited voting rights for employees through the Filene Cooperative Association, which he saw as an opening step to the eventual establishment of a cooperative enterprise owned and controlled by its employees, an example of what Filene's attorney and adviser (and future Supreme Court Justice) Louis D. Brandeis called industrial democracy. In fact, the workers used their power merely to achieve such short-range goals as fewer hours and more holidays; they never moved to assume control of the store. But fear of an employee takeover led some of those who had bought into the company to begin a struggle for control in 1911 that culminated in 1928, after prolonged litigation, when Edward Filene was deprived of all voice in the store's management, although he retained the title of president.

Filene's social views found more direct expression in a lifelong involvement in civic affairs. His public service, like his business dealings, was inspired by his faith that people who are well informed will act rationally in their own self-interest. During a fight over streetcar franchises in the 1890s, he was dismayed by the fragmentation of Boston's business groups, and took the lead in organizing the Boston and U. S. Chambers of Commerce; the Boston City Club; and the Good Government Association. In 1909 he engaged journalist Lincoln Steffens, an authority on urban problems, to help formulate a five-year plan for the improvement of Boston. The resulting "1915 Movement," which sought to mobilize and unite the energies of all classes, made some progress in education and public health but failed in its broader purpose, mainly because business groups were unwilling to support any but the conventional kinds of reform, but also because of Filene's limitations as a leader. He was too arbitrary and dictatorial, too impatient to explain his ideas adequately to those with lesser minds, and too harsh in his criticism to be effective in political affairs.

In other forms of public service Filene made significant contributions. Many of the addresses he made to policy-making groups in which he was very influential were widely circulated. He served the U.S. government as a dollar-a-year man in World War I, and helped raise funds for the League to Enforce the Peace. An inveterate traveler with many influential acquaintances in Europe, he helped to persuade French and German leaders to accept the provisions of the Dawes Plan for the economic rehabilitation of Germany.

Filene's hope for the evolution of a single producer-consumer class born out of what he called "companionate prosperity" continued for most of his life. In 1919 he founded and endowed the Cooperative League, later called the Twentieth Century Fund, to undertake by research into economic and social problems, and ultimately left it most of his fortune. In 1935 he established the Consumer Distribution Corporation to promote consumer cooperatives, particularly department stores, and in 1936 the Good Will Fund to conduct research and educational projects in cooperatives and other public-affairs enterprises. A lifelong Democrat, he was a strong supporter of Franklin D. Roosevelt's New Deal. During the presidential campaign of 1936, when Roosevelt was running for reelection, he broke openly with the U.S. Chamber of Commerce, increasingly disillusioned by what he considered the unenlightened and self-destructive behavior of the business class, which he had expected to take the lead in social betterment. Now this feeling of defeat, similar to that of many progressive reformers, was added to his sense of failure at being unable to pass his business on to his employees.

Edward Filene, who never married, lived unostentatiously in a house on Otis Street, but was something of a dandy in his dress. He has been variously described, with some accuracy in each case, as "a maimed and cheerless personality" and the "philosopher of our machine economy." In 1937 while on one of his many

European visits he contracted pneumonia and died in the American Hospital in Paris. At his direction, his ashes were returned to America and scattered over Boston harbor.

Significance

Edward Filene, renowned to his business acumen, also, in the words of Yankl Stillman (*Jewish Currents*, September 2004) "played a pivotal role in passing America's first Workmen's Compensation law in 1911. He favored paying workers a 'buying' wage instead of a marginal 'living' wage. He initiated profit-sharing, health clinics, paid vacations, and welfare and insurance programs. He also established minimum wages for female workers and introduced a five-day, 40-hour work week. In the early 1900s, ideas like these were revolutionary."

Further Reading:

The Autobiography of Lincoln Steffens, 1931

Brandeis: A Free Man's Life, 1946

The Dictionary of American Biography

The Filene Store, 1930

Jewish Currents, 2004

Liberal's Progress, 1948

Speaking of Change, 1939

Anita Roddick

Businesswoman and social activist

Anita Roddick—"the queen of green"— was the founder of the Body Shop chain of stores, which offers eco-friendly cosmetics and toiletries that are manufactured without cruelty to animals.

Areas of Achievement: Retail, ethical consumerism, writing

Born: October 23, 1942; Littlehampton, England

Died: September 10, 2007; Chichester, England

Early Life

Anita Roddick was born on October 23, 1942 in England, the daughter of Italian immigrants. The chief source of the original knowledge she brought to the founding of the Body Shop was her international traveling as a young adult, when, in such places as Tahiti, the New Hebrides, New Caledonia, and the Australian outback, she noted the efficacy of the beauty rituals of indigenous women using freely available natural ingredients such as cocoa butter and tea-tree oil. Such ingredients from renewable sources—along with vitamins—became the core components of the products she created with the assistance of an herbalist. Unlike traditional cosmetic manufacturers, she tried to offer women not overpriced chemical creations promising unattainable glamour but, essentially, a line of relatively affordable creams, shampoos, and other products designed to "cleanse, polish, and protect the skin and hair." (She would later add a great variety of other items, including makeup, bath items, and fragrances.) In addition, she was able to boast that none of her products had been tested on animals. Having been taught by her mother to recycle everything possible—and originally experiencing a shortage of the plastic bottles in which she sold her wares—she first ventured into environmental activism on a small scale by offering to refill bottles brought back by customers. She opened her first Body Shop in Brighton, England in the spring of 1976 and her second in Chichester the following September. Her husband, Gordon Roddick, joined her in the business as CEO in 1977. The couple began franchising in 1978.

Life's Work

Within 30 years there were more than 2,000 Body Shop stores in 51 markets across 12 international time zones. In 1984 the company went public. In the mid-1980s the Body Shop became the first cosmetics company to establish a direct business relationship with suppliers of cocoa butter and other natural ingredients through a program called Community Trade. Community Trade began with one supplier in India and in time provided essential income to 15,000 people across the globe, from Brazil to Zambia. Anita Roddick brought the Body Shop's clout to the aid of Nigerians seeking justice against Shell Oil in 1993. In stepping down as managing director of the Body Shop in 1998 and as co-chair in 2002, she freed herself to work more fully in her many causes and charities. Those included Amnesty International, Greenpeace, Human Rights Watch, the Nuclear Age Peace Foundation, the Hepatitis C Trust, Friends of the Earth, and the National Coalition to Free the Angola 3. She also supported organizations or projects promoting the development of alternative energy, the protection of battered women, fighting slave-labor sweatshops in Bangladesh, and capital punishment anywhere. She founded Anita Roddick Publications, published the autobiography *Business as Usual* (2000) and edited *Take It Personally* (2001), a book attacking globalization and the World Trade Organization, and 2003's *A Revolution in Kindness*. She also founded the organization Children on the Edge, to help children in distress or at risk internationally, and Body & Soul, to help families living with or affected by HIV or AIDS, and she co-founded the magazine the *Big Issue*, produced and sold by homeless people. Queen Elizabeth II made her a Dame of the British Empire in 2003. The Body Shop was sold to the L'Oreal Group in 2006.

Significance

Dame Anita Roddick, who suffered from hepatitis C, died in St. Richard's Hospital in Chichester, England, after suffering a major brain hemorrhage. Her survivors included her husband and her two daughters, Samantha and Justine.

Roddick was not only one of Britain's most successful retailers, but also a foremost pioneer in turning the once-fringe ideals of entrepreneurial social conscience and ethical consumerism into mainstream corporate concerns. As she envisioned, the Body Shop was dedicated to "using our stores and our products to help communicate human rights" and to pursue "social and environmental change."

Further Reading:

Current Biography, 1992, 2007
New York Times, Sept. 12, 2007

Selected Books:

Business as Usual, 2000
Take It Personally [ed.], 2001
A Revolution in Kindness [ed.], 2003

Julius Rosenwald

Businessman and philanthropist

Julius Rosenwald was a leader in the world of retail business, running Sears, Roebuck and Co. He was a civic leader and a generous philanthropist, who supported African American causes.

Areas of Achievement: Retailing, philanthropy

Born: August 12, 1862; Springfield, Illinois

Died: January 6, 1932; Chicago, Illinois

Early Life

Julius Rosenwald grew up in Springfield, Illinois, the son of Samuel and Augusta Rosenwald, a German Jewish immigrant couple. His father was the president of the Springfield Jewish Congregation, and Rosenwald received religious instruction along with public school education. He left high school after two years, and he joined relatives who operated a clothing store in New York City. In 1884, he opened his own store, but the enterprise struggled.

In 1886, his father bankrolled a wholesale operation, selling lightweight suits, which was located in Chicago. Business success, marriage to Augusta Nusbaum, and the birth of five children followed. The business survived the devastating depression of 1893 because of Rosenwald's frugality and his shrewd decision to concentrate on low-cost clothing lines. Rosenwald was a successful merchant and well prepared to move on to business operations on a grand scale.

Life's Work

A relative introduced Rosenwald to Richard Sears, one of the founders of Sears, Roebuck and Co. Sears had been working as a railroad station agent, and his retail career began when he acquired watches wholesale and sold them to other station agents. Sears was ambitious, and the modest start soon developed into a mail-order business featuring products aimed at rural families. Sears, a visionary in the field of marketing, moved the operation from Minneapolis to Chicago. His schemes often resulted in cash-flow problems, and Rosenwald invested $37,500 in the firm in 1895. This investment soon gave Rosenwald a major role in the daily operations and the long-term planning of the company. For years the different styles and skills of Sears and Rosenwald complemented one another. The economic downturn of 1907 led to a serious rift between the two, with Sears bent on major expansion and Rosenwald in favor of prudent consolidation. Sears cited declining health as the reason for his retirement in 1908, and from 1906 until 1924 Rosenwald guided Sears, Roebuck and Co. to retail greatness.

Rosenwald made major changes at Sears, Roebuck and Co., reducing the large array of patent medicines for sale and canceling other products whose advertising claims were shaky. He also set a ceiling for the marketing budget, trusting quality to sell products for Sears. He was a leader in advancing corporate policies that aided employees, but in 1911 he endured strident criticism from the Illinois legislature, which charged that entry-level female employees at Sears, Roebuck and Co. worked for near sweatshop wages. With the exception of that episode, Sears and Rosenwald were cited as role models of enlightened corporate policy.

While building Sears, Roebuck and Co. and raising a family, Rosenwald continued his observance of Judaism as a follower of the Reform rabbi Emil Hirsch. Hirsch urged his congregation to give back to the community with time and money, and Rosenwald took those obligations seriously. He donated to the Tuskegee Institute, Fisk University, and Howard University, which served African Americans, and he provided challenge grants to construct what were called "Colored YMCAs," which promoted sports teams for African Americans, in several major American cities.

His best-known effort was the construction of thousands of Rosenwald Schools throughout the rural South. Rosenwald required local African Americans and state departments of education to contribute to the project. The program was controversial. Some scholars charged that the schools helped perpetuate segregation and that they were intentionally inferior to local white schools. Another controversy arose from the decision by Rosenwald in 1920 to strip Tuskegee Institute of supervision of the project and turn it over to a white director. Rosenwald cited administrative problems as the basis of his decision, but the widow of Booker T. Washington, the renowned African American activist with whom Rosenwald had worked closely, claimed that the decision was a blow to the African American quest for autonomy. Rosenwald put a premium throughout his life on efficiency: There is no solid evidence that his decision was racially motivated. As for the charge of segregation, Rosenwald was a pragmatist who wanted to get children in school and educated. The fact that African American literacy soared in the South from 1910 to 1940 is an indisputable tribute to his vision.

In Chicago, Rosenwald helped establish two housing projects and the rental apartments known as the Michigan Boulevard Garden Apartments. He also contributed to numerous museums and performing arts groups, and for decades he was a generous donor to the University of Chicago and served on its board of trustees.

In religion, Rosenwald worked to close the gap between Reform and Orthodox Jews in Chicago. He succeeded in getting the groups to consolidate their charity efforts into one organization. He also donated to an agricultural station in Palestine, although he did not consider himself a Zionist, and he played a major role in soliciting funds for a project to resettle Soviet Jews on farms in the 1920s. He resigned from Sears, Roebuck and Co. in 1924 because of the poor health of his wife and because of his desire to spend more time on philanthropy. He died of heart and kidney ailments on January 6, 1932.

Significance

Rosenwald had a long and distinguished career as a business executive and philanthropist. He took Sears, Roebuck and Co. from its early days and made it into a model of corporate efficiency. He was a leader in offering employee-benefit programs. His numerous philanthropic undertakings, including generous support of educational and athletic programs for African Americans, showed his belief in progressive civic principles and traditional Jewish charity.

Further Reading:

Ascoli, Peter. *Julius Rosenwald: The Man Who Built Sears, Roebuck and Advanced the Cause of Black Education in the American South* (Bloomington: Indiana University Press, 2006).

Hoffschwelle, Mary. *The Rosenwald Schools of the American South* (Gainesville: University Press of Florida, 2006).

Weil, Gordon. *Sears, Roebuck U.S.A.* (New York: Stein and Day, 1977).

Werner, M. R. *Julius Rosenwald* (New York: Harper Brothers, 1939).

David Sarnoff

Broadcast pioneer

As chairman of the board of the Radio Corporation of America (RCA), David Sarnoff controlled one of the country's largest communications enterprises. Sarnoff was remembered as the young Marconi operator who in 1912 picked up the first news of the sinking of the Titanic and was the first to receive the list of survivors. In 1915 he came forward with the idea of the modern radio set, and in 1926 he was a leader in the launching of NBC. As president of RCA from 1930 to 1947 he inspired important experimental work in the field of television. During World War II Sarnoff served with distinction as General Dwight D. Eisenhower's communications consultant and was decorated with the Army's Legion of Merit and the President's Medal for Merit.

Areas of Achievement: Broadcasting, media

Born: February 27, 1891; Uzlian, Russia

Died: December 12, 1971; New York City

Early Life

David Sarnoff, eldest of five children was born February 27, 1891, in Uzlian, a small Jewish community not far from the Russian city of Minsk. His father, Abraham Sarnoff, hoped that his first-born would become, like his own forebears, a trader. On the other hand, the boy's mother, the former Lena Privin, wished him to be a scholar: thus, when in 1895 the elder Sarnoff departed alone to the United States, she "promptly packed" young David "off to her uncle, a rabbi" (*Time*, July 23, 1951). There, during the next five years David Sarnoff was set to studying the Talmud for fifteen-hour stretches. He had reached the point where he could memorize 2,000 words a day by the time his father, whose health had become seriously impaired, sent for his family to join him in America in the summer of 1900. Sarnoff later wrote in an autobiographical article "Every Chance in the World" (*American Magazine*, April 1948): "My mother, two younger brothers, and I had arrived in the New World via steerage to Montreal and rail to Albany.... Two days later I was peddling papers in the streets ... to help support my family." Two months later he began attendance at a New York City grade school, rising each morning at four to deliver his copies of the *Jewish Morning Journal* or to run errands for a butcher before school hours. Subsequently he had his own newsstand, which he operated in the early mornings, late afternoons, and evenings, and also earned money as a boy soprano in a synagogue.

Abraham Sarnoff died when his eldest son was fifteen, leaving two American-born children in addition to his widow and his earlier offspring. In 1906 David left school and became a messenger boy for the Commercial Cable Company. With the first money he could save he bought a telegraph instrument, learned the Morse code, and six months later (September 30, 1906) applied to the Marconi Wireless Telegraph Company of America for a job as an operator. It was, however, as an office boy that he was engaged. In his spare time he studied technical books, worked during weekends in the company's experimental shop, and in 1908 at the age of seventeen, was sent as a

$60-a-month junior operator to the Marconi station at Siasconset on Nantucket Island. The station, isolated and therefore unpopular with full-fledged operators, nevertheless had a superior technical library of which young Sarnoff made good use. A year later he applied for and received a transfer to Sea Gate, Coney Island, New York, a station within easy traveling distance of the Pratt Institute in Brooklyn, where he took a special course in electrical engineering. Later still (1911) he acquired practical experience as a marine radio operator, working aboard the *S.S. Beothic* on an Arctic sealing expedition, on the *S.S. Harvard* between Boston and New York, and on the American Line's *S.S. New York*, sailing to Southampton, England.

When John Wanamaker of Philadelphia decided to install the most powerful radio station yet designed atop his New York store, young David Sarnoff applied for and was given the post of operator. Alone at his instrument on April 14, 1912, he picked up the message, "S.S. Titanic ran into iceberg, sinking fast," and for the next 72 hours was occupied in receiving and giving out the news of the disaster and the names of survivors. For this Sarnoff was rewarded by the Marconi Company with appointment as a radio inspector and an instructorship at the Marconi Institute. In the following year (1913) he became chief radio inspector and assistant chief engineer, and then in 1914 was promoted to contract manager.

Life's Work

In 1915 Sarnoff submitted to the Marconi Company's general manager the idea of what he called a "radio music box." His suggestion, as summarized by S. J. Woolf in *the New York Times*, was for "sending music over the air which could be picked up by a simple radio arranged for different wave lengths and 'which would be changeable by the throwing of a switch or the pressure of a single button.'" Circumstances at the time did not permit experimentation with this forerunner of the modern radio receiving set, but thereafter Sarnoff's advancement was rapid. In the same year he was appointed assistant traffic manager of the American Marconi Company, and two years later became commercial manager, continuing as such when the newly formed Radio Corporation of America, headed by Owen D. Young, absorbed American Marconi in 1919. When he was appointed general manager of RCA on April 29, 1921, he submitted his "music box" idea to Young, who was impressed. "But," stated *Time*, "RCA's directors were willing to risk only $2,000. Sarnoff gave a demonstration that woke them up. He borrowed a Navy transmitter and helped give a blow-by-blow broadcast of the 1921 Dempsey-Carpentier world championship fight. It created a sensation: about 200,000 amateur wireless operators and others with homemade sets heard it. RCA began the manufacture of receiving sets, and on September 8, 1922, elected Sarnoff a vice-president; within three years sales of sets amounted to $83 million. In 1926, largely for the purpose of widening still further the market for sets, the National Broadcasting Company was launched under the guidance of Sarnoff, who subsequently also originated the idea of the combination radio and phonograph cabinet and negotiated the acquisition of the Victor Company.

Later to be cited by the Television Broadcasters Association as "the father of American television," Sarnoff foresaw the possibilities of this new medium as soon as Dr. Vladimir Zworykin invented the iconoscope in 1923. Five years later, in 1928, he set up a special NBC station (B2XBS) to experiment with what eventually became TV. In 1929 Sarnoff went to Europe with Owen Young to help set up the so-called "Young Plan" for German World War I reparations, and shortly after his return was named president of the Radio Corporation of America on January 3, 1930. (He had become executive vice-president one year previously). A firm believer in the importance of broadcasting as a cultural agency, Sarnoff initiated a music appreciation hour conducted by Walter Damrosch, pioneered the broadcasting of grand opera from the stage of the Metropolitan in New York, and in 1937 established the NBC Symphony Orchestra under Arturo Toscanini.

The first public demonstration of television was made by the National Broadcasting Company at the opening of the New York World's Fair on April 30, 1939, when Sarnoff himself was seen and heard uttering the words, "Now at last we add sight to sound". Two years later (1941) NBC started commercial telecasting from Station WNBT in New York, but thereafter development of the new medium was delayed by the demands of America's World War II preparedness program on RCA's resources. Sarnoff, who had been commissioned a lieutenant colonel in the Army Signal Corps in 1924 and was promoted to full colonel seven years later, was himself called to active duty on March 20, 1944. About a month later, or shortly before the launching of the Normandy invasion, he went overseas to become General Dwight D. Eisenhower's communications consultant. For his services while on General Eisenhower's staff he was promoted to brigadier general in the United States Army. He was also decorated with the Legion of Merit on October 11, 1944, the accompanying citation especially commending his "great diplomacy in the handling of French citizens."

Meanwhile, commercial black-and-white television had become a reality, and the development of commercial color television had advanced—another area of his concern and interest.

The title "General" fit Sarnoff well: He was an imposing, dominating figure, and an active Cold Warrior. Sarnoff "vigorously opposed communism," to the extent of proposing "dropping millions of radios and compact phonographs on the Communist Bloc to broadcast pro-democracy propaganda, and influenced the formation of the Voice of America broadcasting network." (*American Experience* Web site)

Significance

David Sarnoff's vision was extraordinarily far-reaching. He oversaw the expansion of radio from a fledging medium into the huge force that shaped American life and communications. In 1939 he introduced RCA's new electronic television system, which broadcast from the New York World's Fair. He was equally central to television's exponential growth and spearheaded the development of accessible color television, which—although hard to envision today—was considered a major technological breakthrough. David Sarnoff's contributions can be felt in almost every sphere of America mass media.

Further Reading:

Adv & Sell Mar. 1948

American Magazine May 1936; Apr. 1948

American Men of Science 1949

Business Executives of America, 1950

Etude Sept. 1936

Fortune Jan. 1938

International Who's Who, 1951

New York Herald-Tribune Apr. 11, 1940; Jan. 3, 1951

New York Times Magazine Feb. 23, 1941

Newsweek Dec. 5, 1949

Science Illustrated Oct. 1946

Time Jul. 23, 1951

Who's Who in America, 1950–51

Who's Who in American Jewry, 1938–39
Who's Who in Engineering, 1948
World Biography, 1948

Jack I. Straus

Department store executive

Jack I. Straus was the chief executive of what had been described as the "world's largest store" and the third in successive generations of the Straus family to head R. H. Macy & Company, Inc. Associated with the New York store since his graduation from college, Jack Straus became its president in 1940.

Areas of Achievement: Retail, civic affairs

Born: January 13, 1900; New York City

Died: September 19, 1985; New York City

Early Life

Jack Isidor Straus was born in New York City on January 13, 1900, one of three children of Jesse Isidor and Irma (Nathan) Straus. He was the grandson of Isidor Straus, who in 1854 came as a small boy to the United States from Rhenish Bavaria, worked as a supply agent for the Confederacy in 1863, and in 1866 joined his father and his brothers, Nathan and Oscar Solomon Straus, in forming the firm of L. Straus and Sons, importers of pottery and glassware. (Isidor Straus and his wife perished on the *Titanic* in 1912.) In 1888, with his brother Nathan, he became one of the partners of the R. H. Macy & Company department store in New York City and later a member of the firm of Abraham & Straus of Brooklyn. Jack I. Straus's father, Jesse Isidor Straus, was also an executive of Abraham & Straus and from 1919 to 1933 was president of R. H. Macy & Company. During the last few years of his life he was United States Ambassador to France. Other members of the Straus family have also been business executives, have held government positions, and have been directors of philanthropic societies. In this environment of business and philanthropy the member of the third generation of Straus executives spent his early years.

For his secondary education Jack Straus attended the Westminster Preparatory School in Simsbury, Connecticut, graduating in 1917. He then entered Harvard College, of which his father was an alumnus, and chose English as his major study. At Harvard Straus was a member of the Hasty Pudding Club and the Delta Kappa Epsilon fraternity. He also joined the Reserve Officers' Training Corp in 1918, receiving his commission as second lieutenant in the United States Army the next year and in 1923 becoming a member of the United States Army Reserve. In 1921, with his Harvard B.A., he entered the family business as a member of Macy's training squad. From this he passed through executive posts in the other departments of the firm. For a while he was assistant general sales manager, then a buyer, and then merchandise councilor. In 1926 he became executive vice-president in charge of the merchandise division and two years later a member of the board of directors.

Life's Work

From 1929 to 1933 he also served as secretary of the board and at the end of that time was appointed vice-president. He held the latter title until 1939, when, as acting president, he was placed in charge of all operations of the 34th

Street store. In 1940, when Percy Straus, a member of the second generation of the family and president for the previous seven years, became chairman of the board of directors, Jack I. Straus was elected president.

The company over which Straus presided was founded in 1858 by Rowland H. Macy, a whaler from Nantucket who in that year opened a retail store in New York City, innovating aggressive advertising and cash sales as the guiding principles for success. Some thirty years later, members of the Straus family became associated with the firm and held the controlling interest in what was generally agreed to be one of the most important mercantile firms in the United States. The main store, occupying almost the entire area between Broadway and Seventh Avenue and 34th and 35th Streets in New York City, was at that time physically the largest store in the world, with approximately 2,150,000 square feet, and containing departments which in themselves were larger than many individual stores specializing in these items. Reorganized in 1919 as R. H. Macy & Company, Inc., the firm began gradually acquired ownership of large department stores nationwide.

The Straus executives closely adhered to the original Macy policies of wide-scale advertising and cash sales. To facilitate cash sales, Macy's actually had its own bank, with Straus as a director and vice-president, into which customers could deposit money and from which they drew as they make their purchases.

During his presidency Straus has held fast to the low-price policy. In May 1946 he urged retention of the Office of Price Administration and the next spring, at a press conference and in full-page advertisements in leading New York papers, he asked for a general reduction in the prices of consumer goods, warning of a business recession if manufacturers and distributors did not cooperate in such reductions. He suggested that the increase in industrial efficiency be translated "into lower prices rather than into additional profits," advised the public of the availability of most consumer items, and, according to a report of the conference in the *New York Herald Tribune*, concluded that "the only way we [Macy's] know to retain prosperity for the nation and business is to keep full production going by producing more units at lower prices." The next year at a conference of the Alumni Association of the Harvard Business School he again spoke for lowered prices: "We must fight for a lower level of prices on which depends the maintenance of a standard of living adequate to support a prosperous United States.... Price-fixing and price-maintenance are devices aimed at keeping prices up and, as such, are dangerous to the community and inimical to the interests of the consumer" (quoted in the *New York Times*, June 13, 1948). When, in the spring of 1951, the United States Supreme Court ruled that nonsigners of fair trade agreements were not bound by state fair-trade laws, Straus was able to put into practice his theories by announcing reductions in the prices of the "fair-trade" items. Other retailers joined in the price cutting and for some ten weeks a price war prevailed, in which many items were sold not only below the manufacturer's list price but below wholesale prices.

Also active in civic affairs, Straus was a member in 1937 of Mayor Fiorello La Guardia's Traffic Commission, from 1940 to 1947 a member of the Mayor's Business Advisory Commission, for a period during World War II a member of the New York City Council of Defense, and from 1935 to 1949 a member of the board of trustees of the Jewish Board of Guardians. In 1951 Belgium awarded him the Cross of Officer of the Order of Leopold II and the same year he was named Chevalier in the French Legion of Honor. In 1973 Straus and Robert K. Straus, his brother, endowed a chair at the Harvard Business School in honor of their father.

Significance

Jack I. Straus's reputation was such that he appeared on the cover of *Time* magazine in 1965. Straus became honorary chairman and director emeritus of Macy's in 1977, positions he held until his death in 1985. At the time of his death there were nearly 100 Macy's stores in 14 states, with annual sales totaling $4.4 billion.

Further Reading:

Current Biography, 1952

New York Post May 1, 1940

New York Times Jun. 13, 1948; Sept. 20, 1985

Who's Who in America, 1950–51

Who's Who in Commerce and Industry, 1951

Who's Who in New York, 1947

Geraldine Stutz

Business executive

Geraldine Stutz turned Henri Bendel, the elegant women's specialty store, into one of the most successful retail operations in New York City.

Areas of Achievement: Fashion, retail

Born: August 5, 1924; Chicago, Illinois

Died: April 8, 2005; New York City

Early Life

Of Irish and German descent, Geraldine Veronica Stutz, the older of the two daughters of Alexander H. and Estelle (Tully) Stutz, was born in Chicago, Illinois on August 5, 1924. Her father was a contractor; her mother, who held an executive position with the Du Pont Chemical Company before her marriage, eventually returned to work as a medical secretary. Stutz's sister, Carol Hopkins, was a professor at Chicago's Loyola University. Reared in a middle-class Catholic household, Geraldine Stutz attended St. Scholastica School for Girls in Chicago, after which she entered Mundelein College, a Roman Catholic college in the city, on a drama scholarship. She had intended to become an actress, but after concluding that she was, in her words, "an enthusiastic amateur actress, but not a professional one," she switched her major to journalism. To help pay her tuition, she took a part-time job as a model for Marshall Field, Chicago's best-known department store. She graduated cum laude in 1945. Commenting years later on her parochial education for a *New York Daily News* profile (August 26, 1980), Stutz, no longer a practicing Catholic, told Helen Dudar: "My kind of training laid great stress on discipline and control and performance. I am a total product of that system."

Life's Work

Shortly after her graduation from Mundelein, Stutz went to work as the assistant to the director of Chicago Fashion Industries, a public relations organization. About a year later, she moved to New York City so that she could "go to the theatre more often." There, she landed a job as the fashion editor of four movie magazines, even though she "didn't know beans about the fashion business," as she candidly admitted to Sheila John Daly, who interviewed her for the *Saturday Evening Post* (April 13, 1963). In 1947, while working for a magazine distributed by a hotel chain, Stutz chanced to meet the editor in chief of *Glamour* magazine, which was at the time suffering from a personnel shortage. Hired on the spot as an associate fashion editor, she was first assigned to cover shoes. Putting her journalistic skills to good use, she researched the subject thoroughly, talked to shoe designers, visited shoe factories, and within a short time earned a reputation as an authority on the shoe market. During her seven years with *Glamour*, Geraldine Stutz also reported on accessories, sportswear, and French haute couture collections, but it was her knowledge of the shoe industry that led to her next job, as fashion and publicity director for Mademoiselle Shoes, a subsidiary of the Carlisle Shoe Company.

When the General Shoe company (the company eventually shortened its name to Genesco) purchased I. Miller, the noted shoe manufacturer in 1954, W. Maxey Jarman, the company's president, recruited Stutz to serve as fashion coordinator of I. Miller's wholesale branch. The following year Jarman defied an industry-wide unspoken rule against women executives to name Stutz general manager and vice-president of I. Miller's 17-store retail division. Her first task was to revive sluggish sales. Convinced that women were more likely to buy fashionable shoes than comfortable ones, Stutz pushed pointed-toe and T-strap styles in eye-catching advertisements designed by Andy Warhol, then an unknown commercial artist. Under her direction, sales figures for I. Miller shoes rose more than 20 percent.

Jarman was so impressed by her ability to turn a failing operation around that he decided in 1957 to install Geraldine Stutz as president of Genesco's latest acquisition, Henri Bendel, the staid New York women's specialty store. It took Jarman five months to persuade her to undertake the task of resuscitating the financially troubled 60-year-old store, whose most recent balance sheet showed a loss of some $850,000 on a $3.5 million sales volume. She agreed only after Jarman assured her that she would have a free hand, full financial backing from Genesco, and five years to put the store in the black. In his public announcement of her appointment to the presidency, as quoted in the *New York Times* (November 15, 1957), Jarman enumerated Stutz's qualifications as "enthusiasm, a spirit of leadership, and, most importantly, the talent of developing other people's talents." Geraldine Stutz herself attributed her rapid rise to the top in the hotly competitive, male-dominated world of retail merchandising at least partly to Jarman's unwavering confidence in her. "Did I have the ability? Yes," she said in an interview for *Working Woman* (September 1981). "But could I have done it without him? No....Maxey was the only tycoon of his time who held the philosophy that businesses directed at women would be better run by women."

Geraldine Stutz's first action as president of Henri Bendel was to make a two-month personal survey of the other women's stores in New York City. Realizing that what the city needed was not another "mini Bonwit's" or "little bitty Bergdorf's," to use her own words, but a specialty shop in the original sense of the term—a store with "individualistic" taste, distinctive ambiance, and perhaps most important, "impeccable" service, she resolved to radically change Bendel's somewhat dowdy image. "I wanted to create a new store character—an old time specialty shop done in a contemporary style," she explained to Dan Dorfman in the *New York Herald Tribune* (October 31, 1965). "I had my eyes on a specific shopper—the big city woman leading a sophisticated life who wanted clothes that were chic and elegant... a woman with a good figure, a strong sense of individuality, and a woman you could pick out in a room of twenty." Instead of stocking something for everyone, the new Henri Bendel would concentrate on offering everything to one particular customer: the svelte, sophisticated, "snappier" woman. "She's twenty to sixty, depending on her point of view," Stutz once said, "but she's hip." The prototype for that hypothetical shopper was none other than the slim and stylish president herself, and it was her understated elegance and individual flair that influenced Bendel's fashion collections. "I look the way I like to look and that looks like Bendel's," she told one reporter. Named to the list of Best-Dressed Women in the Fashion Industry in 1959, 1963, and 1964, she was elected to the Hall of Fame in the best-dressed category for professionals in 1965.

The first step in Bendel's facelift was the conversion of the vast ground-floor selling area into a "street" of nine individual boutiques for accessories and gifts in a wide range of prices. In its architecture and decor, the "Street of Shops," which was designed by H. McKim Glazebrook, Bendel's innovative display director, was reminiscent of European luxury shopping arcades. Opening off a piazza paved with white marble bricks, each shop was decorated in a different style. For example, the Bagatelle, which carried handkerchiefs, stoles, and scarves, had a baroque facade; the Bag Shop, featuring small leather goods imported from France and Italy, was distinguished by Corinthian columns; the Gift Shop was tastefully decorated in the style of Louis XVI; and the Glove Shop was furnished in the Directoire style. Then an adventurous concept in retailing, the "Street," which opened to customers in September 1959, was at first ridiculed in the press as "the Street of Flops" and "Gerry's Folly." It was "my talking dog," Geraldine Stutz told Sheila John Daly. "It brought in the curious. They came and bought." Eventually the "Street of Shops" accounted for about 10 percent of Bendel's sales.

Moving on to update the other floors, Stutz installed a modish beauty salon, complete with a resident podiatrist, on the sixth floor, and she redecorated the second floor, which housed the high-priced Parisian couturier collections, to resemble a luxurious townhouse. Lured by Bendel's new look, shoppers flocked to the store in record numbers, and by 1963 Bendel's boasted a modest profit. In the same year, Geraldine Stutz was counted by the editors of *Life* magazine as among the "One Hundred Most Important Young People" in the country because she managed to "put the fancy but frail fashion emporium solidly in the black with her lively merchandising."

Henri Bendel enjoyed the biggest sales increase in its history in 1964, when volume jumped a full 10 percent to $5.5 million. In recognition of her remarkable achievement, the fashion consulting firm Tobe Associates presented Stutz with its special award for "creative merchandising in fashion retailing" at the annual convention of the National Retail Merchants Association in January 1965. The store showed "a dandy profit," as Stutz put it, in fiscal 1965, and over the next several years, sales figures continued to climb steadily. In April 1967 the jubilant president told a meeting of the Young Women's Financial Association that Bendel's sales had doubled since she took over in 1957 and that the store "now pays its own way." Bendel's fiscal pretax profit in 1980 was an impressive $1.4 million on sales of $15 million. According to *People* magazine (October 13, 1980), the figures were unrivaled to that date.

In her single-minded drive to give Bendel's a unique personality by providing its clientele with what she called "offbeat, but not kooky offbeat clothes," Geraldine Stutz introduced the French yé-yé and British mod styles that swept the country in the mid-1960s. For the well-heeled customer in search of the unusual, she opened a trendy boutique in 1963—the Fancy—featuring one-of-a-kind garments, which were produced locally by small manufacturers working from patterns originated by Bendel's. In the mid-1960s such designers as Donald Brooks and John Weitz began offering Henri Bendel exclusive collections, and in 1967 Stutz established the Bendel Studio to manufacture clothes from the store's own designs. Bendel's was also the first retailer in the United States to carry the prêt-à-porter collections of the innovative young European designers Jean Muir, Cacharel, Chloe, and Sonia Rykiel.

Since Geraldine Stutz defined fashion as "what the Bendel customer is interested in—and not simply a matter of what a person wears," she always invited artisans and craftsmen as well as designers to Bendel's weekly open house for new talent. Among the trendsetting designers who got their first big breaks from Geraldine Stutz were Mary McFadden, Stephen Burrows, Ralph Lauren, Holly Harp, Kosey, and John Kloss. She discovered comparable talents for promotion, marketing, advertising, and display among the ranks of her employees. Given a free rein, Bendel's ingenious window dressers regularly created crowd-attracting window displays. Department buyers with certified aptitudes for anticipating fashion trends and with entrepreneurial instincts were often rewarded with potentially lucrative leasing arrangements for shops on the main-floor "Street." "My gift, if I have one, is choosing terrific talent and providing the atmosphere for them to do their best work..." Stutz told Shirley Clurman, who interviewed her for a *People* magazine (October 13, 1980) profile. "When you can't afford to have the best, you hire the young who are going to be the best."

Henri Bendel's emergence as a leader in the retail fashion business was, to a great extent, the result of Geraldine Stutz's ongoing personal involvement in the store's operations. "I'm part and parcel of every transaction," she told Marilyn Mercer of the *New York Herald Tribune* (March 3, 1960). "I go to the market with the buyers. I know every piece of stock in the store. Like old Henri Bendel, I make a point of knowing the steady customers." It was at least partly because the store's success was, in the words of one Genesco executive, "dependent largely, if not entirely, on one person" that the financially ailing conglomerate decided to sell Bendel's, the last of its women's specialty store holdings. On July 18, 1980 Genesco announced that Stutz, with the backing of a Swiss-based international investment consortium, had purchased the store for an estimated $7 million in cash. The legal owner of 30 percent of the operation, Stutz acted as managing partner.

According to Geraldine Stutz, as quoted in the *New York Times* (July 21, 1980), the flagship store itself would not change, "except as it has always changed, keeping up with what goes on in the world within the framework of our character."

Geraldine Stutz's preferred recreation was reading, especially the novels of F. Scott Fitzgerald and Jean Rhys. A self-described "professional theatregoer," she rarely missed a Broadway opening. She entertained regularly at her six-room duplex apartment on Manhattan's Upper East Side or at her weekend rural retreat in Roxbury, Connecticut. Her twelve-year marriage to David Gibbs, the British abstract painter, ended in divorce in 1977. "Marriage is a linchpin in many women's lives, but many other things can create a satisfying life," she told Shirley Clurman. "I adore my career. It stretches every physical, emotional, and intellectual muscle I have. Plus, I've invested all my money in this. It's called taking a chance on love."

The first woman to be named to the board of directors of the venerable Fifth Avenue Association, she also served on the boards of New York's Reality House, the First Women's Bank, and the Tobe-Coburn School for Fashion Careers. After her career in retail ended, Stutz, according to her April 9, 2005 *New York Times* obituary, "worked as a publisher with Random House.... She also continued to consult with designers and retailers..."

Significance

Geraldine Stutz did not simply transform Henri Bendel from an understated retail outfit into a commercial powerhouse, but transformed fashion itself by bringing in elements of lifestyle choice, art, and film, as well as launching the career of Andy Warhol, Ralph Lauren, and a huge number of other major talents.

Further Reading:

Fortune Aug. 25, 1980
New York Daily News Jul. 21, 1980; Aug. 26, 1980
New York Herald Tribune Mar. 3, 1960; Oct. 31, 1965
New York Times Jul. 21, 1980; Apr. 9, 2005
People Oct. 13, 1980
Saturday Evening Post Apr. 13, 1963
Time Nov. 18, 1957; Sept. 5, 1980
Who's Who in America, 1978–79
Working Woman Sept. 1981

Sam Walton

Corporate executive and retailer

Sam Walton was the chairman of Wal-Mart Stores, the largest retail chain in the United States, and was also the richest man in the country. His chain of Wal-Mart discount outlets, which began in 1962 with one store in Rogers, Arkansas, grew at an astronomical rate. Unlike his principal competitors, Walton focused from the beginning on small cities and towns, believing that such communities represented the last untapped resource for American retailers.

Areas of Achievement: Retailing, merchandising

Born: March 29, 1918; Kingfisher, Oklahoma

Died: April 5, 1992; Little Rock, Arkansas

Early Life

Born in Kingfisher, Oklahoma on March 29, 1918, Samuel Moore Walton was the older of the two sons of Thomas and Nancy Walton. In 1923 Thomas Walton, a farm-mortgage broker, moved his family to his native state of Missouri, where they lived in a succession of rural communities for three years and then settled in the medium-sized university town of Columbia. Thanks to his hard work and keen business sense, Thomas Walton managed to have a fairly large nest egg put aside by the time the bottom fell out of the American economy in 1929; his family therefore suffered less during the Great Depression of the 1930s than did most of their neighbors.

As a student at Hickman High School in Columbia, Sam Walton made a name for himself as a quarterback on the school football team, captain of the basketball team, class president, and student council president. He was also a member of the track team and the star of the senior play, *Growing Pains*. The Hickman High School yearbook of 1936 described him as having distinguished himself in "leadership, service, and ability." At the University of Missouri, Walton studied economics and was a member of the Zeta Phi fraternity and president of his senior class.

After receiving his B.A. in 1940, Walton took his first retailing job—at a J. C. Penney store in Des Moines, Iowa, where he was a sales trainee. In an interview with John Huey for *Fortune* (September 23, 1991), Walton recalled the day that James Cash Penney, the company's founder, paid a visit to the Des Moines store: "He taught me how to tie a package with very little twine and very little paper and still make it look nice," Walton remembered. Drafted into the United States Army in early 1942, Walton served as a communications officer in the Army Intelligence Corps, an assignment that enabled him to remain stateside for the duration of World War II.

When he was released from military service in 1945, Walton had aspirations of obtaining an M.B.A. from the University of Pennsylvania's prestigious Wharton School of Finance, but his lack of funds forced him to return to his trainee's job at J. C. Penney. In that year, however, Walton used his savings and a loan to buy a Ben Franklin variety store in Newport, Arkansas. Although he built the store into a major success, his landlord refused to renew his lease when it expired in 1950, forcing Walton to turn over the store to the landlord's son. Walton then moved to Bentonville, Arkansas, where he and his younger brother, James, became franchisees of the Ben Franklin variety store chain. They eventually controlled 15 stores in Arkansas and Missouri.

Life's Work

During his days as a Ben Franklin franchisee, Walton traveled throughout the East and Midwest, studying large retail chains such as Korvette, Caldor, and Zayre. While on those trips, Walton observed that the big discount chains always situated their stores in or near large cities, obviously out of a conviction that small towns could not generate enough business to make a large store profitable. But Walton saw things differently. "I thought that larger stores could be put in smaller towns than anyone had tried before," he later explained. "There was a lot more business in those towns than people ever thought." When he broached the idea to Ben Franklin's management, he received no encouragement whatsoever. Undeterred, Walton took on the project himself, and in 1962 he opened the first Wal-Mart Discount City, in Rogers, Arkansas.

The early years were trying ones for the Wal-Mart chain. The grand opening of the second Wal-Mart, in Harrison, Arkansas, was, by coincidence, attended by David Glass, then the head of a drug retailing chain and eventually Wal-Mart's chief executive officer. "It was the worst retail store I had ever seen," Glass told John Huey. "Sam had brought a couple of trucks of watermelons in and stacked them on the sidewalk. He had donkey rides out in the parking lot. It was 115 degrees, and the watermelons began to pop, and the donkeys began to do what donkeys do, and it all mixed together and ran all over the parking lot. And when you went inside the store, the mess just continued. He was a nice fellow, but I wrote him off. It was just terrible."

"The Wal-Mart strategy was to target rural areas," Louis W. Stern, a professor of marketing at Northwestern University, told Jon Bowermaster for the *New York Times Magazine* (April 2, 1989). "That proved to be very smart. They understood rural America perfectly. The other thing they did was to avoid going head to head with K Mart, which existed mostly in bigger towns and cities."

From that inauspicious start, the Wal-Mart empire grew slowly but steadily for the next eight years, and by 1970, there were 25 stores. It took only two more years for the chain to grow to 64 stores, and by the end of 1972, sales had mushroomed to $125 million. Wal-Mart grew at a startling rate ever since; in 1981 alone, it opened 161 stores and by 1983 the chain had become the eighth-largest retailer in the United States, with 642 stores in 19 states and annual sales of $4.2 billion. In that same year, *Forbes* magazine estimated Walton's net worth to be $2.15 billion, making him the second-richest person in the United States, behind only oil magnate Gordon P. Getty. It was also around this time that Wal-Mart veered slightly from its rural concentration, opening stores in such medium-sized cities as Little Rock, Arkansas; Springfield, Missouri; and Shreveport, Louisiana, as well as in the suburbs of several large cities, including Kansas City, Missouri and Dallas, Texas. By 1987 Wal-Mart had 1,108 stores, located from Colorado to Virginia, with sales of over $20 billion and by 1989 there were 1,326 stores, with sales of almost $26 billion.

In April 1983 Walton launched the first Sam's Wholesale Club. Aimed at small-business owners and others who wished to buy merchandise in bulk, these warehouse outlets had few employees and offered goods at only 8 to 10 percent over cost. By 1991 there were more than 200 Sam's Clubs; by 2012 there were over 600. Walton introduced another retailing innovation in December 1987, when he opened the first Hypermart USA store in Garland, Texas. Encompassing some 220,000 square feet of retail space (about four times the size of the standard Wal-Mart store), these "malls without walls" devoted approximately the same amount of space to food and nonfood products. Wal-Mart Supercenters, still another Walton innovation, ranged from

97,000 square feet to 211,000 square feet and featured both a supermarket and a regular Wal-Mart under the same roof.

Walton studied his competitors assiduously and underpriced them whenever possible. "There aren't many secrets in this industry," he said, as quoted in *U.S. News & World Report* (July 9, 1990). "I walked into more competitors' stores than anyone.,...We learned from everyone else's book and added a few pages of our own." Walton often slipped into rival stores to check their prices on a specific item. If the price in any of them was lower than that being charged by the local Wal-Mart, he ordered his store manager to reduce the price.

From the beginning, Sam Walton devoted a significant portion of his time to visiting his stores and talking with employees (or in Wal-Mart's parlance, "associates") and customers. Walton visited every store at least once a year, but the chain's incredible growth eventually made that impossible. Still, in 1991, Walton estimated that he had made at least one trip to all but about 30 of the more than 1,650 stores and 200 Sam's Wholesale Clubs in the chain at that time. "This is still the most important thing I do, going around to the stores, and I'd rather do it than anything I know of," Walton told John Huey. "I know I'm helping our folks when I get out to the stores. I learn a lot about who's doing good things in the office, and I also see things that need fixing, and I help fix them. Any good management person in retail has got to do what I do in order to keep his finger on what's going on. You've got to have the right chemistry and the right attitude on the part of the folks who deal with the customers."

Described by one interviewer as "a militantly unglamorous, religiously cost-conscious mass merchandiser," Walton had a modest, homespun style that made him an American folk hero of sorts. "He is an old-fashioned promoter in the P. T. Barnum style," John Huey wrote in *Fortune* (January 30, 1989). "But he is more than that. He's a little bit Jimmy Stewart, handsome with halting, 'aw shucks' charm. He's a little bit Billy Graham, with a charisma and a persuasiveness that heartland folks find hard to resist. And he's more than a little bit Henry Ford, a business genius who sees how all parts of the economic puzzle relate to his business. Overlaying everything is a lot of the old yard rooster who is tough, loves a good fight, and protects his territory."

Walton traveled from town to town in a twin-engine Cessna that he piloted himself and simply showed up at a store unannounced, often surprising his employees by knocking on the front doors before the store opened for business in the morning. Once inside, Walton, wearing his trademark Wal-Mart baseball cap and name badge, drank coffee with the night receiving crew, chatted with his employees (using a microcassette recorder to note their ideas for improving sales), talked to customers, and examined the books. He also held pep rallies, during which he led employees in the Wal-Mart cheer, and he often took groups of them to a local restaurant for lunch.

In addition to maintaining one-on-one contact with his employees, Walton encouraged them to work hard through profit sharing, stock purchase plans, and incentive bonuses, one of which furnished a check to workers if "shrinkage" (losses from theft and damage) was held below the corporate goal. If a store exceeded the profit goal set for it by the company, part of the additional profit was shared by the employees. "What sets us apart is that we train people to be merchants," Walton explained to John Huey. "We let them see all the numbers so they know exactly how they're doing within the store and within the company; they know their cost, their markup, their overhead, and their profit. It's a big responsibility and a big opportunity."

Unlike most executives, Walton worked out of a small cubicle, and when one of his cherished bird dogs died, he wrote a mournful poem entitled "Ol Roy" that was printed in the company newsletter. After Wal-

Mart stock reached an all-time high in 1984, Walton celebrated by going to the floor of the New York Stock Exchange, where, dressed in a hula skirt, he danced and sang his high school song. Walton insisted that his associates called him by his first name and that every Wal-Mart store have a "people greeter," an employee who welcomes customers as they entered the store.

Sam Walton and Wal-Mart were not without their detractors. In addition to manufacturers and suppliers who considered Wal-Mart's buyers to be the toughest, most demanding, and most arrogant in the business, the many small-town retailers driven out of business by the giant chain also have little of a positive nature to say about the company. Although the arrival of a Wal-Mart was ordinarily hailed by local chambers of commerce because of the jobs and tax revenues it generated, Main Street merchants often cringed, knowing that they would be unable to compete with Wal-Mart's enormous variety and "everyday low prices." "Wal-Mart just cannibalizes Main Street," Jack D. Seibald, a retail analyst at Salomon Brothers, told Jon Bowermaster. "They move into town and in the first year they're doing $10 million. That money has to come from somewhere, and generally it's out of the small businessman's cash register."

With an estimated net worth of $2.8 billion, Sam Walton reached the top of *Forbes* magazine's list of wealthiest Americans in 1985. He remained in the number-one spot in 1986 ($4.5 billion), 1987 ($8.5 billion), 1988 ($6.7 billion), 1989 ($8.7 billion), 1990 ($13.3 billion), and 1991 ($18.5 billion). (The figures for 1990 and 1991 were for the entire Walton family.) For his part, Walton despised the richest-American tag, believing it detracted from his working-class and populist image. As he told John Huey, "All that hullabaloo about somebody's net worth is just stupid, and it's made my life a lot more complex and difficult."

By 1987 Wal-Mart had become the third-largest retailer in the United States, trailing only Sears, Roebuck and Company and the K Mart Corporation. In February 1988 Walton announced that he was handing over the duties of chief executive officer to David Glass, Wal-Mart's president and chief operating officer, but would continue to serve as chairman of the company. At Wal-Mart's annual meeting in June 1990, Walton predicted that the company's revenues would quintuple to $125 billion over the next decade, and in November of the same year, Wal-Mart edged out K Mart to become the nation's second-largest retailer. Within a year, Wal-Mart had surpassed Sears to become number one. Not content to rest on its laurels, Wal-Mart expanded its empire into the northeastern quadrant of the United States in 1991, when it opened two stores in New Jersey. As of 1992 Wal-Mart had stores in forty-three states.

Wal-Mart also expanded its food operations in 1990 and 1991, acquiring McLane Company, a grocery distributor; making a deal with Cifra S.A., Mexico's largest retailer, to open a chain of warehouse-style stores in Mexico that would sell a wide range of products, including stationery and electronics equipment as well as food; acquiring Phillips Companies, a small Arkansas grocery chain; stepping up efforts to sell fresh foods at the Sam's Warehouse Clubs; selling its own version of cola, cookies, and juice in some stores; and expanding its Supercenter stores.

Unlike many highly successful men, Sam Walton shunned publicity. Despite that aversion, he had been the subject of many newspaper and magazine articles and two notable books: Vance H. Trimble's *Sam Walton: The Inside Story of America's Richest Man* (1990) and Austin Teutsch's *The Sam Walton Story: The Retailing of Middle America* (1991). Walton's autobiography, *Sam Walton: Made in America*, which he wrote in collaboration with John Huey and for which he received more than $4 million from Doubleday, was published in 1992.

Sam Walton and his wife, the former Helen Robson, were married from February 14, 1943 until his death in 1992. They had four children—three sons, Rob, John, and Jim, and a daughter, Alice. The Waltons lived in a modest house in Bentonville, where Sam tooled around in a pickup truck, ate breakfast most mornings with friends at the local Ramada Inn, and attended potluck suppers at the Presbyterian church. Walton, who neither drank nor smoked, listed tennis and quail hunting as his favorite hobbies. He devoted about 80 percent of his time to visiting stores and the other 20 percent to meetings at corporate headquarters. Those sessions customarily began with the singing of "The Star-Spangled Banner." Among the honors Walton received were the National Retail Merchants Association's gold medal for the most distinguished retailing performance of the year (1988), *U.S. News & World Report*'s Excellence Award in Business (1990), and *Advertising Age*'s Adman of the Year Award (1991). On March 18, 1992 President George Bush traveled to Wal-Mart's headquarters in Bentonville, Arkansas, to present Sam Walton with the Presidential Medal of Freedom, the United States government's highest civilian award.

Significance

Sam Walton died in 1992, the most successful merchant of his era. According to 2014 data from *Forbes* magazine, Wal-Mart employs more than two million people and has greatly expanded its scope to encompass "money orders, prepaid cards, wire transfers, check cashing and bill payment." Its 2014 revenue was an astronomical $476 billion.

Further Reading:

Forbes Web site

Fortune Jan. 30. 1989; Sept. 23, 1991

Maclean's Dec. 7, 1987

New York Daily News Nov. 17, 1985

New York Times Magazine Apr. 2, 1989

The Sam Walton Story, 1991

Who's Who in America, 1990–91

John Wanamaker

Retailing pioneer

John Wanamaker created the first modern department store. He was also a respected religious leader and philanthropist, donating thousands of dollars and several buildings to Young Men's Christian Association (YMCA) chapters worldwide and funding the campaign for a national Mother's Day.

Areas of Achievement: Retailing, philanthropy

Born: July 11, 1838; Philadelphia, Pennsylvania

Died: December 12, 1922; Philadelphia, Pennsylvania

Early Life

John Nelson Wanamaker (WAHN-ah-may-kehr), the oldest of seven children, was born on July 11, 1838 in Philadelphia. His father, Nelson, owned a small brickyard. Young Wanamaker helped turn bricks out of molds so they could dry in the family's backyard. He attended school for three years, starting at age nine. As a teenager, he worked in men's clothing stores, becoming a manager by age nineteen. He quit this job for health reasons and spent his savings traveling the country. In 1858, Wanamaker became the secretary of the Philadelphia Young Men's Christian Association (YMCA), earning $1,000 a year. Wanamaker married Mary Brown on September 27, 1860.

Wanamaker and his brother-in-law, Nathan Brown, each invested $2,000 to start Oak Hall, a men and boys' clothing store. Their store opened on April 8, 1861, just days before the start of the Civil War. The store was small, located on the first floor of a building at Sixth and Market Streets in Philadelphia. The first day the partners sold $24.67 worth of merchandise. However, business improved after the two men acquired a contract to manufacture military and customs uniforms. Wanamaker and Brown also advertised special sales, a rare practice at the time. Customers were curious to test the honesty and accuracy of these advertisements. In its first year, Oak Hall's total sales amounted to $24,125.62; by the end of the 1860s, annual sales had climbed to more than $2 million

Life's Work

A year after Brown died, Wanamaker opened a second store in Philadelphia under the name John Wanamaker and Company. In 1875, he purchased an abandoned train depot for $505,000 and began renovating it in January 1876, so it could open as a store in time for the nation's centennial celebration. Wanamaker focused his advertising for his Grand Depot store on out-of-town tourists. The two-acre store opened on May 6, 1876, four days before the centennial celebrations began.

In order to keep sales from falling, Wanamaker decided to create a new kind of store. In addition to men and boys' clothing, the store began selling women's merchandise. He made a more controversial addition to the store in early 1877, when he started to sell dry goods. Wanamaker eventually expanded his retail space to eight acres and installed an air-cooling system. By 1884, the Grand Depot was the largest retail store in America. The following year, the

Grand Depot was generating more than $10 million in sales. Wanamaker sold his two smaller stores to his brothers, who had been managing them.

Beginning in 1889, Wanamaker served in President Benjamin Harrison's cabinet as postmaster general. In this position, he extended free mail delivery to all Americans, not just those living in cities.

Wanamaker opened a store in New York City in 1896. This venture paid off, allowing him to take a long European vacation within three years. In 1906, construction began on a 16-story addition across the street from the New York store, with an overhead walkway connecting the two sites. Wanamaker also opened stores in London and Paris.

Wanamaker loved music and purchased a large pipe organ that was used at the 1904 World's Fair. He later had the organ installed in the Grand Depot, and immediately began enlarging it. Customers were treated to organ music every day for eighty years. The Grand Depot also was the site of public concerts featuring symphonies and organists from around the world. In the twenty-first century, the organ remained in the Wanamaker Building in Philadelphia.

He was also a philanthropist. When Anna Jarvis petitioned to make Mother's Day a national holiday, Wanamaker financed her campaign from 1908 to 1914. He also gave money to YMCA branches wordwide.

John Wanamaker died in 1922, leaving his estate, estimated at $100 million, to his three surviving children.

Significance

"Wanamaker, a devout Presbyterian, represented many of the conflicts between commerce and piety produced by the new consumer culture," David Sullivan wrote in the *Encyclopedia of Greater Philadelphia*. "His advertising—he is credited with the first full-page newspaper ad—emphasized the goods on sale but often contained moral aphorisms he wrote…" A new, giant store, opened in 1911, was dedicated by none other than President William Howard Taft.

One of the keys to John Wanamaker's success was his commitment to his customers. He used the innovative practice of attaching price tags to all of his merchandise, believing that all customers should pay the same price. Wanamaker guaranteed his merchandise in writing, upheld the promises in his stores' advertisements, gave cash refunds, and allowed customers to return items.

Further Reading:

Biswanger, Ray. *Music in the Marketplace* (Bryn Mawr, PA: Friends of the Wanamaker Organ, 1999).

Ershkowitz, Herbert. *John Wanamaker: Philadelphia Merchant* (Cambridge, MA: Da Capo Press, 1999).

Gibbons, Herbert. *John Wanamaker* [reprint] (Whitefish, MONT: Kessinger, 2003).

Hepp, John Henry, IV. *The Middle-Class City* (Philadelphia: University of Pennsylvania Press, 2003).

Sullivan, David. "Department Stores." *The Encyclopedia of Greater Philadelphia*.

Zulker, William. *John Wanamaker, King of Merchants* Wayne, PA: Eaglecrest Press, 1993).

Bibliography

Bisciotti, Steve

Battista, Judy. "The Man behind the Ravens' Curtain." *New York Times,* January 30, 2013, p. B15.

Hensley, Jamison. *Flying High: Stories of the Baltimore Ravens.* New York: Sports Publishing, 2014.

Jordan, Gregory. "Executive Life; N.F.L. Ownership, on the Installment Plan." *New York Times,* December 28, 2003.

King, Peter. "The Ray Rice Fallout." *Sports Illustrated*, July 25, 2014.

Macur, Juliet. "Another Explanation for Ineptitude? Save It." *New York Times,* September 23, 2014, p. B10.

Maese, Rick. "For Ravens, What a Difference a Year Makes." *Baltimore Sun,* January 22, 2009.

Maese, Rick. "Ravens Owner Bisciotti Prefers to Stay behind Scenes." *Washington Post,* February 1, 2013.

Maese, Rick. "Ravens Owner Steve Bisciotti Defends Team." *Washington Post*, September 22, 2014.

Matte, Tom, with Jeff Seidel. *Tales from the Baltimore Ravens Sideline: A Collection of the Greatest Ravens Stories Ever Told.* New York: Sports Publishing, 2014.

Murray, Ken. "Big Picture, Not Snapshot, Focus of Bisciotti's Vision. *Baltimore Sun,* January 31, 2007.

Walker, Childs. "Steve Bisciotti Faces Worst Crisis of His Ravens Ownership." *Baltimore Sun,* September 23, 2014.

Branson, Richard

Brenner, Joel Glenn. "Virgin Galactic SpaceShipTwo Wreckage Found 35 Miles from Crash Site." *Washington Post*, November 4, 2014.

Frons, Marc, with Mark Maremont. "All Richard Branson Wanted to Be Was a Magazine Editor." *BusinessWeek*, June 30, 1986.

Goodman, Fred. "The Virgin King." *Vanity Fair*, May 1992.

Bravo, Rose Marie

Bravo, Rose Marie. "Think Tank: Rose Marie Bravo on CEO Challenges for 2013." *WWD*, January 14, 2013.

Delson, Susan. "Managing: Rose Marie Bravo." *Forbes* 182, no. 11 (November 19, 2008).

"Face Value: Rose Marie Bravo, the American behind Burberry's Revival." *Economist,* February 9, 2001.

Fletcher, Richard. "Brava, Bravo!" *London Sunday Telegraph*, October 5, 2003.

Horyn, Cathy, with Suzanne Kapner. "Burberry Finds a Fountain of Youth." *New York Times*, July 12, 2002.

Zimbalist, Kristina. "Turning Plaid into Profits." *Time*, February 9, 2004.

Custin, Mildred

Brady, James, "Who's Minding the Store?" *Crain's New York Business* 18 (February 4, 2002): 9.

Custin, Mildred. "Retailer Mourns Bonwit's Closing." *New York*, May 28, 1979, p. 7.

Schiro, Anne-Marie. "Mildred Custin, 91, Retailer; Made Bonwit's Fashion Force." *New York Times*, April 1, 1997.

Diebold, John

Bayot, Jennifer. "John Diebold, 79, a Visionary of the Computer Age, Dies." *New York Times*, December 27, 2005.

Kleinschrod, Walter A. "'Automation' Thirty Years Later: A Conversation with John Diebold." *Administrative Management* 43 (October 1982): 24 ff.

Krass, Peter. "Diebold's Bitter Pill." *Information Week* 262 (March 19, 1990): 17 f.

Malone, Robert. "Cybershock." *Omni* 6 (December 1983): 92 ff.

Taylor, Thayer C. John Diebold on PCs in Marketing: The Best Is Yet to Come." *Sales and Marketing Management* 1939 (July 1987): 42.

Drexler, Millard "Mickey"

Amed, Imran, and Lauren Sherman. "At Work with Mickey Drexler." *Business of Fashion* Web site, April 30, 2014.

Barmash, Isadore. "Gap Finds Middle Road to Success." *New York Times*, June 24, 1991.

Cuneo, Alice Z. "Marketer of the Year: The Gap; Apparel Retailer Remakes Itself as a Brand by Integrating Marketing into Merchandise Licensing." *Advertising Age* 68, no. 50 (December 15, 1997): 11 ff.

Ebankamp, Betty. "Mickey Drexler (Marketer of the Year)." *Mediaweek* 19, no. 32 (September 14, 2009): 20 f.

Gordon, Meryl. "Mickey Drexler's Redemption." *New York*, May 21, 2005.

Liu, Betty. *Work Smarts: What CEOs Say You Need to Know to Get Ahead.* Hoboken, NJ: Wiley, 2014.

Mitchell, Russell. "From Dirty Towels to the Top of the Heap." *Business Week,* March 9, 1992, p. 63.

Mitchell, Russell. "The Gap: Can the Nation's Hottest Retailer Stay on Top?" *Business Week*, March 9, 1992.

Munk, Nina. "Gap Gets It." *Fortune* 138, no. 3 (August 3, 1998): 68 ff.

O'Neil, William J. *Business Leaders and Success: 55 Top Business Leaders and How They Achieved Greatness.* New York: McGraw-Hill, 2003.

Tosh, Mark. "Gap's Drexler Saluting Old Navy." *WWD* 170, no. 82 (November 1, 1995): 20.

Van Meter, Jonathan. "Fast Fashion." *Vogue*, June 1990.

Duke, Michael

Bullock, Diane. "Most Influential CEOs: Walmart's Mike Duke Grows a Greener Operation." *Minyanville*, May 28, 2010.

Clifford, Stephanie. "More Dissent Is Expected over a Wal-Mart Scandal." *New York Times,* June 6, 2013, p. B1.

Clifford, Stephanie. "Discontent With Chief Is Seen in Votes by Wal-Mart Shareholders." *New York Times,* June 10, 2013, p. B6.

Forseter, Murray. "New Wal-Mart Leader to Focus on Domestic Domination." *Chain Store Age* 84, no.13 (December 15, 2008): 106.

Hazel, Debbie. "Retail's Power Players." *Chain Store Age* 89, no.1 (January 2013): 12 ff.

Morgenson, Gretchen. "Moving the Goal Posts on Pay." *New York Times,* May 7, 2011, p. BU1.

Palmeri, Christopher. "For Exiting Wal-Mart CEO, a Victory Lap." *Business Week*, November 24, 2008.

Tharpe, Jim. "Wal-Mart CEO's Journey Began in Georgia." *Atlanta Journal-Constitution,* September 26, 2009.

Eyler, John Jr.

Canedy, Dana. "Schwarz Sues Chief for Move to Toys 'R' Us." *New York Times,* February 18, 2000.

Hays, Constance. "Toys 'R' Us Plans To Lay Off 1,900 and Close 64 Stores." *New York Times,* January 29, 2002.

Newman, Anne. "Is Toys 'R' Us Back in the Game?" *Business Week,* March 20, 2000.

Palmieri, Jean E. "Hartmarx: Re-storing the Specialty Group." *Daily News Record* 21, no. 23 (February 11, 1991): 10 f.

Prior, Molly. "Eyler Arrival Boosts Morale." *DSN Retailing Today* 42, no. 19 (October 2003): 32.

SpendSmart Networks Inc. "Former Toys "R" Us Chairman and CEO John H. Eyler Jr. Joins SpendSmart Board of Directors" [press release]. BusinessWire, November 26, 2014.

Story, Louise. "Two to Leave Toys 'R' Us If Investors' Takeover Is Completed." *New York Times,* June 22, 2005.

Strom, Stephanie. "FAO Schwarz Appoints a New President." *New York Times*, May 14, 1992.

Filene, Edward

Berkcley, George E. *The Filenes.* Wellesley, MA: International Pocket Library, 1998.

Johnson, Gerald W. *Liberal's Progress* (New York: Coward-McCann, 1948).

La Dame, Mary. *The Filene Store* (New York: Russell Sage Foundation, 1930).

Lisicky, Michael J. *Filene's: Boston's Great Specialty Store.* Charleston, SC: Arcadia Publishing, 2012. [Images of America series]

Mason, Alpheus Thomas. *Brandeis: A Free Man's Life* (New York: Viking, 1946).

Marcus, Morton. "Brothers Set Example for Today's Execs." *Indianapolis Business Journal* 26, no. 20 (July 25, 2005): 13.

Stillman, Yankl. "Edward Filene: Pioneer of Social Responsibility." *Jewish Currents*, September 2004.

Wright, John S., and Parks B. Dimsdale Jr., eds. *Pioneers in Marketing: A Collection of Twenty-Five Biographies of Men Who Contributed to the Growth of Marketing Thought and Action.* Atlanta: School of Business Administration, Georgia State University, 1974.

Fudge, Ann

Alleyne, Sonia. "A Commercial Success: Ann Fudge Takes the Helm as the First African American to Head a Major Advertising Agency." *Black Enterprise* 33, no. 12 (July 2003): 19.

Beale, Claire. "The Networkers: Ann Fudge." *Campaign,* March 26, 2004, p.28.

Carr, Ashley. "The Sweet Success of Ann Fudge." AAUW [American Association of University Women] Website, March 31, 2009.

Clarke, Caroline V. "Meeting the Challenge of Corporate Leadership." *Black Enterprise,* 26, no. 1 (August 1995): 156 ff.

Dobrzynski, Judith. "Way Beyond the Glass Ceiling." *New York Times*, May 11, 1995.

Elliott, Stuart. "Chief to Pass Reins of Y. & R., the Agency." *New York Times,* April 18, 2005.

Elliott, Stuart. "Marketer to Lead Division of Big Agency Company." *New York Times,* May 13, 2003.

Reynolds, Rhonda. "Brewing Success." *Black Enterprise*, August 1994.

Gass, Michelle

Adamy, Janet. "At Starbucks, Low-Key Vet Plots Course." *Wall Street Journal*, March 18, 2008.

Allison, Melissa. "She's Giving Seattle's Best Coffee a Jolt; Starbucks' Michelle Gass." *Seattle Times*, May 22, 2011.

Davis, Stacy Vogel. "New Kohl's Executive Gass, Hired from Starbucks, Is Company's Highest-Paid Exec in 2013." *Milwaukee Business Journal*, March 24, 2014.

Goudreau, Jenna. "Starbucks' Secret Weapon." *Forbes*, November 21, 2011.

Macarthur, Kate. "Women to Watch 2007: Michelle Gass." *Advertising Age*, June 1, 2007.

McCluskey, Eileen. "Life in the Espresso Lane." *Transformations*, spring 2005.

"Passion Play." *Foster Business Magazine*, fall 2008.

Skelton, Kathryn. "Lewiston Native Helps Lead Starbucks." *Lewiston Sun Journal*, November 28, 2011.

Zmuda, Natalie. "Starbucks Exec Michelle Gass Jumps to Kohl's As Chief Customer Officer." *Advertising Age*, May 23, 2013.

Gorman, James

Angelova, Kamelia. "The Legendary Career of John J. Mack." *Business Insider*, September 14, 2009.

Bowley, Graham. "Morgan Stanley Tries on a New Psyche." *New York Times*, January 16, 2010.

Currie, Antony, and Rob Cox. "Morgan's Effort to Cut Risk Appears to Pay Off." *New York Times*, July 22, 2010.

Currie, Antony. "Morgan Stanley and Bank of America, Five Years On." *New York Times*, December 18, 2014.

Mathieson, Clive. "New Master of the Universe: A Straight-Talking 'Native of Australia.'" *The Australian*, September 12, 2009.

Thomas, Landon Jr. "Homecoming at Morgan Stanley." *New York Times*, July 1, 2005.

Thornton, Emily. "Mack Attack." *BusinessWeek*, July 2, 2006.

Gorman, Leon

Anderson, J. Craig. "L.L. Bean's Chairman Hangs Up His Boots." *Portland* (Maine) *Press Herald*, May 20, 2013.

Berman, Phyllis. "Trouble in Bean Land." *Forbes*, July 6, 1992.

McWilliams, Gary. "Strategies for the New Mail Order." *Business Week*, December 18, 1994.

Prokesch, Steven E. "Bean Meshes Man, Machine." *New York Times,* December 23, 1985.

Richardson, Whit. "Leon Gorman, L.L. Bean's Leader for 45 Years, Steps Down as Chairman." *Bangor* (Maine) *Daily News*, May 20, 2013.

Ivey, Susan

Adams, Brent. "Reynolds American CEO a Fiery Competitor." *Business First*, November 15, 2007

Martin, Edward. "A Woman's Work." *Business North Carolina*, April 2005.

Sellers, Patricia. "Tobacco CEO Susan Cameron Can't Quit." *Forbes,* October 6, 2014.

Business North Carolina Apr. 2005

Kamprad, Ingvar

Dreifus, Claudia. "Talking Shop." *New York Times Magazine,* April 6, 1997.

Trotman, Andrew. "IKEA Founder Ingvar Kamprad Moves Back to Sweden After 40 Years in Switzerland." *Telegraph*, June 26, 2013.

Webb, Sam. "The Frugal Billionaire." *Daily Mail*, March 29, 2013.

Kanter, Rosabeth Moss

Curtis, Charlotte. "Corporate Populist." *New York Times,* February 28, 1984, p. C11.

Deutsch, Claudia H. "If at First You Don't Succeed, Believe Harder." *New York Times*, September 19, 2004.

Frons, Marc. "Rosabeth Kanter: From Flower Child to Management Guru." *Business Week* (May 26, 1986): 65.

Hodgetts, Richard. "A Conversation with Rosabeth Moss Kanter." *Organizational Dynamics* 24, no. 1 (Summer 1995): 56 ff.

Hodgetts, Richard. "Rosabeth Moss Kanter: World-Class Thinker." *Management Review* 84, no. 12 (December 1995): 25 ff.

Kanter, Rosabeth Moss. "The Organization Woman: An Interview with Author Rosabeth Kanter." *Boston Magazine* 72 (December 1980): 177 ff.

McHenry, Susan. "Rosabeth Moss Kanter." *Ms. Magazine* 13, January 1985): 62 ff.

Pickett, Les. "Managing Change." *Journal of Corporate Management* 44, no. 4 (July/August 1992): 173 ff.

Walker, David. "Doctor of Corporate America; Rosabeth Moss Kanter, the guru of Business School Theorists." *Times Higher Education Supplement,* no. 1034 (August 28, 1992): 15.

Kao, John

Bandyk, Matthew. "Keeping America's Edge in Innovation." *U.S. News & World Report*, October 29, 2007.

Benson, Heidi. "A Man with Innovation on His Mind." *San Francisco Chronicle*, November 24, 2007.

Davidson, Andrew. "Ealing's Big Picture." *Management Today,* April 1, 2001.

Dean, Cornelia. "Where the Whole Agenda Is Innovation." *New York Times*, June 24, 2008.

Henkoff, Ronald. "*Jamming*: The Author Argues That to Compete, Companies Need to Form Free-flowing Workplaces That Emulate Late-night Jazz Sessions." *Fortune*, September 9, 1996.

Lampert, Edward

Bailey, Jeff. "Shake-up at the Top at Sears." *New York Times*, September 9, 2005.

Chandler, Susan. "Memo to Sears Staff: Work Really Hard or Move On." *Chicago Tribune*, March 25, 2005.

Fromson, Brett D. "How to Make a Million." *Washington Post*, September 10, 1995.

Guy, Sandra. "Sears Chief Authorizes Stock Buyback in First Big Move." *Chicago Sun-Times*, September 15, 2005.

Kimes, Mina. "At Sears, Eddie Lampert's Warring Divisions Model Adds to the Troubles." *Businessweek*, July 11, 2013.

Rudnick, Michael. "Is There a New 'Oracle of Omaha' in the Making?" *HFN*, September 20, 2004.

Sorkin, Andrew Ross, and Riva D. Atlas. "The Architect behind Kmart's Surprising Takeover of Sears." *New York Times*, November 18, 2004.

Lazarus, Rochelle

Adelson, Andrea. "Rochelle Lazarus." *New York Times,* November 28, 1994, p. C6, D6.

Elliott, Stuart. "Why Is Ogilvy's Boss One of the Few Women at the Top?" *New York Times,* February 19, 1997.

Elliott, Stuart. "Ogilvy & Mather Names a New York President." *New York Times,* May 23, 1991, p. C15, D8.

Foltz, Kim. "Women Deflate Some Adland Images." *New York Times*, November 17, 1991.

Levin, Gary. "Lazarus Set to Steer O&M's Flagship." *Advertising Age* 62, no. 22 (May 27, 1991): 4.

Rigg, Cynthia. "Can Lazarus Revive a Troubled Ogilvy?" *Crain's New York Business* 8, no. 14 (April 6, 1992): 3 f.

Sellers, Patricia. "Women, Sex and Power." *Fortune,* August 5, 1996.

Zara, Christopher. "Ogilvy & Mather's Shelly Lazarus on Leadership, Millennials, the Beauty of Memes, and Why She Doesn't Watch 'Mad Men.'" *International Business*

Times, June 27, 2013.

Comden, Betty. "Shelly Lazarus: the CEO of Ogilvy & Mather Freely Advertises Her Feminity." *People Weekly* 47, no. 17 (May 5, 1997): 89 ff.

Lyne, Susan

Block, Alex Ben. "Susan Lyne: Building the Brand." *TelevisionWeek* 23, no. 23 (June 6, 2005): 10.

Bryant, Adam. "Want to Talk to the Chief? Book Your Half-Hour." *New York Times*, October 3, 2009.

Carmody, Deirdre. "The Media Business: Film Magazine Editor to Lead Disney's Development Effort." *New York Times*, January 3, 1996.

Freeman, Michael. "ABC: Conservative Talk, Bold Actions." *Electronic Media*, September 9, 2002.

Reingold, Jennifer. "The Many Lives of Susan Lyne." *CNN Money*, October 3, 2011.

Rich, Laura. "C.E.O, If Not the Star." *New York Times*, April 24, 2005.

Swisher, Kara. "AOL's Brand CEO Susan Lyne Stepping Down to Run Women-Focused Fund for Company." *Re/code*, September 2, 2014.

McAndrews, Brian

Lashinsky, Adam. "These Go to Eleven: Pandora's Plans for Growth." *Fortune*, November 11, 2014.

Levy, Ari and Andy Fixmer. "Pandora's Stock Rally Isn't Solving Its Problems." *Businessweek*, March 13, 2014.

Sisario, Ben. "Ex-Ad Chief is Named Next Leader at Pandora." *New York Times*, September 11, 2013.

Story, Louise. "Microsoft Takes Aim at Google's Ad Supremacy." *New York Times*, September 26, 2007.

McCann, Renetta

Alleyne, Sonia. "No Commercial Breaks." *Black Enterprise*, September 2002.

Baar, Aaron. "SMG Advances McCann." *Adweek*, August 3, 2004.

Derryberry, Jennifer. "Open-Minded McCann Says Flexibility Essential to Success." *Advertising Age's Business Marketing*, August 1995.

Freeman, Laurie. "Burnett Executive Paves the Way for African-Americans." *Advertising Age*, February 15, 1999.

Lazare, Lewis. "Renetta McCann Rejoins Leo Burnett Agency." *Chicago Business Journal*, September 11, 2012.

Meyrowitz, Carol

Bowers, Katherine. "TJX Taps New Chief amid Data Breach Uproar." *WWD,* January 31, 2007, p. 8.

Grillo, Thomas. "TJX Re-signs CEO for Two More Years." *Boston Herald,* February 2, 2011.

Pollay, Jessica. "Meyrowitz Moving On, Herrman Moving Up At TJX." *Harrisonburg* (Virginia) *Daily News Record,* November 15, 2004.

Williams, Christopher C. "Carol Meyrowitz." *Barron's* 93, no. 12 (March 25, 2013): S24.

Wilson, Marianne, and Connie Robbins Gentry. "The Retail Power 10." *Chain Store Age,* December 17, 2010.

Moreno, Arturo

Basten, Fred E. *Great American Billboards: 100 Years of History by the Side of the Road* (Berkeley, CA: Ten Speed Press, 2007).

Burgos, Adrian, Jr. *Playing America's Game: Baseball, Latinos, and the Color Line* (Berkeley: University of California Press, 2007).

Lewis, Michael. *Moneyball: The Art of Winning an Unfair Game* (New York: W. W. Norton, 2004).

Nightengale, Bob. "As Angels Tumble, Arte Moreno Defends His Turf." *USA Today,* June 24, 2013.

Travers, Steven. *Angels Essentials: Everything You Need to Know to Be a Real Fan* (Chicago: Triumph Books, 2007).

Roddick, Anita

Lyall, Sarah. "Anita Roddick, Body Shop Founder, Dies at 64." *New York Times,* September 12, 2007.

Mariotti, Steve, Mike Caslin, and Debra DeSalvo. *Entrepreneurs in Profile.* Franklin Lakes, NJ: Career Press, 2000.

Paprocki, Sherry Beck. *Anita Roddick: Entrepreneur.* (New York: Chelsea House, 2010.)

Vinnicombe, Susan, and John Bank. *Women with Attitude: Lessons for Career Management.* New York: Routledge, 2003.

Rosenwald, Julius

Ascoli, Peter. *Julius Rosenwald: The Man Who Built Sears, Roebuck and Advanced the Cause of Black Education in the American South* (Bloomington: Indiana University Press, 2006).

Hoffschwelle, Mary. *The Rosenwald Schools of the American South* (Gainesville: University Press of Florida, 2006).

Weil, Gordon. *Sears, Roebuck U.S.A.* (New York: Stein and Day, 1977).

Werner, M. R. *Julius Rosenwald* (New York: Harper, 1939).

Sammons, Mary F.

Dochat, Tom. "Rite Aid CEO Sammons outlines growth strategy. [Harrisburg, PA] *Patriot-News,* 2005 June 24

"Driving Culture Change." *Leaders,* April 2010.

Pikalova, Maria. "Mary F. Sammons, President and Chief Executive Officer of Rite Aid Corporation." *Good2Work,* September 3, 2007.

Meyer, Scot. "Sammons: Proactive, Set to Go." *MMR* 20, no. 9 (May 26, 2003): 58.

"Rite Aid Starts Over." *Retail Merchandiser* 40, no. 8 (August 2000): 19.

"Sammons Honored for Life's Work." *MMR* 28, no. 1 (January 10, 2011): 1f.

Sarnoff, David

Bilby, Kenneth. *The General: David Sarnoff and the Rise of the Communications Industry* (New York: Harper, 1986).

Buchholz, Todd G. *New Ideas from Dead CEOs: Lasting Lessons for the Corner Office.* New York: Collins, 2007.

Dreher, Carl. *Sarnoff, an American Success.* New York: Quadrangle/New York Times Book Co., 1977.

Kressel, Henry, and Thomas V. Lento. *Entrepreneurship in the Global Economy: Engine for Economic Growth.* New York: Cambridge University Press, 2012.

Lewis, Tom. *Empire of the Air: The Men Who Made Radio.* New York: E. Burlingame, 1991.

Lyons, Eugene. *David Sarnoff: A Biography.* New York: Harper, 1966.

Magoun, Alexander B. *David Sarnoff Research Center: RCA Labs to Sarnoff Corporation.* Charleston, SC: Arcadia, 2003.

Sobel, Robert. *RCA.* New York: Stein and Day, 1986.

Stashower, Daniel. *The Boy Genius and the Mogul: The Untold Story of Television.* New York: Broadway Books, 2002.

Tebbel, John W. *David Sarnoff: Putting Electrons to Work.* Chicago: Encyclopaedia Britannica Press, 1963.

Wallace, David. *Capital of the World: A Portrait of New York City in the Roaring Twenties.* Guilford, CT: Lyons Press, 2011.

Sen, Laura J.

Abelson, Jenn. "BJ's Completes $2.8 Billion Deal." *Boston Globe*, June 30, 2011.

Abelson, Jenn. "Returning the Focus to Fundamentals at BJ's." *Boston Globe*, February 8, 2009.

Elton, Catherine. "Queen B." *Boston Globe*, January 9, 2011.

Velders, Christina. "Sen Brings Merchandising Skills to New BJ's Role." *Supermarket News*, February 18, 2008.

Zipkin, Amy. "A Happy Return." *New York Times*, April 25, 2009.

Sinegal, James

Byrnes, Nanette. "The Good CEO." *Business Week*, September 23, 2002.

Chiang, Chuck. "Costco Executive Speaks to Bend, Ore., Business Leaders." *Bulletin*, November 18, 2005.

Heylar, John. "The Only Company Wal-Mart Fears." *Fortune*, November 24, 2003.

Holmes, Stanley, and Wendy Zellner. "Higher Wages Mean Higher Profits." *Business Week*, April 12, 2004.

Schmit, Julie. "Costco Wins Loyalty with Bulky Bargains." *USA Today*, September 24, 2004.

Shapiro, Nina. "Costco: Company for the People." *Seattle Weekly*, December 15, 2004.

Veverka, Mark. "Bigger and Better." *Barron's*, May 12, 2003.

Storch, Gerald

Apgar, Sally. "Dayton Hudson at Crossroads; CEO Ulrich Still Struggling to Jump-start Mervyn's Stores." *Minneapolis Star Tribune*, July 23, 1995.

Barbaro, Michael. "No Playtime at Toy Chain on Its Road to Recovery." *New York Times*, November 19, 2006.

"On Target." *Economist*, May 3, 2001.

Schlosser, Julie. "How Target Does It." CNNMoney.com, October 18, 2004.

Straus, Jack I.

Brady, James. "Saks Changes Hands One More Tome, Rousing Gimbels' Gentlemanly Ghosts." *Crain's New York Business* 14, no. 31 (July 13, 1998): 9.

Brady, James. "Who's Minding the Store?" *Crain's New York Business* 18, February 4, 2002, p.9.

"Fun on Herald Square." *Time* 48, no. 21 (November 18, 1946): 94.

"The Great Shopping Spree." *Time* 85, no. 2 (January 8, 1965). [Cover story.]

Pace, Eric. "Jack I. Straus, 85, Macy's Leader through Four Decades of Expansion." *New York Times,* September 20, 1985, p. 44(N), A20(L).

Stutz, Geraldine

Clurman, Shirley. "Gerry Stutz Is Hardly Just Window Dressing at Bendel's—She Owns the Store." *People Weekly*, October 13, 1980.

Cunningham, Sheila. "She Bought the Place." *Working Woman*, September 1981.

Daly, Sheila John. "Whirlwind of the Fashion World." *Saturday Evening Post*, April 13, 1963.

Silver, Lily Jay. *Profiles in Success*. New York: Fountainhead, 1965.

Wilson, Eric. "Geraldine Stutz Dies at 80; Headed Bendel for 29 Years." *New York Times*, April 9, 2005.

Thomas-Graham, Pamela

Brady, Diane. "A Better Fit at Liz Claiborne?" *BusinessWeek*, October 9, 2005.

Greene, Donna. "Author Explores Issues through Heroine." *New York Times*, July 18, 1999.

Kuczynski, Alex. "A Perpetual Winner." *New York Times*, May 2, 1999.

Roach, Ronald. "Black Ivy Mysteries." *Black Issues in Higher Education*, May 14, 1998.

Shakespeare, Tonia. "Million Dollar Advice." *Black Enterprise*, October 1996.

Walton, Sam

Bergdahl, Michael. *What I Learned from Sam Walton: How to Compete and Thrive in a Wal-Mart World*. Hoboken, NJ: Wiley, 2004.

Blumenthal, Karen. *Mr. Sam; How Sam Walton Built Wal-Mart and Became America's Richest Man*. New York: Penguin, 2011.

Bowermaster, Jon. "When Wal-Mart Comes to Town." *New York Times Magazine*, April 2, 1989.

Buchholz, Todd G. *New Ideas from Dead CEOs: Lasting Lessons for the Corner Office*. New York: Collins, 2007.

Huey, John. "Wal-Mart: Will It Take Over the World?" *Fortune*, January 30, 1989.

Huey, John. "How Sam Walton Does It." *Fortune*, September 23, 1991.

Ortega, Bob. *In Sam We Trust: The Untold Story of Sam Walton, and How Wal-Mart Is Devouring America*. New York: Times Business, 1998.

Packer, George. *The Unwinding: An Inner History of the New America*. New York: Farrar, Straus and Giroux, 2013.

Sidey, Hugh. "The Two Sides of the Sam Walton Legacy." *Time* 139, no. 16 (April 20, 1992): 50 ff.

Slater, Robert. *The Wal-Mart Decade: How a New Generation of Leaders Turned Sam Walton's Legacy into the World's #1 Company*. New York: Portfolio, 2003.

Teutsch, Austin. *The Sam Walton Story: The Retailing of Middle America* (Austin, TX: Golden Touch Press, 1991).

Trimble, Vance H. *Sam Walton: The Inside Story of America's Richest Man*. New York: Penguin, 1990.

Vance, Sandra S., and Roy V. Scott. *Wal Mart: A History of Sam Walton's Retail Phenomenon*. New York: Twayne, 1994

Wanamaker, John

Biswanger, Ray. *Music in the Marketplace*. Bryn Mawr, PA: Friends of the Wanamaker Organ, 1999.

Ershkowitz, Herbert. *John Wanamaker: Philadelphia Merchant* (Cambridge, MA: Da Capo Press, 1999).

Gibbons, Herbert. *John Wanamaker* (Whitefish, MONT: Kessinger, 2003).

Hepp, John Henry, IV. *The Middle-Class City* (Philadelphia: University of Pennsylvania Press, 2003).

Sullivan, David. "Department Stores." *Encyclopedia of Greater Philadelphia*.

Zulker, William. *John Wanamaker, King of Merchants* Wayne, PA: Eaglecrest Press, 1993).

Welch, Jack

Banks, Howard. "General Electric: Going with the Winners." *Forbes*, March 26, 1984.

Baum, Stephen H., with Dave Conti. *What Made Jack Welch Jack Welch: How Ordinary People Become Extraordinary Leaders*. New York: Crown Business, 2007.

Davis, L.J. "Did RCA Have to Be Sold?" *New York Times Magazine*, September 20, 1987.

Flax, Steven. "The Toughest Boss in America." *Fortune*, August 6, 1984.

Heller, Robert. *Jack Welch*. New York: Dorling Kindersley, 2001.

Krames, Jeffrey A. *The Jack Welch Lexicon of Leadership*. New York: McGraw-Hill, 2001.

Krames, Jeffrey A. *Jack Welch and the 4Es of Leadership: How to Put GE's Leadership Formula to Work in Your Organization.* New York: McGraw-Hill, 2005.

Lane, Bill. *Jacked Up: The Inside Story of How Jack Welch Talked GE into Becoming the World's Greatest Company.* New York: McGraw-Hill, 2008.

Lowe, Janet. *Welch: An American Icon.* New York: Wiley, 2001.

Norman, James R. "General Electric Is Stalking Big Game Again." *Business Week*, March 16, 1987.

O'Boyle, Thomas F. *At Any Cost: Jack Welch, General Electric, and the Pursuit of Profit.* New York: Knopf, 1998.

Petre, Peter. "What Welch Has Wrought at GE." *Fortune*, July 7, 1986.

Slater, Robert. *The GE Way Fieldbook: Jack Welch's Battle Plan for Corporate Revolution.* New York: McGraw-Hill, 2000.

Slater, Robert. *Jack Welch and the GE Way: Management Insights and Leadership Secrets of the Legendary CEO.* New York: McGraw-Hill, 1999.

Tichy, Noel M., and Stratford Sherman. *Control Your Destiny or Someone Else Will,* rev. ed. New York: HarperBusiness, 2001.

Wexner, Leslie

Barr, Elizabeth. "Limited's Wexner Urges More Retail Involvement in Politics." *Daily News Record* 23, no. 13 (January 21, 1993): 3.

Baumgold, Julie. "The Bachelor Billionaire; On Pins and Needles with Leslie Wexner."

New York, August 5, 1985, p. 28 ff.

Born, Pete. "Leslie H. Wexner: Shopkeeper's View." *WWD* 191, No. 113 (May 26, 2006): 4.

Born, Pete. "Leslie H. Wexner; Uneasy Rider." *WWD* 149, February 27, 1985, p. 54 ff.

Feinberg, Samuel. "Leslie Wexner Has Some Fresh Ideas for Retailing." *WWD* 142, August 12, 1981, p. 22 f.

Mayer, Caroline E. "The Limited's Wexner Sets No Limits; Called 'Retail Genius.'" *Washington Post,* March 31, 1985, p. F1.

Meyers, William H. "Rag Trade Revolutionary." *New York Times Magazine*, June 8, 1986.

O'Reilly, Brian. "Leslie Wexner Knows What Women Want." *Fortune* 112 (August 19, 1985): 154 ff.

Silverstein, Michael J., Neil Fiske, and John Butman. *Trading Up: Why Consumers Want New Luxury Goods—and How Companies Create Them,* rev. ed. New York: Portfolio, 2005.

Wall Street Journal Eds. *Boss Talk: Top CEOs Share the Ideas That Drive the World's Most Successful Companies.* New York: Random House, 2002.

Wawro, Thaddeus. *Radicals and Visionaries.* Irvine, CA: Entrepreneur Press, 2000.

Woertz, Patricia

Berfield, Susan. "From One Male Bastion to the Other." *Business Week*, May 14, 2006.

Birger, Jon. "The Outsider." *Forbes*, October 19, 2006.

Diesenhouse, Susan, and Michael Oneal. "ADM's Focus Clear with Choice of CEO." *Chicago Tribune*, April 29, 2006.

Jones, Del. "ADM's New CEO Has Energy Expertise." *USA Today*, April 28, 2006.

Kennedy, Lucinda. "First Lady of Oil Knocks Chevron into Shape." *London Sunday Times*, August 22, 2004.

Kinsman, Michael. "ADM's Top Exec Is Not Shy When Opportunities Knock." *San Diego Union-Tribune*, June 4, 2006.

Sachdev, Ameet, and Mark Skertic. "Skills Refined in Oil's Ranks." *Chicago Tribune*, April 30, 2006.

Zander, Edward

Burrows, Peter. "The Man Who 'Dot.commed' Sun." *Business Week*, December 13, 1999.

Flynn, Laurie. "Coming from the Shadows." *PC Week* 12, no. 41 (October 16, 1995): A8.

Flynn, Laurie J. "Motorola Replaces Chief with an Insider." *New York Times,* December 1, 2007, p. C3(L).

Hamilton, David P. "Sun Microsystems' Operating Chief, Zander, Is Adding Position of President." *Wall Street Journal Western*

Edition, April 22, 1999, p. B11(W), C23(E).

Johnsson, Julie. "Motorola Chief on Treasure Hunt; Review of Business Units May Yield Surprising Nuggets." *Crain's Chicago Business* 27, no. 2 (January 12, 2004): 3.

Kirkpatrick, David. "The New Player." *Fortune,* April 17, 2000.

Strahler, Steven R. "Zander Faces Next Test; Motorola Chief under Pressure to Make Deeper Cuts in Costs." *Crain's Chicago Business* 30, no. 20 (May 14, 2007): 2.

Strahler, Steven R., and Paul Merrion. "CEO on Razr's Edge with Wall St." *Crain's Chicago Business* 30, no. 13 (March 26, 2007): 2.

Selected Works

Branson, Richard

Branson, Richard. *Business Stripped Bare: Adventures of a Global Entrepreneur*. London: Virgin, 2008.

Branson, Richard. *Like a Virgin: Secrets They Won't Teach You at Business School*. New York: Portfolio/Penguin, 2012.

Branson, Richard. *Losing My Virginity: How I've Survived, Had Fun, and Made a Fortune Doing Business My Way*, rev. ed. New York: Crown Business, 2011.

Branson, Richard. *Reach for the Skies: Ballooning, Birdmen, and Blasting into Space*. New York: Current, 2011.

Branson, Richard. *Screw Business as Usual*. New York: Portfolio/Penguin, 2011.

Branson, Richard. *Screw It, Let's Do It: Lessons in Life*, rev. ed. London: Virgin, 2007.

Branson, Richard. *The Virgin Way: Everything I Know about Leadership*. New York: Portfolio/Penguin, 2014.

Bravo, Rose Marie

Bravo, Rose Marie. "What Will Keep CEOs Up at Night in 2013? *WWD* 205, no. 9 (January 14, 2013): 1.

Diebold, John

Diebold, John. *Automation: The Advent of the Automatic Factory*. New York: Van Nostrand, 1952.

Diebold, John. *Automation: Its Impact on Business and Labor*. Washington, DC: National Planning Association, 1959.

Diebold, John. "'Demand Pull' Policy Would Top 'Supply Push.'" *Computerworld* 26, no. 42 (October 19, 1992): 33.

Diebold, John. *The Innovators: The Discoveries, Inventions, and Breakthroughs of Our Time*. New York: Dutton, 1990.

Diebold, John. *Making the Future Work: Unleashing Our Powers of Innovation for the Decades Ahead*. New York: Simon & Schuster, 1984.

Diebold, John. "Midsize Companies Competing from Strength." *Infosystems* 34 (September 1987): 26f.

Diebold, John. "The Next Revolution in Computers." *Futurist* 28, no. 3 (May–June 1994): 34ff.

Filene, Edward

Filene, Edward. *The Model Stock Plan*. New York: McGraw-Hill, 1930.

Filene, Edward. *Morals in Business*. Berkeley: Committee for the Barbara Weinstock Lecture, University of California, 1935.

Filene, Edward. *Speaking of Change*, ed. by Sherman F. Mittell. Freeport, NY: Books for Libraries. 1971.

Filene, Edward. *The Way Out: A Business-Man Looks at the World*. London: Routledge, 1925.

Filene, Edward, and Charles W. Wood. *Successful Living in the Machine Age*. New York: Simon & Schuster, 1931.

Gorman, Leon

Gorman, Leon Leonwood. *Hunting, Fishing, and Camping*, with updates by great-grandson Bill Gorman. 100th anniversary ed. Rockport, ME: Down East, 2011.

Gorman, Leon Leonwood. *L.L. Bean: The Making of an American Icon*. Boston: Harvard Business School Publications, 2006.

Kanter, Rosabeth Moss

Kanter, Rosabeth Moss. *America the Principled: Six Opportunities for Becoming a Can-Do Nation Again*. New York: Crown Publishers, 2007.

Kanter, Rosabeth Moss. *The Change Masters: Innovation for Productivity in the American Corporation*. New York: Simon & Schuster, 1983.

Kanter, Rosabeth Moss. *Commitment and Community: Communes and Utopias in Sociological Perspective.* Cambridge, MA: Harvard University Press, 1972.

Kanter, Rosabeth Moss. *Confidence: How Winning Streaks and Losing Streaks Begin and End.* New York: Crown Business, 2004.

Kanter, Rosabeth Moss. *Corporate Entrepreneurs at Work.* 1983; reprint, London: Allen & Unwin, 1989.

Kanter, Rosabeth Moss. *Men and Women of the Corporation.* 2d ed. New York: Basic Books, 1993. [New ed., New York: Basic Books, 2008, in electronic format.]

Kanter, Rosabeth Moss. *Rosabeth Moss Kanter on the Frontiers of Management.* Boston: Harvard Business School Press, 1997.

Kanter, Rosabeth Moss. *Supercorp: How Vanguard Companies Create Innovation, Profits, Growth, and Social Good.* New York: Crown Business, 2009.

Kanter, Rosabeth Moss. *When Giants Learn to Dance: The Definitive Guide to Corporate Success.* New York: Simon & Schuster, 1989.

Kanter, Rosabeth Moss. *World Class: Thriving Locally in the Global Economy.* 1995; reprint, Touchstone, 1997.

Kanter, Rosabeth Moss, Barry Stein, and Todd Jick. *The Challenge of Organizational Change: How Companies Experience It and Leaders Guide It.* New York: Free Press, 1992.

Kanter, Rosabeth Moss, John Kao, and Fred Wiersema, eds. *Innovation: Breakthrough Thinking at 3M, DuPont, GE, Pfizer, and Rubbermaid.* New York: HarperCollins, 1997.

Kao, John

Kanter, Rosabeth Moss, John Kao, and Fred Wiersema, eds. *Innovation: Breakthrough Thinking at 3M, DuPont, GE, Pfizer, and Rubbermaid.* New York: HarperCollins, 1997.

Kao, John J. *The Entrepreneur.* Englewood Cliffs, NJ: Prentice-Hall, 1991.

Kao, John J. *The Entrepreneurial Organization.* Englewood Cliffs, NJ: Prentice-Hall, 1991.

Kao, John J. *Innovation Nation: How America Is Losing Its Innovation Edge, Why It Matters and What We Can Do to Get It Back.* New York: Free Press, 2007.

Kao, John J. *Jamming: The Art and Discipline of Business Creativity.* New York: HarperBusiness, 1996.

Kao, John J. *Managing Creativity: Text, Cases, and Readings.* Englewood Cliffs, NJ: Prentice-Hall, 1991.

Lazarus, Rochelle

Woods, John, comp. *The Quotable Executive: Words of Wisdom from Warren Buffett, Jack Welch, Shelly Lazarus, Bill Gates, Lou Gerstner, Richard Branson, Carly Fiorina, Lee Iacocca, and More.* New York: McGraw-Hill, 2000.

Roddick, Anita

Roddick, Anita. *Body and Soul: Profits with Principles, the Amazing Success Story of Anita Roddick and the Body Shop.* New York: Crown, 1991.

Roddick, Anita. *Body Shop Book: Skin, Hair and Body Care.* New York: Dutton, 1994.

Roddick, Anita. *Business as Unusual.* London: Thorsons, 2000.

Roddick, Anita. "Profits and Principles," in *Going Green.* Boston: Harvard Business School Pub., 2008.

Roddick, Anita. *A Revolution in Kindness.* Chichester: Anita Roddick, 2003.

Roddick, Anita, et al. *Take It Personally: How to Make Conscious Choices to Change the World.* Berkeley, CA: Conari Press, 2001.

Sarnoff, David

Sarnoff, David. *Looking Ahead: The Papers of David Sarnoff.* New York: McGraw-Hill, 1968.

Sarnoff, David. 'Our Next Frontier…Transoceanic TV,' from *Look,*" in *Mass Communication and American Social Thought; Key Texts, 1919–1968,* ed. by John Durham Peters and Peter Simonson. Lanham, MD: Rowman & Littlefield, 2004.

Sarnoff, David. *Pioneering in Television, Prophecy and Fulfillment; Excerpts from Speeches and Statements.* 3d ed. New York: Radio Corporation of America, 1948.

Sarnoff, David. *Principles and Practices of Network Radio Broadcasting.* New York: RCA Institutes Technical Press, 1939.

Sarnoff, David, et al. *The Fabulous Future: America in 1980, as Seen by David Sarnoff.* 1956; reprint, Freeport, NY: Books for Libraries Press, 1971.

Walton, Sam

Walton, Sam, with John Huey. *Sam Walton: Made in America.* New York: Doubleday: 1992.

Welch, Jack

Lowe, Janet. *Jack Welch Speaks: Wit and Wisdom from the World's Greatest Business Leader,* rev. ed. Hoboken, NJ: Wiley, 2008.

Welch, Jack, with Suzy Welch. *Winning.* New York: HarperBusiness, 2005.

Welch, Jack, with Suzy Welch. *Winning: The Answers.* New York: Collins, 2006.

Welch, Jack, with John A. Byrne. *Jack: Straight from the Gut.* New York: Warner Books, 2001.

Woods, John, comp. *The Quotable Executive: Words of Wisdom from Warren Buffett, Jack Welch, Shelly Lazarus, Bill Gates, Lou Gerstner, Richard Branson, Carly Fiorina, Lee Iacocca, and More.* New York: McGraw-Hill, 2000.

Profession Index

―――――――

Activist

Filene, Edward Albert

Roddick, Anita

Advertising Executive

Lyne, Susan

McAndrews, Brian

McCann, Renetta

Business Executive

Bravo, Rose Marie

Drexler, Millard S.

Filene, Edward Albert

Fudge, Anne M.

Gorman, James P.

Gorman, Leon A.

Ivey, Susan M.

Kao, John J.

Mcyrowitz, Carol M.

Roddick, Anita

Rosenwald, Julius

Sammons, Mary

Straus, Jack I.

Stutz, Geraldine

Thomas-Graham, Pamela

Walton, Sam

Wexner, Leslie H.

CEO

Duke, Michael T.

Eyler, John

Lazarus, Rochelle

McAndrews, Brian

Sen, Laura J.

Sinegal, James D.

Storch, Gerald L.

Welch, John F.

Woertz, Patricia A.

Zander, Edward J.

Chairman

Branson, Richard

Storch, Gerald L.

Consultant

Kanter, Rosabeth Moss

Kao, John J.

Welch, John F.

COO

Zander, Edward J.

Educator

Kanter, Rosabeth Moss